Straight Talk About GAYS in the Workplace

Creating an Inclusive, Productive Environment for Everyone in Your Organization

Liz Winfeld and Susan Spielman

amacom

American Management Association

New York • Boston • Chicago • Kansas City • San Francisco • Washington, D.C.
Brussels • Mexico City • Tokyo • Toronto

Library of Congress Cataloging–in–Publication Data

Winfeld, Liz.
    Straight talk about gays in the workplace: creating an inclusive,
    productive environment for everyone in your organization/Liz
    Winfeld and Susan Spielman.
        p.   cm.
    Includes bibliographical references (p.   ) and index.
    ISBN 0–8144–0305–0
    1. Gays—Employment.   2. Lesbians—Employment.   3. Diversity in
    the workplace.   4. Employee fringe benefits.   5. Sexual orientation.
    I. Spielman, Susan.   II. Title.
    HD6285.W56   1995
    658.3′045—dc20   95–23800
                                                              CIP

Printing number

10   9   8   7   6   5   4   3   2

This book is dedicated with love to
Bev and **Sid Winfeld,**
and
Amy and **Les Spielman,**
who taught us all about pride
long before it was fashionable.

"I am not an advocate for frequent changes in laws and constitutions, but the laws and institutions must go hand in hand with the progress of the human mind. As that becomes more developed, more enlightened, as new discoveries are made, new truths discovered and manners and opinions change with the change in circumstances, institutions must advance to keep pace with the times."

—Thomas Jefferson

"This above all, to thine own self be true."

—Shakespeare, from *Hamlet*

Contents

Acknowledgments

Common Ground, our consulting/education company, would not exist if Banyan Systems, Inc., of Westboro, Massachusetts, had not stood up for what it believes is equitable and just plain good business by implementing a full program of employee benefits to cover domestic partners and their dependents. Special thanks to (then) Vice President of Human Resources Robin Schwartz and her staff. Special thanks also to "benefits co-conspirator" Suzanne Turner; to Jenny Pollak for all the slides; and to Lauri Bachofner for always helping us out.

Thanks also to the keepers of the "gay information superhighway" in such electronic places as GLB-Digest, QueerPlanet, and the Domestic List. Thanks to Brian McNaught, educator; Laura Gold, Polly Laurelchild-Hertig, and Helen Berry at Lotus; Liz Parrish at Intel; Ronni Sanlo at University of Michigan; Jane Moyer at Xerox; Kim Cromwell at Bank of Boston; Don McNerney at HR Focus; Garrett Hicks at Disney; Judith Yarrow at GilDeane; William Padilla at UNM; Bill Mayo in New Jersey; Julie Netherland and everyone else at GLAD in Boston; Deb Dellapiana at Millipore; Andrea Sigetich and Carolyn G. Rose at Novell; Ron Woods; The National Gay/Lesbian Task Force; Stacia Cooper; Dr. Cynthia Burke; Daniel Sonnenfeld and Sally Gottleib at Apple; The Human Rights Campaign Fund; Harneen Chernow of Local 285, Boston; Susan Moir of the Gay/Lesbian Activists Network; Bob Lewis from The Prudential; Ken McDonnell at the Employee Benefits Research Institute; Brian Hobbs at Hewlett-Packard; Dr. Richard Williams at Polaroid; Sheila Landers at AT&T; Frank Finamore at the EPA; Maura Pershak of the Healthy Boston Coalition; Scott Fearing in Minneapolis; Jason Cohen at OAW in Chicago; Phil James at AGOG in San Francisco; and all the people who contributed but asked us not to print their full names, especially Michael, and L. Here's hoping that won't always be necessary.

Special thanks also to Adrienne Hickey of AMACOM for opening her door and for the excellent debates and guidance, and to Maggie Stuckey in Portland, Oregon, for lending her considerable editorial talents to this manuscript.

Most of all, thanks to all the gay, transgendered, bisexual, and heterosexual women and men working openly or behind the scenes for the inclusion of sexual orientation issues at their organizations and schools. You are not alone.

Prologue

Certain truths in this life are inescapable. One of them is that humans, as animals and as a race, individually and in groups of varying size, possess certain characteristics that are inherent to their being. Their skin color, their eye color, and their gender are examples. This book is about another of those inherent traits.

People who share this trait are not in the majority, which seems to make them automatically suspect and somehow deficient. Estimates of their actual number as a percentage of the world's population usually range from 4 to 10 percent. There is strong evidence that a subset of all other animals also share this characteristic in similar proportion to their species.

Throughout history, people who demonstrate the trait we're discussing have been subject to prejudice, humiliation, discrimination, and negative preconceptions never substantiated by fact. The English words associated with these people are familiar to most, and there are similar words in French, German, Spanish, Latin, Russian, Polish, and just about every other language. Almost without exception, the words are derogatory in nature and origin.

Religion and superstition in particular have both been extremely hard on this type of person for centuries. These people have been, and in some instances still are, called the devil incarnate, responsible for everything from natural disasters to devastating diseases. In many of the books of the Bible, they are singled out for being the personification of evil and contrary to everything that is holy and sacrosanct.

The authors of this book share this trait, and as such bear part of the burden foisted on us by others who are hateful or fearful or just honestly ignorant of the facts. People tried to change us when we were younger because they thought we chose to be as we are. People like us are likely to die nine years sooner than other types of people. We are more likely to develop diabetes, epilepsy, thyroid problems, sleep disorders, and auto-immune illnesses. We are women who, with others like us, must daily find the courage to confront societal inequities and bias by stating simply that, despite all the difficulties, we are proud to be lef..t-handed.

The English word for *left* is derived from the Anglo-Saxon *lyft,* which means "weak or broken." The *Oxford English Dictionary* defines *left-handed* as "crippled, defective, inept, characterized by underhanded dealings, illomened, and illegitimate." In French, the word for *left* is *gauche,* which means "crooked and uncouth." In German it's *linkisch,* which means "clumsy and maladroit." Italians say *mancino,* which comes from *mancus,* meaning "crooked, maimed, dishonest, and deceitful." And in Latin, the word for *left* is *sinister,* from *sinistrum,* which means "evil."

Among superstitious people, left-handedness is not a positive attribute. In Scotland, in Morocco, among gypsies, and in parts of North America, if your right palm itches, it is said you will soon receive money. But if it's your left palm, you are certain to lose money. In North Africa, if your right eye twitches, you will be reunited with someone you love; twitches in your left eye signify that someone close to you is going to die. And why do we throw salt over our left shoulder? Because it is over our left shoulder that the devil is said to lurk. Furthermore, check any depiction of Satan in books or on Tarot cards, and you'll see that he is most decidedly left-handed.

In Judeo-Christian tradition, right is always good and left is always bad. In the Old Testament, in Leviticus for example, left-handedness is singled out as a "blemish" a priest cannot have. And in the Roman Catholic, Eastern Orthodox, Lutheran, and Anglican churches of Christianity, all rites are performed with the right hand. To do so with the left is considered very unlucky. Finally, it is said that the thief crucified with Christ to his right ascended to heaven, while the thief on Jesus's left descended to hell.[1]

By offering this analogy, it is our intention to demonstrate a correlation between being left-handed and being homosexual. If you think that this comparison, while perhaps interesting and compelling, is also ridiculous, you are not alone. Very few people would get up in spite of all you've just read and all the other semantic, superstitious, or religious "truths" we could offer about left-handedness, and declare that left-handed people are unfit to be parents, teachers, doctors, engineers, soldiers, or anything else on the basis of the inherent trait of handedness. But in fact, until the early twentieth century, people were beaten, discriminated against, and in some cases put to death simply for being left-handed. Being left-handed was considered without exception to be evil, a matter of choice, and a weakness that the individual could overcome.

However, over time, discrimination against left-handed people has been overcome by rational examination of genetics, by logic, and by reason. It is our position that discrimination based on sexual orientation will be similarly defeated. And in this book we hope to show that, for reasons of increased organizational productivity and profitability, it is in the absolute best interest of all workplaces to end discrimination based on sexual orientation.

People say that gays* make choices. That's true. All people make choices, but not about their sexual orientation. For gay people, the actual choice is weighing economic survival and survival in general against hostility, humiliation, and fear. For straight** people, the choice is whether to reexamine deeply ingrained beliefs. For employers, a big choice faced daily is how to treat all their employees. Only one thing is certain in this triangulation of choice: It must never be personal beliefs that are at issue in the workplace, only personal behavior. Or to put it another way, the right of every individual to work in a safe environment should not be dependent on highly subjective beliefs or opinions.

Ultimately, we base this entire book on the fact that sexual orientation is as inherent a characteristic as handedness, skin color, or eye color, and therefore should not be subject to any form of discrimination. It is not a choice any more than heterosexuality is a choice. People say we have no proof of this. Our reply is that Sue, Liz, and all other gay people by their very existence are proof of this.

All straight people who say "gays choose to be gay" should ask themselves whether they chose to be straight. The question is not, "How do you choose to behave?" The question is, "Who are you?"

---

*We intend the word *gay* to include lesbians and gay men. It is also meant to include bisexual and transgendered people whenever appropriate to the discussion of so-called sexual minorities.
**The word *straight* is commonly accepted slang for heterosexual people and will also be used throughout the book.

Note

1. Stanley Coren, *The Left-Hander Syndrome: The Causes and Consequences of Left-Handedness* (New York: Free Press, 1992).

1

Issues of Sexual Orientation at Work: Problem or Opportunity?

Those charged with the management of any organization do not typically address a problem until two things happen. First, they become reasonably sure that a problem exists, and second, they become convinced that trying to solve the problem will be good for business. Case in point: diversity.

In 1988 a training practices study of corporations employing more than one hundred people showed that not one even listed diversity among its top forty training topics. But by 1992, a Towers-Perrin survey showed that three-quarters of all companies either had started or planned to start diversity-targeted training programs.[1] Somewhere in those four years, diversity became a recognizable issue that people decided was worthy of attention. By 1994, estimates were that 30 to 50 percent of major corporations and government agencies had diversity programs up and running. Apple, Avon, DuPont, Hughes, the IRS, and others have made workforce diversity an explicit goal.[2]

Why is diversity in the workplace attracting so much attention? The reason, as with so many things, can be traced directly to simple economics. The composition of the workforce is changing whether employers like it or not. And regardless of what the workforce looks like, employers must do whatever they reasonably can to exact everybody's best effort. Attention to and management of issues of diversity are, above all else, matters of productivity and profitability.

By the year 2000 the workforce will be dominated by women and members of racial and ethnic minority groups, so adjustments must be made now. These are not just adjustments to make the workplace seem "friendlier" to these emerging constituencies. They are changes to enhance the competitive edge of the corporation through proactive development and integration of the strengths of these people.

Diversity management is now viewed more as a business issue and less as strictly a human resources issue. The distinction is a crucial one. Although management has not doubted that proper management and support programs are important, those programs have not been hard-wired to the bottom line. Some shadowy relationship between taking care of your people and their resulting performance has always been acknowledged, but it was never considered an empirical cause and effect. That is changing.

What This Book Is About

Just by reading this book, you demonstrate an interest in managing workforce diversity, and either you have a particularly focused interest in including sexual orientation as part of your model, or you're trying to decide whether you should include it. This book is specifically about why you should include sexual orientation in your diversity management initiatives and programs, and how to go about doing so. This first chapter sets the stage for you.

If the point of your diversity management efforts is to create a harassment-free, satisfactory, cooperative, productive, and profitable workplace for all, then you must include sexual orientation as a diversity factor. Make no mistake about it: By including sexual orientation, you are taking a very progressive stand. But this should not be confused with taking a leadership position on gay issues in the workplace. You may rest assured that the leader-

---

If the point of your diversity management efforts is to create a harassment-free, satisfactory, cooperative, productive, and profitable workplace for all, then you must include sexual orientation as a diversity factor. Make no mistake about it: By including sexual orientation, you are taking a very progressive stand. But this should not be confused with taking a leadership position on gay issues in the workplace; doing that makes people uncomfortable. You may rest assured that the leadership position has been assumed by others. Yours is an opportunity to participate in this movement toward total inclusion of all people, specifically gay people, and to benefit greatly by doing so.

ship position has been assumed by others. Yours is an opportunity to participate in this movement toward total inclusion of all people, specifically gay people, and to benefit greatly by doing so.

Progressiveness Pays

It is a matter of record that companies with progressive, people-oriented strategies experience better results in terms of customer satisfaction, profitability, and global competitiveness.[3] The stock of the companies listed in *The 100 Best Companies to Work for in America* consistently and dramatically outperformed the *Standard and Poor's 500* stock price average over a ten-year period.[4] The book *The Change Masters* by Rosabeth Moss Kanter compared forty-seven companies chosen by human resources professionals for their progressive policies to comparable firms of equal size in their industries. The progressive companies were more profitable and enjoyed greater growth and return on investment over a twenty-year span than those with which they were compared.[5]

Progressiveness is reflected by a slight but palpable shift from a reactive (let's-avoid-the-negatives) to a proactive (what-can-we-do-before-the-competition-does?) mind-set. By finding ways to get ahead of a problem or a potential problem, companies can enhance their profitability. The potential benefits include gaining market share, improving their competitive advantage for labor and patronage, and taking full advantage of their greatest resource— all the people, gay and straight, who work for them.

Gaining Market Share

Customer loyalty is an enormous factor in the continued profitability of an enterprise, but customers, being people, are fickle. People may very well refuse to patronize a particular store or manufacturer, or they may choose to boycott a city or state as isolated acts of protest against some perceived wrong. But they are even more likely to actively and steadily support a company that they feel does business in the right way all across the board.[6] Building a loyal customer base cannot be done as an add-on; it must be intrinsic to the business because it is inexorably tied to profitability. Increased customer loyalty translates into greater market share and bigger revenues.

Customers are people who come in all genders, races, ethnic groups, social standings, faiths, educational backgrounds, and sexual orientations. Successful companies will logically be the ones that reflect as much diversity in their programs and policies as possible. There is almost no evidence to suggest that adopting progressive policies and programs on the basis of sexual orientation costs companies anything in terms of revenue or patronage. In fact, quite the opposite is true. Companies like Saab, IKEA Furniture, Absolut, Levi Strauss, Northwest Airlines, and others are extremely vocal about the patronage they are enjoying from the gay community in exchange for corporate support of gay issues and policies.

A company is like a politician. It cannot hope to succeed in a marketplace that it does not understand or accurately represent. Therefore, it must publicize its programs and policies to let people know where it stands. If a company loses touch with its market, it will lose everything.

Improving the Competitive Advantage for Skilled Labor

The next benefit of progressive policies lies in attracting and retaining employees. This is another area that is no longer solely a human resources issue. Hiring policies and employee programs are also clearly matters driven by economics.

In order for people to land high-paying jobs, they must possess skills that ordinarily are the result of a great deal of education. That requires an investment by the individual. By the same token, in order to obtain and keep employees who make such a significant investment in themselves, the employer must also make investments that encourage all employees to feel satisfied and able to be fully productive. Any decisions reflected overtly in published hiring policies or covertly in the initiatives of the company to provide only for a certain race, gender, or orientation will result in an enormous loss of competitive positioning for that company. As more organizations offer protection and equitable benefits, people working in less progressive companies will find the strength to move.

Look at it this way. If any corporation tried to turn back the clock to the year 1940 or so and told all its black employees that they were unwelcome to use the same toilets or eat in the same cafeteria as whites, that organization could reasonably expect trouble in the form of lowered morale, lessened productivity, and loss of profitability. Most if not all of its black employees would walk out the door. Or if any corporation publicly stated that no woman working within it should expect to rise in the ranks higher than administrative assistant or assistant professor, the organization could not feign surprise if the women working there either gave less than their all or left altogether. Either scenario would probably lead to public outrage and boycotting of the company's products as well.

By breaking down barriers for women and minorities in the workplace, we have learned that a policy of inclusion results in more creativity, greater productivity, and a larger applicant pool from which to draw qualified candidates. It is vitally important to eliminate barriers that keep people out of the workforce for reasons unrelated to their basic abilities.

Many corporations, colleges and universities, and religious, political, civil, professional, and scientific groups already realize the importance of being gay-supportive. For businesses and corporations, a supportive stance results in becoming an employer of choice for many people—not just gay people, but for all concerned about a fair, equitable, and nonhostile work environment.

Taking Full Advantage of All Your Human Resources

Finally, progressive companies benefit from the ability to take full advantage of the skills and knowledge of all of their employees. A big part of this benefit is felt in allowing each person to perform to his or her greatest potential, unfettered by fear of prejudice, but it is demonstrated in another way as well. Members of a given group understand the customs, practices, and requirements of that group better than people who are not members. Therefore, tapping into the cultural expertise and knowledge of a certain employee constituency can pay rich dividends. Books on diversity are full of examples of American companies that lost big deals in the developing markets of the Pacific Rim because they did not understand how to do business in that part of world. Worse, they did not even ask the Asian-American members of their staffs, who might have provided valuable insights, for help.

With this in mind, it is ironic that when gay employees ask that their concerns be taken into consideration, they are often asked for quantifiable evidence that including them will be good for the business. This double standard, which we call the "Quantifiable Quandary," is very unlikely to occur when the petitioning group is any other employee minority. Only gays are likely to be told something to the effect that the organization is generally in agreement that discrimination is bad, but that it wants quantifiable evidence that discrimination against gays is bad. Women, people of color, and ethnic minorities seldom have to provide reams of statistics to bolster their position that including them will be good for everyone.

Another significant factor is the very real issue of productivity. Work is a task, but it is also a social activity. People need and expect to be able to express themselves to the fullest, and when they can't, they are unhappy. That unhappiness eventually sabotages the efforts of the work group and by extension drags down the performance of the whole organization. As Laura Gold, director of diversity strategy for Lotus Development Corporation, explains:

We are trying to offer the broadest possible menu of programs that can help people feel stable and secure at work. This thinking enables employees to be more productive because it streamlines their ability to keep their lives in order, and it communicates that the company cares about them as whole people.

Why Act Now?

Once you accept the premise that inclusion of all kinds of people is crucial to the continued productivity and prosperity of the enterprise, then you must identify exactly what classifications of people you are going to include, recruit, and solicit.

Gay people must be included in the diversity mix for a number of reasons. There are three that stand out: matters of law, matters of profitability, and matters of common sense.

Matters of Law

The legal landscape in relation to gay rights changes continually. As of this writing, gay rights are not protected by the U.S. Constitution. There is no federal job protection for gays in the United States. An act to provide such protection, the Employment Non-Discrimination Act (ENDA), was introduced to Congress in 1994 but has yet to get out of committee (see Chapter 3 and Epilogue). However, nondiscrimination provisions do exist in this country. Nine states (California, Connecticut, Hawaii, Massachusetts, Minnesota, New Jersey, Rhode Island, Vermont, and Wisconsin) specifically include gays in civil rights protection that typically extend to employment, public accommodations, private employment, education, housing, credit, and union practices. Between fifteen and eighteen others cover some degree of gay rights with very tenuous executive orders. Eighty-seven cities and counties have civil rights ordinances for gays, and thirty-eight others have proclamations banning discrimination.

These laws and ordinances carry varying weight, but each represents a building block upon which precedents are being set. Many of these precedents have implications for employers. For example:

- In New Jersey, specific language in the nondiscrimination law refers to benefits. There is a lawsuit ongoing (as of spring 1995) to win these benefits at Rutgers University on the basis of this language.
- In Rhode Island, the nondiscrimination executive order specifically

> Organizations can expect more of their gay employees to in-
> sist upon discrimination protection and equitable benefits in
> the workplace. And those organizations would do well to lis-
> ten. The reason is simple. In those places where the law does
> not protect and provide for inclusion of sexual minorities, gay
> people work under enormous strain. They cannot perform at
> their best under these oppressive circumstances. In many
> cases discrimination is unlawful; it is always unproductive and
> unprofitable.

states that no state agency or organization that does business with the
state may discriminate in any way on the basis of sexual orientation.

- In Alaska, where discrimination is outlawed on the basis of marital
  status, two gay employees of the University of Alaska won a decision
  by a superior court judge mandating medical benefits for their partners.
- In Vermont, a petition to win full benefits for the unmarried partners
  of all state employees was successful on the basis of that state's gay
  civil rights laws.

If your company operates in a state, city, county, or town that has a
nondiscrimination law or order specifically inclusive of sexual orientation,
and it does not specifically include sexual orientation as a protected characteristic in its nondiscrimination policy, then it is breaking the law and can be
sued or brought before your state's human rights commission.

Organizations can expect more of their gay employees to insist upon discrimination protection and equitable benefits in the workplace. And those organizations would do well to listen. The reason is simple. In those places
where the law does not protect and provide for inclusion of sexual minorities, gay people work under enormous strain. They cannot perform at their
best under these oppressive circumstances. In many cases discrimination is
unlawful; it is always unproductive and unprofitable.

Matters of Profitability

Another reason for organizations to take proactive measures goes straight to
the bottom line. We have spoken in general terms of the positive potential for
expanded market share and increased patronage by companies with pro-

gressive policies. On the other side of the coin, there is also a great deal to suggest that adopting discriminatory policies is detrimental to economic health.

We have already seen it in the public sector. Williamson, Texas, demanded in 1994 that Apple stop giving domestic partner benefits or lose tax incentives. The result was that Williamson lost thousands of potential jobs—in a time and place where jobs were at a premium—when Apple refused to back down. After passing Proposition 2 prohibiting "special rights" for homosexuals, Colorado lost almost $120 million in convention and tourism revenues. Portland, Oregon, lost $15 million in convention business after an anti-gay initiative was put on the ballot, even though the initiative was eventually defeated in the election. Cobb County, Georgia, lost an estimated $10 million when gay activists pressured the United States Olympic Committee to move the 1996 volleyball competition elsewhere. In the private sector, Coors Brewing Company and L.L. Bean both found themselves fighting boycott efforts because of the publicizing of anti-gay remarks made by family members of both family-owned companies. The Cracker Barrel Company, Domino's Pizza, and Allstate Insurance have also found themselves battling well-organized and publicized protests by the gay community and gay allies seeking nondiscriminatory treatment.

Human rights are never far divorced from economics. As the twentieth century winds down, gay people—and all those who care about equitable treatment of all citizens—are fighting for equitable policies with economics as their first weapon. Companies and organizations that support gay employees and their requirements will be rewarded, and those that resist inclusion will see the results in the bottom line.

Matters of Common Sense

Perhaps the most compelling reason for including gay workers in your diversity mix is this simple fact: They are already there. About 10 percent of the population is gay, and so about 10 percent of any workforce consisting of more than ten people is statistically likely to include at least one gay person. Anywhere from 7 million to 21 million gay people live and work in the United States alone. In fact, some studies estimate that they are the single largest minority in the workforce.[7] They don't need or want affirmative action or special rights. They need and want the quite ordinary freedom of visibility without reprisals.

Your workforce already includes gay workers, closeted* or not, in whom

---

* "The closet" is a term commonly used to describe how a person hides his sexual orientation. To say that someone is closeted is to say that the person does not freely reveal that he or she is gay. "Coming out" or "out of the closet" refers to the act of being honest about one's sexual orientation.

you have made and continue to make a significant investment. Pretending they don't exist or asking them to pretend about who they are is ridiculous and wasteful.

The Question of Leadership

All organizations have it within their power to take a progressive position on nondiscrimination and to proactively ensure that all members understand the dynamics of the nondiscrimination policy. The reason for doing so is simple: Unless companies take a proactive stance, they can be sure that they will lose customers, and talented employees, to competitors who have. Inclusion is a very small price to pay for profitability.

And yet we must acknowledge that some are hesitant or want to avoid this subject altogether. Some organizations fear that they will lose market share if they take a progressive stance in policies of workplace inclusion, specifically in relation to gay people. They are afraid that having an inclusive policy will be interpreted as giving tacit approval, and that customers who hold the opposite view will withdraw their business. This perception problem is probably the number one concern of corporations everywhere when it comes to sexual orientation in the workplace (whether they'll admit it or not). The answer is simple: Acknowledgment of and education about something does not equal endorsement of it. Providing for the concerns of a particular constituency in your workforce does not mean that you endorse the members of that constituency, their behavior, or their beliefs. It simply signals that the organization is committed to all of its employees with no exceptions.

In fact, many believe that taking a leadership position is the profitable thing. In 1993, John M. Conley and William M. O'Barr, anthropologists at Duke University, responded to a hypothetical situation presented in the *Harvard Business Review*.[8] In this scenario, a valued employee of a financial services firm notifies his boss that he intends to bring his same-sex partner to an upcoming corporate function at which clients would be present. The boss worries that in making his homosexuality known at a company function, the employee may put some client relationships in danger.

Conley and O'Barr maintain that it is neither economically necessary nor morally justifiable for organizations, even conservative ones, to "conform to the meaner aspects of their clients' cultures." For a long time, they point out, elite law firms insisted that the exclusion of women and racial minorities was justifiable because their clients just wouldn't stand for female or black lawyers. But in fact firms did start to diversify and the clients did stand for it.

An organization should not, according to Conley and O'Barr, make the mistake of underestimating its customers. If institutions use their predictions of another's response as an excuse not to do what they know to be right, they are missing the boat on their enormous opportunity to exercise the influence that can shape a culture and grab more market share. "We believe," wrote Conley and O'Barr, "that the history of elite law firms suggests that, in the long run, the moral choice is the lucrative one as well. When major changes in cultural values take place, it pays to be ahead of the trend rather than running behind making excuses."

Employers, Employees, and Families

Progress on so-called gay issues (even though not only gay people benefit from them) is being made in the workplace faster than in any other segment of society. Since 1990 the number of companies, colleges and universities, and municipal employers that offer any form of domestic partner benefits has gone from five to over two hundred. In a June 1994 article, *Time* pointed out that hundreds more companies are implementing specific policies prohibiting discrimination based on sexual orientation.[9] At the time of this writing, one to three new workplaces per week are adding some level of benefits or nondiscrimination protection for employees based on sexual orientation.

Employers are recognizing that the dynamics of "the family" are changing, and that these changes result in different economic and social realities and requirements for their workforce. This has profound implications for the organization's family-based programs and policies. The traditional family has long been defined as a wage-earner husband/father, his homemaker wife/mother, and their two children under age 18 living under one roof. This construct of the family has not been in the majority in the United States since World War II. It has not existed among the poorer segments of our society for much longer than that because rarely did the wives/mothers in lower-income families have the option of being homemakers.

Today, nontraditional families far outweigh the traditional units. In the 1994 Census Bureau analysis of households, the "traditional" nuclear family (a heterosexual married couple with children under age 18 living at home) accounted for just under 25 percent. The balance of the 1994 census was "other."

What is "other"? Gay people have a lot of allies in the battle for validation and representation of their families: unmarried straight couples, single parents, intergenerational families, adoptive and foster families, and members of the disabled community who care for each other as family, to name a few. The definition of "family" is only going to get harder to pinpoint as time goes on. The structure of the family is changing because the family is, and always has been, a dynamic unit. The British Broadcasting Corporation (BBC), in a program about the role of the family in society, said "the family must be learned, practiced, and rehearsed. It is not a force of nature; it is a work of art."

The workforce too is a work of art—a living, functioning, vital entity that each organization creates from a magnificent palette: the human race. The workforce comes from and is a reflection of the same forces shaping and reshaping the family. It is more than logical to conclude that if less than one-quarter of all family units are traditional in nature, then fewer than one-quarter of all workers are bringing traditional family backgrounds and requirements into the workplace.

Gay people and gay families are in the minority: About that there is no argument. Gay families function in exactly the same way that heterosexual families function: About that the argument has raged for centuries. It's vital to the success of all organizations that this argument be resolved because "the family" continues to serve as the foundation for many human resources policies and workplace benefits and programs. If the yardstick by which the family is measured is no longer a valid one, than the possibility exists that many employees are not being equitably compensated.

Opportunity Is Knocking

The balance of this book is dedicated to providing you with the tools for getting ahead of tomorrow's progress today. The key elements are laid out for you in the pages that follow. They involve:

- Fully understanding the sexual orientation aspects of the "whole self" and the "work self."
- Confronting the misconceptions about gay people that are often at the heart of workplace conflicts.
- Identifying specific strategies to defeat homophobia and promote cooperation.
- Understanding the elements of education that effectively deal with sexual orientation at work.
- Understanding all the elements of, and implementing, domestic partner benefits.
- Providing education about HIV/AIDS and other sexually transmitted diseases (STDs) to ensure that these issues do not become more widely disruptive.

- Understanding the answers to questions related to orientation education, benefits, and health education.

In the chapters ahead, you will find strategy upon strategy to help make your organization the most productive, profitable, and satisfactory organization it can be.

The idea must be to do everything possible to expand both the customer base and the employee pool, and then to pay attention to the diverse groups inside and outside the organization—*all* of them. Purposely neglecting one type of person in favor of another, either in the way you attract or try to retain your employees, or in the way you market your products, will shrink your organization's resource and market potential. That is simply bad business.

Notes

1. Sara Rynes and Benson Rosen, "What Makes Diversity Work," *HR Magazine* (October 1994).
2. Frederick R. Lynch, "Demystifying Multiculturalism," *National Review*, February 21, 1994.
3. Steven Lyndenberg, Alice T. Marlin, and Sean O. Strub, *Rating America's Corporate Conscience: A Proactive Guide to the Companies Behind the Products You Buy* (New York: Addison-Wesley, 1986).
4. Ibid.
5. Ibid.
6. Frederick F. Reichheld, "Loyalty Based Management," *Harvard Business Review* (March/April 1993).
7. Alistair D. Williamson, "Is This the Right Time to Come Out?" *Harvard Business Review*, July/August 1993.
8. Ibid.
9. Henry, William A., "Pride and Prejudice: Bumping Up Against the Limits of Tolerance," *Time* (June 27, 1994).

2

Homophobia and Heterosexism: Facts and Myths

Discrimination against people because of sexual orientation is wasteful in every sense. To counteract this, we must first understand it. And to fully understand it, we must face head-on the condition called homophobia and its pervasiveness as an excuse against progressive and equitable workplace policies for gay people. Homophobia—irrational fear and hatred of gay people—underlies a spectrum of emotions and misconceptions that are destructive in the workplace and in society at large.

Homophobia if translated literally means "fear of sameness." Semantics can be delightfully ironic. It is the fact that gays are the same as heterosexuals, save their erotic attractions, that most confounds straight people. Homophobia is irrational because it manifests itself as a hatred of (irrelevant) differences in people.

Homophobia is not just destructive to homosexuals. It hurts everyone:

- It inhibits the ability of straight people to form close relationships with people of their own sex, for fear of being labeled gay.
- It locks people into rigid gender-based roles that squelch creativity and self-expression.
- It compromises human integrity by pressuring people to treat others badly, actions that are contrary to their basic humanity.
- Combined with AIDS-phobia, it results in the lack of forthright sex education in business and in schools. These phobias are killing people.

- It prevents some gay people from developing an authentic self-identity and adds to the pressure to marry, which in turn places undue stress and trauma on themselves, their spouses, and their children.
- It inhibits appreciation for other types of diversity, making it unsafe for everyone who has a unique trait not considered mainstream or dominant.[1]

Exactly What Is Homophobia?

Homophobia, according to the Campaign to End Homophobia, comes in four types: personal, interpersonal, institutional, and cultural.[2] By combining these homophobia types with its three causes as described by Dr. Gregory Herek of the University of California—experiential, defensive, and symbolic[3]—it is possible to put together a description of homophobia in all its manifestations.

Personal Homophobia

An individual's belief that gay people are sick, immoral, inferior to straights, or incomplete as men or women is called *personal homophobia*. People who are personally homophobic do not have to be straight. Many people with a homosexual orientation are intensely homophobic. This phenomenon is called "internalized homophobia," and it occurs in gay people who have been battered by their families or society for so long that they come to believe that they really are somehow deficient.

Personal homophobia is caused by what Herek calls "defensive attitudes." When people believe that the image they project does not satisfy that of a "real man" or a "real woman" (whatever those terms mean to those particular individuals) and that they might be labeled gay because of it, this makes them defensive and leads to homophobic behavior.

Interpersonal Homophobia

The fear, dislike, or hatred of people believed to be gay is called *interpersonal homophobia*. It is likely to show itself in the form of name-calling, verbal and physical harassment, or widespread acts of discrimination.

Let's deal briefly with violent harassment first. Homophobia is frequently referred to as the last acceptable prejudice, and incidents of violence against homosexuals ("gay-bashing") are not going away and may very well be increasing. In 1994, several surveys reported that hate crimes against homosexuals were up and were occurring in greater numbers than racial crimes or violent crimes against women.

The virulence with which homophobia is sometimes expressed is astonishing. When the Regional Civil Rights Committee of the National Forest Service prepared its 1992 report to support the need for policy changes and specific protections for its gay employees, it included some of the following statements from employees:

- "As a lesbian I live in fear daily."
- "On the rural districts I work on, I've heard male employees talking about the enjoyment of inflicting bodily harm on homosexuals."
- "We are afraid for our jobs, careers, and lives."
- "A female Forest Service employee was murdered by her husband, also a Forest Service employee; given a minimal sentence, he was subsequently hired back by the Forest Service. When the District Ranger who hired him was questioned about the rehire, he stated that the murder was insignificant, because after all she (the victim) was a lesbian."[4]

In a study of 3,000 students in New York in 1992, *The New York Times* reported that although teenagers were reluctant to discuss racial or ethnic hatred, they were emphatic about their hatred of gay women and men. The *Times* concluded that gays are perceived as legitimate targets for attack. Herek interpreted these results to suggest that many gay-bashers consider hating gays a litmus test for being a moral person. In attacking gays, they are attacking evil.[5] These kinds of attitudes are taught, and they can be untaught.

It's important to point out that most people act out their interpersonal homophobia in ways that are not physically violent. But the violence they perpetrate on gay family members and friends is no less devastating. Relatives who shun or vilify their gay children, parents, siblings, other relatives, or close friends wreak devastating emotional cruelty.

Herek believes that a primary cause of interpersonal homophobia—whether expressed violently or nonviolently—is experiential attitude. Experiential attitude arises when a person who has had a bad experience with any type of person projects that experience to all people of the same type. In other words, if a woman is approached in a way by a female friend or acquaintance that makes her feel uncomfortable, she may assume from that point on that all gay women will try to approach her that way. To understand how illogical this reaction is, she has only to think of her experience with men. In all likelihood she has at some point spurned the inappropriate advances of a male without concluding that all men will approach her in similarly inappropriate ways.

The second possible cause of interpersonal homophobia is symbolic attitudes, which are driven by a belief that homosexuality destroys closely held values and belief systems. Our values and belief systems help each of us get through this life, and we can react badly to whatever we feel threatens them. Symbolic attitudes drive some organizations' efforts to scapegoat all gay people. These organizations would be better served, and would better serve humanity, if they would focus their attention on things like the divorce rate (gay and straight) and its role in breaking up families, the increasing phenomenon of youth having babies, the need for accurate and responsible sex education, and the lack of parental attention to their children's education.

. In late 1994, Beverley LaHay, president and founder of Concerned Women for America (CWA), sent out a fund-raising letter accusing the Gay and Lesbian Victory Fund (which is a political action group that raises money for gay candidates and those who support gay issues in government) of being a "militant homosexual group demanding special rights."

The Victory Fund was inundated with messages from some of the 600,000 members of CWA. Here's a sample of what could (barely) be reprinted:

- "Dear Faggots and Faggees—I am eagerly watching for the resumption of gay-bashing as a national pastime."
- "I have one wish as a mother, to stop and kill your organization."
- "You may argue that homosexuality is natural in the animal world, but drinking out of the toilet is natural in the animal world as well."

What is particularly disturbing about interpersonal homophobia, whether it is attributable to experiential or symbolic attitudes, is that—like most other forms of prejudice—it is continually propagated upon a minority. People are not automatically suspect, guilty, evil, sick, immoral, or inferior just because there are fewer of them.

Interpersonal Homophobia in the Workplace

Gay people, those thought to be gay, or people of any sexual orientation who are or are thought to be HIV-positive or AIDS-affected are victimized in the workplace with disturbing regularity. The harassment they endure (or don't endure) runs the gamut from mental cruelty to out-and-out violence. It is not unusual for these people to receive hateful electronic mail or telephone messages. It is not unusual for gay people to read hate-filled graffiti in washrooms, or to have such messages deface their offices, cars, or other possessions. It is not unusual for gay employees to be shunned by their coworkers, or to be quietly but continually verbally harassed.

During the Congressional hearings in 1994 to discuss the implementation of the Federal Employee Non-Discrimination Act, many gay people gave testimony about the harassment they've suffered on the job. One postal worker from Detroit described his experience of being nonviolently harassed for close to a year until he was one day beaten half to death by a co-worker, whose assault of him went unpunished. This occurred in a city that has a nondiscrimination ordinance to protect people on the basis of their orientation.

A young man named Ron Woods of Chrysler Corporation saw his career there go from one of outstanding reviews and promotions to degradation and fear literally from one day to another when his co-workers learned he was gay. He was forced to push a heavy cart filled with his tools from one end of the giant Chrysler plant to another. Each day, his work location was changed to be as far away as possible from the place he had worked the day before. This harassment was condoned by his management. Co-workers physically attacked him on three occasions, shoved fingers in his face, threatened to beat him up more, plastered his workspace with obscene graffiti targeting him by name, and went so far as to sabotage his work. Woods was forced to relocate within Chrysler literally to save his life, while those who harassed him continued to work unimpeded and unreprimanded.

Institutional Homophobia

There are many ways in which government, business, churches, and other institutions of society discriminate against people because of their sexual orientation. This phenomenon is known as *institutional homophobia*. The organizations and institutions set policies, allocate resources, and maintain both written and unwritten standards for their members. In terms of the workplace, not specifically listing sexual orientation in a nondiscrimination policy is homophobic. Not giving equal access to benefits and resources of the organization to (same-sex) domestic partners is homophobic. Not using inclusive language such as *partner* or including the unmarried significant (same-sex) others in invitations to corporate events is homophobic. Insisting that perceived cost increases, administrative complications, or outsiders (like insurance companies or governments) are blocking the implementation of domestic partner benefits when in fact they are not is homophobic.

Cultural Homophobia

Heterosexism is another term for *cultural homophobia*, a largely unstated but prevalent belief that everyone is straight or ought to be. This standard is reinforced in almost every TV show or print advertisement, where virtually every character is straight and every sexual relationship involves a man and a woman. In the workplace, heterosexism is at the root of many of the molehills that become mountains in the minds of people who think that progressive policies toward their gay employees will be detrimental to the organization.

History proves that no system of government or commerce—from slavery in ancient Egypt to slavery in nineteenth-century North America—survives if it is based on the misguided belief that one group is superior to another. It cannot because people who are discriminated against are unable to give their tasks their full effort and concentration. Nor are they able to reap the full benefits of their labor. And no group of people will put up with these inabilities indefinitely, especially when it becomes clear to them that they can initiate change. For gay people, this is becoming clearer every day.

Orientation Does Not Equal Behavior

"Coming out," or making one's sexual orientation known, is discussed in detail in Chapter 4, but it bears mention here when discussing heterosexism in the workplace. In almost all our Common Ground education sessions about sexual orientation in the workplace, someone will ask us, "Since sexual behavior has, or should have, nothing to do with work, why do gays have to come out?" This is a heterosexist question that deserves a straight (pun intended) answer. Sexual behavior does not and should not have anything to do with work. Sexual orientation, however, is not sexual behavior. Orientation is who a person is, not what a person does.

Heterosexuality is constantly on display in the workplace from straight people chatting about their vacations with lovers or spouses and families, to the pictures of spouses or opposite-sex partners on their desks, to the freedom straight people feel to bring their spouses or dates to a company function, to the wearing of wedding rings, to the display of baby pictures, to explanations about why a rough divorce is making it hard to concentrate at the office.

When straight people do any of these things, no one accuses them of flaunting their sexuality or making an issue of their sexual behavior. Heterosexuality is the standard, so people are free to be heterosexual. Heterosexism manifests itself in the homophobic belief that all gay people are about is their sex lives. If being straight is much more than sexual behavior, why is being gay not accepted as much more than sexual behavior?

These Conditions Are Expensive

Homophobia and heterosexism in the workplace are destructive because, among other things, they cause conflict and they cost dearly. Work is a social activity as well as a serious task because it is performed by people, and people are social animals. Business relationships are the product of personal relationships, and personal relationships are the by-product of trust and camaraderie.

If homophobia and heterosexist attitudes within a workplace make gay employees feel unable to be honest and open with co-workers about themselves or their lives, it will have a negative impact on those employees' ability to function as members of the team. They will simply not be trusted. This lack of trust will affect the productivity and profitability of the work group and eventually the entire organization. Homophobia also contributes to such workplace problems as substance abuse, harassment, absenteeism, and turnover. These things cost money.

Facing Up to the Facts

Ask any human resources professional dealing with workplace diversity today what is the most difficult classification of people to include in company programs and policies, and you will be told that it is the gay employee population. In 1995 the desire of gays to be wholly recognized and included in workplace policies puts them in direct conflict with some of their fellow employees. These areas of conflict are usually centered around three things:

Ask any human resources professional dealing with workplace diversity today what is the most difficult classification of people to include in company programs and policies, and you will be told that it is the gay employee population. In 1995 the desire of gays to be wholly recognized and included in workplace policies put them in direct conflict with some of their fellow employees. These areas of conflict are usually centered around three things: anger, fear, and religion.

anger, fear, and religion. For some people, one or all of these factors make it impossible for them to extend the benefits of honest labor to gays.

Dealing With Anger

Anger is a common reaction to gay people, to gays "coming out" and making their needs known in the same manner that all minorities eventually do. A failure to understand the exact nature of both homophobia and heterosexism is a big part of this anger. Another part is less acknowledged: discomfort.

The two things workplace diversity programs leave out for as long as possible are issues of sexual orientation and of physical disability. These are two very different things, both neglected for the same reason. People get angry when confronted with things that have the potential to make them feel uncomfortable. If we are confronted with a person in a wheelchair, we might feel compassion for her but we also feel uncomfortable around her. We don't know what to say to her, we don't know whether we should plainly acknowledge her disability or pretend to ignore it, we don't know whether we can ignore it, we don't know whether we're staring...we are uncomfortable. It is easier for some people to get angry and strike out at those things that make them uncomfortable than to confront their own limitations and figure out why they are uncomfortable.

Dealing With Fear

Another common reaction to gay people is fear. People like absolutes, they don't like ambiguity, and they fear things they don't understand. That's why coming out is the best weapon against homophobia and discrimination. When a vehemently homophobic person finds out that a family member whom he loves or a friend or acquaintance whom he respects happens to be gay, homophobia almost always disappears along with the debilitating fear of the unknown. "Individuals," someone once said, "are the enemy of stereotypes."

Dealing With Religion

Last, and most difficult, is religion. People hold tight to their religious convictions with the same fervor as they hold tight to the people they love. It is our opinion that people's religious convictions are to be respected, even when those religious convictions are at someone else's expense, as long as no discrimination, violence, or harassment are the result of those beliefs. Kim

Cromwell, senior consultant of diversity and change for Bank of Boston, explains it this way:

> If a group forms to discuss their religious convictions at work, that's okay. But if they form to oppress the beliefs of another group, then that is not appropriate in the workplace. We can't mandate acceptance, but we can have expectations about behavior at work because we have a responsibility as an employer to create an atmosphere where everyone feels safe.

There are no simple answers to discrimination based on religious dogma, or values, or standards of morality; these are very personal things. In discussing them, in dealing with them, the employer walks a fine line. The only way to make sure that balance is not lost is to remember that the focus must be solidly fixed on behavior and not on beliefs.

Where beliefs are concerned, however, we offer these opinions. First, it is religion and not sexual orientation that is a matter of choice. People can choose to adopt a religion, change their denomination or affiliation, or reject religion altogether. And they can change their minds about religion as often as they like.

Employers must find the courage to overcome the difficulties inherent in the issue of sexual orientation for two reasons. First, sexual orientation is of itself morally neutral. Second, the inequitable treatment of gay people in the workplace and the danger of sabotaging the efforts of the organization because of benign or blatant discrimination demand action.

Replacing Myth With Fact

It is our experience that most of the difficulties inherent in introducing sexual orientation issues into workplace settings are because of misconceptions held by heterosexual people about those with a nonheterosexual orientation. These misconceptions are directly attributable to myths about gays that cause some to form opinions that can lead to discrimination against gay people.

Because so many gay people continue to hide who they really are, many of these myths are attributable to other people's lack of honest exposure to gay human beings—exposure that all by itself would go a long way in breaking the cycle of bias.

Myth: Being gay is a choice.

Fact: Being gay is not a choice any more than being straight is a choice. Being gay is the same as being left-handed versus right-handed or being blue-eyed versus brown-eyed. There is no choice involved in any of these things.

For reasons of genetics—and, if you wish, because our Creator deemed that some individuals will have differing inherent characteristics, including sexual orientation—some people are simply gay, some straight, and some bisexual.

According to Chandler Burr's book on biology and homosexuality, all evidence to date strongly implicates genetics and biology as the basis for all sexual orientation. Burr's finding are based in part on work done by Bailey and Pillard, who have done studies on homosexual twins and siblings. Research continually indicates that sexual orientation is a matter of genetics.[6]

A person's sexual orientation determines to whom that person will be erotically and emotionally attracted. Homosexual women are attracted to women; bisexual women are attracted to both women and men. Homosexual women are not attracted to *all* other women, just as heterosexual women are not attracted to *all* men.

Whether people *behave* in concert with their sexual orientation is a completely different issue, and one not limited strictly to gays. Straight people make that decision too, as do bisexual or asexual individuals.

Heterosexuality is the standard for human sexual behavior only because, without a doubt, there are more heterosexually oriented people. Being the standard does not, however, make heterosexuality either morally superior or more right than other sexual orientations. It just means that the majority voted itself the standard, as majorities are wont to do.

Myth: I don't work in fashion, entertainment, or the arts, so I don't work with any gays.

Fact: More homosexuals work in science and engineering than in social services. Forty percent more are employed in finance and insurance than in entertainment and the arts. Ten times as many work in computers as in fashion.[7]

There are no "gay jobs." Some people theorize that gay people were and are drawn to certain professions, like acting for gay men or athletics for gay women. We believe that such ideas do not stand up to scrutiny, especially today.

The thinking is, or at least was, that gays would migrate to such professions or areas where gender boundaries were more easily crossed. However, sexual orientation and gender identity or gender role have nothing to do with each other. Sexual orientation does not affect a person's interests, capabilities, strengths, or talents any more than any other inherent characteristic of that person might. What you are good at, what you like to do, what you are interested in intellectually are products of many things of which sexual orientation may be but one. Gay people do not choose their professions based on their sexual orientation any more than straight people do.

Myth: Gays don't want to mix with other people.

Fact: Gay people are human, and humans are social animals. All people, as individuals, have their own style. Some are very social and prefer to work in groups; other prefer to work alone. Whether a person is gay or straight has nothing to do with how she or he prefers to socialize.

It is obviously easier for a gay person to socialize in a safe environment than in one that is or can turn hostile. For example, imagine that every Monday morning at a given place of work, there is a group that drifts over to the coffee machine to catch up with one another and discuss how they spent their weekend. Nancy is talking about her date with John, Kenny is telling about his shopping expedition with his wife for baby furniture, and Halette just got back from a vacation with her husband, Andy.

Lauri, a gay woman who is not openly out at work about her sexual orientation, is walking to the coffee machine and hears the conversation unfolding. Her company has no nondiscrimination protection for gays, and she lives in a state that similarly has no civil or legal protection for gay people. She has heard her boss repeat a homophobic joke now and again, and she occasionally hears homophobic comments from others too.

Lauri just had a great weekend with her partner, Kathy, celebrating their fifth anniversary. Walking to get her coffee, she must decide whether to continue on to the machine and join the conversation or turn away and wait for everyone to disperse. Or she could go for her coffee and either pointedly not get involved in the conversation, or get involved while completely suppressing her weekend, her partner—in short, her life.

Lauri doesn't want to lie or ignore her co-workers, so she chooses to return to her desk and get coffee later. Had the environment been a safe one, Lauri could have felt more comfortable approaching her co-workers and participating in the conversation to whatever extent she deemed appropriate. As it is, her co-workers regard her as antisocial and not a team player. Teamwork and productivity are absolutely—and unnecessarily—negatively affected.

Whether or not a person wants to mix with other people is a matter of individuality and personality. Sexual orientation plays a role, usually a destructive one, in cases when gay people feel completely unsafe in bringing their whole selves to work.

Myth: The gay lifestyle is immoral because it is forbidden by the Bible.

Fact: This myth must be broken down into its three parts in order to be addressed correctly. First, there is no such thing as a "gay lifestyle." Sexual orientation is not indicative of a lifestyle, nor does it indicate a "sexual preference." A lifestyle is an indication perhaps of how much money a person has and how he or she chooses to spend it. A preference is a statement of liking one thing more than another. A lifestyle is determined by choice, by effort, and by circumstance. A preference is determined by experience and by choice. Sexual orientation is inherent; it is not chosen, it is not the result of effort, and it is not determined by circumstance.

Next, morality is not determined by religion, nor is it legislated by government. Morality is a matter of individual conscience. We each decide for ourselves what is moral.

Last, the Bible is a collection of stories and essays written by men (and only by men) influenced by their culture and individual interpretations of things in their time, which was a very long time ago. The Bible has been interpreted by people the world over who also bring their own experiences, thoughts, beliefs, biases, and prejudices to the exercise. This is unlikely to change. In short, there is no one official interpretation or any absolutes concerning the Bible as it relates to homosexuality or to anything else. Following are some of the interpretations that run contrary to the myth that the Bible says homosexuality is immoral.[8]

Certain Biblical citations are bound to come up when discussing homosexuality and religion. Three of them, I Kings 14:24, I Kings 22:46, and II Kings 23:7, forbid not homosexuality, but prostitution by men or by women. Two citations, Leviticus 18:22 and Deuteronomy 23:17, do not refer to homosexuality either. Rather, they speak of "kedesh" or "cult prostitutes," who were seen as unclean and were forbidden in purity codes. These same purity codes also outlaw such things as the consumption of pork, shellfish, or rabbit; hybridization as in clothing of more than one fabric; and the cutting of one's beard or hair. These are some of the laws that instruct Jews on how to "keep kosher."

There is no mention of homosexuality in any of the four Gospels of the New Testament, and Jesus himself never spoke of the subject, at least not to anyone who wrote it down. In the references continually cited from St. Paul (Romans 1:26–2:1, I Corinthians 6:9–11, and I Timothy 1:10), Paul was concerned with human sexuality only insofar as a "secular sensuality" conflicted with his Judaic-Christian spirituality. It was lust that Paul objected to, limiting himself to neither homosexual nor heterosexual lust or sensuality. To Paul, any individual interest placed ahead of God was condemned.

Further interpretation of Romans 1:27–29 also suggests, according to Dr. Ide in *Zoar and Her Sisters: The Bible, Homosexuality and Christ*, that St. Paul also strenuously objected to heterosexuals who engaged in homosexuality as a perversion, defined as a conscious choice to act with disregard for their true heterosexual nature. Paul did not, according to Ide, object to homosexuality resulting as a process of *inversion*, defined as innate, biological composition.

Are any of these interpretations fact? Yes and no. Each person's interpretation is fact as he or she sees it. That is the beauty of religion, of law, of philosophy, and of all rational thought. The same Bible some use to bash gay people is used by other people to honor gay people. The same Bible used by some to justify segregation of black and white was held up by Dr. Martin Luther King to integrate us all. The same principles used by some to keep gays closeted for fear of God are used by others to encourage gay people to accept their nature and responsibility in Christ and to demand that their fellow Christians do so as well.

As for religions other than Catholicism, which by their very existence represent other interpretations of the Bible, there are more positions to consider. Orthodox Jews consider homosexuality an abomination (the act, not the people) and encourage homosexuals not to indulge in this behavior. However, Reform Jews have special outreach programs for gays and have also accepted gay women and men publicly into rabbinical associations. In the middle are Conservative Jews, who accept gays into their congregation but will not allow them to be rabbis.[9]

In the Episcopal Church, at conventions held in 1994, the Dioceses of Washington, D.C., and Newark, New Jersey, reaffirmed their support of the rights of gays both within the church and in society. Similarly, in a recent issue of *The Lutheran*, the Evangelical Lutheran Church of America addressed homosexuality within a broader discussion of human sexuality.[10] It said in part that "...in recent times, many Christians have questioned the churches' traditional teachings about homosexuality. These people argue that gay men and women are by nature attracted to persons of the same gender.... The issues at stake are important, complex and deeply emotional.... This Church commits itself to continuing deliberation in the face of this dilemma."

Amen to that.

Myth: Gays are economically and educationally elite and therefore don't need or deserve special treatment.

Fact: When Joseph Brodiss of the Catholic League for Religion and Civil Rights attempted to make this particular argument in front of the Senate subcommittee that was evaluating the Employment Non-Discrimination Act, Senator Paul Wellstone replied:

> As a Jew, I have a real problem with what you say. That's precisely the argument made in Germany in the 1930s. Gays, you say, are not a group of people that need special protection because they do well economically. They are an elite. That is precisely the argument made on behalf of the worst kind of discrimination mankind has ever seen. What is the difference, sir?[11]

Assuming for the moment that issues of elitism do make a difference, then it's worth offering more than indignation as a response. The important principle for business is, "It's not what you earn, it's what you keep." Today, there are fewer children in gay households and both partners tend to work. Therefore, advertisers can and do project greater disposable income in gay families.

However, in 1994 an independent study released by the University of Maryland at College Park found that the gay population is as economically and socially diverse as any other group of people. Sexual orientation does not equal higher income, more education, or any other class-related characteristic. The study reported an average annual income of $26,321 for gay men and $15,056 for gay women, concluding that they earn 11 percent to 27 percent less than straight men and 5 percent to 14 percent less than straight women, respectively.

Also in 1994, Yankelovich Partners, Inc., in Connecticut asked more than 2,000 people whether they were gay. Seven percent indicated that they were. The average annual household income for gay men was $37,400, compared to $39,300 for their heterosexual counterparts. The average for gay women was $34,800, compared to $34,400 for straight women.

Until 1994, the only demographic data about gays came from gay marketing firms or gay publications whose results were skewed by the higher-than-average education level common to those who subscribe to national publications (true for both heterosexual and homosexual people). But the University of Maryland study and the Yankelovich surveys managed to get beyond this very particular subset of gay people and reflect reality as experienced by the silent gay majority. A gay sexual orientation does not make you smart or rich any more than skin color, eye color, or handedness.

Myth: All gays have AIDS, and if we let them work here, we'll get AIDS too.

Fact: The majority of gay women and men neither have AIDS nor are HIV-positive. Although once in the highest risk group for AIDS, gay men no longer claim that dubious distinction. As of February 1995, AIDS is responsible for more deaths among people ages 25 to 44, regardless of sexual orientation. Furthermore, heterosexual transmission of the disease is now more likely than homosexual transmission in many parts of the United States, with straight women, all minorities, and young adults at the highest risk.

The other essential fact to remember is that AIDS can be transmitted only in certain very specific ways, none of which are likely to occur in most work environments. (For more about HIV and AIDS in the workplace, see Chapter 7.)

Myth: Gays are more comfortable in the closet, and it's better for everyone if they hide.

Fact: A closet is a small, dark space where things are stored and the door is usually closed to keep them out of sight. The closet may be big enough to keep everything out of absolutely everyone's sight at all times, or it may be just big enough to keep some things from some people. Some people have different closets to hide different things from different people under various circumstances. It can be quite a handful to manage.

Are gays happier in the closet? Ask these questions of yourself instead. Would you be happy always having to monitor your actions to make sure that you aren't revealing your sexual orientation in any way? Would you like to hide important events and feelings in your life from family, friends, and co-workers? Would you like to agonize over whether the truth revealed would cost you the embrace of your family, the welcome of some of your friends, the ability to succeed at work, or maybe your very life? Do you think you would be happy having to mentally censor everything you say to everyone you know? Would you enjoy constantly rearranging your office, your house, your car, your room, your bookshelves to hide any evidence of your true self, depending on who was coming over or needed a ride?

Gays are not happier in the closet, and that's why more are finding the courage to come out. It's not better for anyone if gays continue to hide. Hiding costs too much. It costs people their sense of self, their self-respect, and their self-esteem. It forces them to lead a double life, to pretend that the things that motivate them to succeed—their partners, their families, their interests—don't exist.

As mentioned earlier, it's not good for the organization for gays to continue to hide either. Hiding takes energy away from the task at hand. Hiding builds invisible walls between co-workers that are detrimental to teamwork, productivity, and profitability. Hiding creates barriers between people who don't understand—aren't given a chance to understand—where another person is coming from. This affects relationships not only between peers, but between management and employees.

Hiding is not good for anyone. The organization may not be able to mandate that all employees be honest about who they are, but it can work to create an environment where it is safe to come out, to be honest, if individuals choose to. And as more organizations become safe, more people will come out until, we believe, by the year 2005, people will be scratching their heads trying to figure out what all the ruckus was about.

Myth: Gays should not work with children under any circumstances.

Fact: There is absolutely no evidence to suggest that gay people should

> Hiding is not good for anyone. The organization may not be able to mandate that all employees be honest about who they are, but it can work to create an environment where it is safe to come out, to be honest, if individuals choose to. And as more organizations become safe, more people will come out until, we believe, by the year 2005, people will be scratching their heads trying to figure out what all the ruckus was about.

not work with children. Homosexuals do not want to recruit children into the "gay lifestyle," and they do not have a secret wish to molest children, any more than most heterosexuals do. In fact, more than 90 percent of sexual abuse and molestation perpetrated against children by adults is by heterosexual adults—usually members of their own families.

Women, especially gay women, almost never sexually molest children.[12] Data also suggest that many men who victimize young boys do not self-identify as gay. In fact, many adult male abusers of boys are married with long heterosexual histories.[13] People's fear of gay people working with children is the result of tabloid sensationalism.

Myth: Gays are not subject to harassment at work and have the same opportunities for advancement as heterosexuals.

Fact: Seventy percent of all Americans don't know that discrimination and harassment of gays is perfectly legal in most of America. Gays can lose their jobs, their homes, their kids, and in some cases their lives on the basis of their sexual orientation, with little or no recourse available to them. There are no federal protections for gay citizens, provided either by the U.S. Constitution or by acts of Congress. As of the end of 1994, just under three-quarters of the *Fortune* 1,000 admitted to having nondiscrimination inclusive of sexual orientation, but only one-third or so of them have put it in writing.

A safe work environment for gays is one that is free of heterosexist, homophobic, and AIDS-phobic behaviors. Such behavior is unfortunately open to a great deal of interpretation. For example, someone telling a homophobic joke in the presence of a gay co-worker might be considered verbal harassment by some but completely ignored by others. Other types of acts, such as removing notices about a group meeting of gay employees, do not directly harass an individual but are discriminatory toward an entire employee group, closeted or not.

In many surveys conducted since 1990, an average of 30 percent of all gay men and 25 percent of all gay women reported that they had experienced employment discrimination at some point in their careers.[14] Threatening phone calls, email messages, and graffiti directed at gay or AIDS-afflicted employees are not uncommon.

As for whether gays have the same opportunities for advancement as straights, most don't think so. The majority of gay women and men who remain closeted at work do so because they are afraid that honesty about their sexual orientation will result in loss of a promotion or other damage to their professional careers. It is extremely difficult to look at any major corporation or high-visibility organization and spot openly gay senior people. Closet doors are bolted very tight at the top in most environments today.

Myth: I can always tell whether a person's gay.

Fact: There are no distinguishing characteristics of gay people that set them apart physically, emotionally, intellectually, or spiritually from straight people. There is no skin color, no hairstyle, no eye color, no fashion, no mannerism or anything else that identifies a person as gay or straight. You cannot tell whether people are gay just by looking at them. The only way to know for sure is if a person tells you her or his sexual orientation.

Similarly, you cannot accurately judge people's potential behavior or abilities by their sexual orientation. To whom a person is erotically attracted also has nothing to do with that person's ability to teach, to police, to be a soldier, to govern, to mop up, to dance, to construct, to play football, or to do anything else.

When we judge someone on the basis of our perception of the presumed characteristics or qualities of a group to which we believe he or she belongs, we are using a shortcut called stereotyping.[15] Stereotyping is not, in and of itself, a bad thing. It permits us to assimilate new information more easily by maintaining a common framework. Stereotyping becomes problematic when we indulge in inaccurate, rigid stereotyping: making false assumptions about others based on incorrect premises, and not revising our assumptions as new evidence comes to light.

There are many stereotypes about gays. Most are negative and are just plain wrong. These negative presumptions are what cause most closeted gays to stay closeted. Most gay people don't fit the stereotypes about them at all, but they continue to hide because they are afraid that if they come out, they will be associated with those stereotypes anyway. The irony is that when gay people do come out, they blow away the stereotypes.

Myth: If a gay person comes out to me and I don't approve, I have to pretend that I do.

Fact: If a person tells you that he is gay, you should respond honestly. If that means that you don't approve, you should feel free to tell him so. If you are able to be supportive of him, you should tell him that. If it is homosexual *behavior* that is problematic for you, you should have no qualms about expressing that opinion in an appropriate way. A great deal of progress can be made if people pay more attention to the fact that although they may have a problem with homosexual behavior, in much the same way that they have a problem with violent behavior, it is the behavior they object to, not the person.

So if you wish to express disapproval of homosexual behavior, it is well within your rights to do so. But you should endeavor to remember that this opinion does not mitigate your responsibility to allow others to be who they are, free from discrimination and irrational hatred, based on an inherent characteristic such as sexual orientation.

Myth: Employing gays or being supportive of gay rights is bad for business.

Fact: There is no evidence to support the notion that public support of gay employees will result in financial loss for the company. There *is* significant evidence to suggest that such support is to the advantage of the organization on many levels: potential gain of market share, greater employee and customer loyalty, increased competitive advantage for skilled labor, increased capacity to take advantage of the strengths of a more diverse workforce, and greater opportunities for teamwork and productivity.

When Lotus Development became the first private-sector company to offer full employee benefits to the unmarried gay partners of its employees, customer reaction to Lotus's action ran 3:1 in favor. In fact, none of the organizations that have since implemented these benefits have suffered a loss of either customers or employees. This myth is covered in detail in Chapter 1. In fact, correcting this misconception is probably the entire point of Chapter 1.

Myth: All homophobic people are straight.

Fact: This is not true. As noted earlier in this chapter, there are homosexuals who suffer a condition known as internalized homophobia, in which they have taken to heart all the myths and stereotypes about gays. Internalized homophobia can cause, and does cause, a minority of gays to be among the most virulent and outspoken opponents of equal opportunity and protection for gay people. These people always rant from the closet.

As more homosexuals make themselves known to their friends and families in the course of everyday life, the myths are destroyed. The myths just can't stand up to reality, and the continued bigotry and hatred are less and less tolerable by people who open themselves up to the facts.

Notes

1. Warren J. Blumenfeld, *Homophobia: How We All Pay the Price* (Boston: Beacon Press, 1992).
2. Cooper Thompson, "A Guide to Leading Introductory Workshops on Homophobia" (Chicago: Campaign to End Homophobia, 1990).
3. Nat Hentoff, "A Case of Loathing," *Playboy,* September 1992.
4. United States Department of Agriculture, "Sexual Orientation: An Issue of Workforce Diversity," a report by the Ad Hoc Committee of the Regional Civil Rights Committee prepared for the Regional Forester (Washington, D.C., September 1992).
5. Hentoff.
6. Eric Marcus, *Is It a Choice: Answers to 300 Most Frequently Asked Questions About Gays and Lesbians* (New York, HarperCollins, 1993).
7. "Gay in Corporate America," *Fortune* (December 1991).
8. Marcus.
9. Ibid.
10. Kim Byham, "Episcopal Dioceses Back Gay Rights," *The Lesbian and Gay Press* (February 7, 1994).
11. Senator Paul Wellman, from "Employment Non-Discrimination Act Hearing," July 29, 1994. Taped in Congress and distributed by the Human Rights Campaign Fund.
12. Warren Blumenfeld, "Speaking Out: A Manual for Speaking on Gay, Lesbian and Bisexual Issues" (Boston Speaker's Bureau, 1993).
13. P. Gebhard, *Sex Offenders: An Analysis of Types* (New York: Harper & Row, 1985).
14. James D. Woods, *The Corporate Closet: The Professional Lives of Gay Men in America* (New York: Free Press, 1993).
15. Stephen P. Robbins, *Organizational Behavior* (Englewood Cliffs, N.J.: Prentice-Hall, 1989).

3

The Choice Is Yours: Strategies for an Inclusive Workplace

The organization can do many things, big and small, cheap or expensive, to secure and maintain the best effort of its employees. In return for these gestures, programs, and policies, the employer has the right to expect dedication, loyalty, self-motivation, and cooperation from all employees at all times. From a gay employee's perspective, the trade is a simple one. Gays want the same as is expected by and granted to heterosexual employees: a safe working environment, equitable benefits, and appropriate public support.

- *A safe work environment* for gay people is demonstrated and encouraged by two things: (1) a nondiscrimination policy that expressly includes sexual orientation and (2) diversity education that includes a comprehensive module on sexual orientation.
- *Equitable benefits* means providing to the partners of gay employees the same benefits, including health coverage, that are accorded the families of other employees.
- *Organizational support* signals that the organization is committed to all of its employees with no exceptions. This support, which can take the form of many programs and initiatives, both internal and external, does not mean that the organization endorses behavior or beliefs, but that it acknowledges the right of all employees to be whoever they are and believe whatever they believe.

To put these basic tenets into concrete reality, the organization has four tools at its disposal:

1. Nondiscrimination policies expressly inclusive of sexual orientation.
2. Education programs and informational resources about sexual orientation.
3. Equitable benefits, compensation, and human resources policies.
4. Programs to protect the health of all employees.

What the Organization Can Do

Here's a look at how a company can approach each of these four areas.

Nondiscrimination Policies

According to the Human Rights Campaign Fund in 1994, 76 percent of Americans support equal employment rights for gay people; 70 percent don't realize that anti-gay job discrimination is still widespread *and predominantly legal*. It's very simple. Since the majority of gay Americans (and gay people the world over) live and work without any form of federal or state protection, it is incumbent upon all employers to send a clear message that harassment and discrimination on the basis of sexual orientation will not be tolerated.

An important first step toward equity in the workplace is a nondiscrimination policy that specifically includes sexual orientation—going on record with the clearest language possible that discrimination will not be tolerated. Without such a policy, gay people have no legal protection against job-related bias. Not having this kind of guarantee makes most gay, lesbian, and bisexual people very nervous and extraordinarily cautious, and this anxiety has enormous impact on productivity.

And the discrimination is real. Since 1980, about two dozen studies have documented hiring, promotion, and compensation practices that discriminate against lesbian and gay workers. In a typical survey conducted in Philadelphia in 1992, 30 percent of gay men and 24 percent of lesbians reported that they had experienced employment discrimination at some point in their careers. Twenty-one percent of both sexes reported that the discrimination had occurred after 1990.[1]

Most companies probably would deny that they have a problem. According to a 1993 survey by the Society for Human Resource Management, 63 percent of respondents said that they have policies that prohibit discrimination based on sexual orientation. But of that number, only 38 percent have it in writing. It is not enough for spokespeople to simply say that the company doesn't discriminate against gays. It has to be spelled out for everyone to see. It sends the message to gay employees that the company cares about them specifically. It also makes the policy clear to any other employee who might have doubts about where the company is coming from. It states clearly for all to see that this is who we are and this is what we believe in.

Further, it's important to use the right words: "sexual orientation," not "sexual preference" and not "lifestyle." A person's orientation has nothing to do with either preferences or lifestyle. Both the words *preference* and *lifestyle* suggest a choice is being made; people do not choose their orientation. This error must be continually corrected because as long as people believe that gays choose to be different and want special treatment because of that choice, homophobia and heterosexism will not be defeated in the workplace and in society.

All Business All the Time?

Many organizations have nondiscrimination policies and yet still find it difficult to adhere to them where sexual orientation is concerned. This is because the organization is no more and no less than a collection of individuals. If each individual does not endorse the content and the spirit of a nondiscrimination policy, then the organization will never, as a whole, be able to adhere to it.

"I'm not denying the importance of the policies for nondiscrimination (inclusive of orientation)," explained Liz Parrish of Intel. "It's a statement of value. But what I've seen is that it's given little more than lip service. It's getting people to act accordingly that's the hard part. Sexual orientation concerns continually come in at number eleven on a list of ten things to consider."

When an enterprise refuses to stand behind its nondiscrimination policies with real actions such as inclusive education, endorsement and support of employee groups (if other types of groups are so endorsed), domestic partner benefits of some sort, or public support of laws like ENDA, it is counting on an unspoken rule of the workplace to mysteriously take effect. This rule is that all the employees will put business before everything and act as though their own opinions, ideals, and beliefs are checked at the door in consideration of the common good. However, such a reaction is rarely if ever the case, especially when the issue at hand is as potentially volatile as sexual orientation.

"We don't separate business from emotion, nobody really does. People are their emotions and their thoughts, feelings, behaviors, and attitudes, and I don't think anybody separates them," said Novell's Sigetich. "None of that gets checked at the door, but there's a time and a place for everything, including emotions, in the workplace. For instance, there are times when it's effective, appropriate and even influential to get angry, and times when it's best to keep anger in check. We each make judgments about how our emotions and opinions will manifest themselves at work, but we can't pretend we don't bring them with us."

Each employee's individuality is an important cog in the organizational wheel. The point is that individuality must be respected if the organization is to succeed. Therefore the organization must be willing in some instances to go an extra mile, spend an extra dollar, and stick its neck out an extra inch to affect positive changes in the behavior of some individuals toward others.

"You have to look at productivity and motivation," explained Robin Schwartz of Banyan Systems. "If you have a workplace team in which two of the people conflict because one is homophobic and the other one is openly and comfortably gay, your challenge is not to change either of their minds. Your challenge is not getting the homophobic person to embrace homosexuality or getting the gay person to accept homophobia. You're faced with a business problem. You would not sit either one down and say, 'You have to learn to like this in him'; you'd say, 'You have to be able to work with him. You don't have to like him, and you don't even have to tolerate him. You just have to do whatever it will take to be able to work with him.' That's the difference between what's appropriate at work and what you might strive for in another part of your life. And maybe a company's policy of education to support its nondiscrimination policy is no more than a mechanism to help its employees reach that behavioral plateau. If so, that's fine."

How does the company reach the point where it can put its muscle behind its nondiscrimination policy inclusive of orientation? By gaining an understanding of the entire issue followed by unrelenting action in support of its understanding.

Education Programs

It is shortsighted of any organization to assume that the concerns of its gay employees do not significantly impact heterosexuals, and vice versa. The truth is that people, regardless of their orientation, have questions about a number of topics that are very new to them—questions perhaps that were never even asked out loud in that particular organization until very recently.

As the 1990s progress, the workplace is becoming the new frontier in the battle for gay rights and equal treatment. This is a fact that has serious repercussions for your business. The best way for the organization to prepare itself and all its employees for the changes it and they will undergo is education. Chapter 5 provides a comprehensive description of effective sexual orientation education for the workplace.

Equitable Benefits

Suppose you have gay employee Suzanne who is in a long-term committed relationship with Jenny. Suzanne shares an office with Kristine who is legally married to Ken. Jenny is a freelance computer engineer with her own business; Ken is a freelance writer. Kristine gets full medical, dental, pension, relocation, company facility use, and other benefits for both herself and Ken. Suzanne gets nothing for Jenny.

Suzanne and Kristine do the same job for the same group at the same pay scale with the same educational background and the same positive history of performance reviews. However, Kristine is being compensated up to 40 percent more than Suzanne (the estimated dollar value of workplace benefits). Suzanne knows this, and she is not happy about it. It distracts her, it makes her angry, and she is actively looking for a company that will treat her and her partner the same as it treats employees' legal spouses. It is becoming easier to find such a company. Between 1990 and 1995 the number of businesses, universities, and municipalities that have chosen to offer domestic partner benefits inclusive of medical benefits has increased from under five to more than two hundred and seventy.[2] And the number that offer employee benefits exclusive of medical coverage is more than that. In 1993, a study by the National Gay/Lesbian Task Force found that even though 70 percent of the Fortune 1000 claim not to discriminate on the basis of sexual orientation, just over 5 percent have domestic partner benefits. These numbers must be brought into better balance.

Our own consulting firm, Common Ground, is often told by companies that they are not able to implement partner benefits because they are just beginning to look at other types of benefits like flexible benefits plans, or tuition reimbursement, or 401(k) plans. These excuses beg the question. If a company is in the process of revamping, expanding, or overhauling its employee benefits programs, then including partner benefits in the mix takes up little in the way of intellectual or monetary bandwidth.

By government estimates, it will cost Suzanne's company five times as much to replace her with another person who could function at a similarly tenured level as it would to implement benefits for her partner. Neither productivity nor profitability are served by denying domestic partner benefits. In fact, both are adversely affected by pushing them aside.

Domestic partner benefits are obviously important to the labor force and are crucial to the concept of equal pay for equal work. As time goes on, more organizations are going to be faced with requests from their gay employees to implement benefits that are completely equal to those granted heterosexual employees and their families. The questions that these requests will raise cover the entire spectrum from the philosophical to the concrete. Chapter 6 provides the answers to all of these questions—and many others—along with strategies and details for implementation.

HIV/AIDS and Sexually Transmitted Diseases Education

There are dozens of reasons why HIV/AIDS and sexually transmitted diseases (STDs) education is appropriate for today's workplace, but two stand out.

First, the misconception that AIDS is a "gay disease" can cause and does cause the sometimes violent harassment of openly gay employees or those who are suspected of being gay. Second, continued ignorance about HIV, AIDS, and other STDs will cause more people—primarily heterosexual people who think they are immune— to contract one or more of them.

In Chapter 7, the relevant parts of HIV/AIDS, and STD education for the workplace are described and explained.

Getting It Done: The Critical Role of the Human Resources Department

It is our opinion that most leaders of most organizations disapprove of discrimination against their gay employees. We also believe that most professionals in the area of human resources/training and development emphatically do not support discrimination against their gay co-workers but that many are hesitant to take a leadership position in *proactively* ensuring that such discrimination does not occur. It is the role of the human resources function, and the HR manager in particular, to take such a proactive stance, especially if the company specifically and expressly disallows discrimination based on sexual orientation. Human resources professionals must stop waiting for problems to occur; they must work to forestall them before they do.

This means fostering active support from senior managers and from departmental managers and supervisors, building coalitions inside and outside the organization, and actively using the many specific tools at the HR department's disposal:

- Communication programs, resource rooms or referrals, and other miscellaneous programs.
- Education programs.
- Mentoring strategies.
- Coming-out coaches.
- Formal and informal management and employee networks and groups.
- Coalitions with community groups and local school systems.

- Equitable benefits implementation and support of federal nondiscrimination.
- Union strategies (to be recognized where appropriate).

But before anything else, it means coming to terms with their own souls and rising above their own biases. Straight or gay, human resources managers must find the courage and personal integrity to lend their support to gay issues and concerns in the same manner they do all others.

Straight human resources personnel owe it to their constituencies to fight their way through any homophobic fears that displaying gay supportive literature in their offices or championing gay concerns will cause others to think that they are gay themselves. And gay human resources personnel owe it to their constituencies and to themselves to be honest about who they are and where they are coming from. They don't have to come out, but they are not entitled to use fear as an excuse to disregard the concerns of others who are out or who are also closeted. There are strategies available that fall well short of avoidance (see Chapter 9). Considering the needs and rights of all employees is the job. Human resources and T&D personnel—straight or gay— who cannot do that for everyone are in the wrong line of work.

Get Management on Board

Laying the groundwork for more progressive policies can be an intimidating prospect for organizations who fear negative consequences. Internally the company, principally through the advocacy of the HR staff, must first solidify management support for these policies. There can be no cracks in the armor. When new programs that any number of employees might find hard to accept are introduced, a unified message of support from senior management or administration that winds its way down through all management levels is absolutely mandatory.

In order for this solid support to gel, senior management must itself be made completely aware of and familiar with the issue. HR personnel have a significant role to play here. Some, for instance, develop a white paper with which senior managers can educate themselves.

For their part, managers and supervisors can support the process by going the extra mile, by availing themselves of education about sexual orientation through the organization's programs, or by attending outside conferences and symposiums. Many professional organizations and universities offer programs that are open to the public.

Managers can lead by example, demonstrating by their daily actions that they will not tolerate discrimination of any kind in their work groups at any time or place. This includes knowing and understanding organizational policies relative to sexual orientation, upholding company behavior standards without exception, and encouraging those within their sphere of influence to take advantage of the resources the organization makes available about these issues.

Senior management in particular should set an example. At Bank of Boston, members of the chairman's office meet regularly with the gay employee group's steering committee and with members of the group individually if necessary. "There is definitely a high level of sophistication here in terms of management's willingness to ask questions and explore gay issues in the workplace in a very open fashion," said Kim Cromwell, consultant to Bank of Boston's HR department. "Senior management is raising questions because there is an acknowledged connection between the welfare of the Bank and its responsibility to its gay members, both employees and customers. The Bank, personified by the chairman's office, is making every attempt to understand all the issues so that it can operate in everyone's best interest."

Most important, each individual in management, regardless of level, can acknowledge and completely accept the fact that, regardless of his or her personal viewpoints, beliefs, or convictions, professionalism demands that the manager put aside individual prejudices to ensure an equitable, fair, and safe working environment for all. It's behavior, not beliefs, that are at issue in the workplace.

Build Coalitions

The HR staff must make sure that all company personnel are engaged in dialogue through informal meetings, education, publicizing new policies via bulletin boards (electronic and otherwise) and in the company newsletter (if one exists). Constant communication of the motivation and intent of new policies and programs is mandatory to winning support for them across the board. Employees tend to take a cynical first view of any new corporate programs. They may think that inclusion of gay issues is a management fad or trend driven by the six o'clock news and not by any real conviction or business purpose. In these cases, selling the program or policy might be best achieved not by launching a program at all, but rather by selling the message, intent, and motivation behind it.[3]

Those who want to see more progressive policies enacted should build coalitions and bridges to other interests within the organization. The message that must be constantly reinforced is that discrimination against even one employee is bad for the entire organization.

Human resources management can also act as a conduit to the community in which the enterprise operates. Whether following existing policies or creating new ones, human resources should make every effort to publicly assert the organization's position, and invite any and all interested and like-minded groups in the community to do likewise. Coalitions can be built with local town government, civic groups, and ad hoc networks of employee groups throughout the region. In fact, several gay employee groups have themselves built coalitions such as Out at Work (or Not) in the Chicago area, or AGOG (A Group of Groups) in northern California, or the Workplace Alliance in Minneapolis. Employers that do not sanction their own employee groups can provide a form of support and relief to gay employees by adding the organization to these groups' mailing lists and keeping its population aware of events and services sponsored by these coalitions.

In its own community, the human resources department can lead the charge for philanthropic efforts or participation in events such as encouraging local multicultural awareness celebrations that include gay issues and by lending public support for Gay Pride Month (June) or National Coming-Out Day (which occurs in October).

At the top of the list, corporate HR can make the effort to build supportive and interactive relationships with local school systems and institutions of higher education to promote learning and fact-dissemination about orientation in order to stop the cycle of homophobia. Corporations can encourage and reward their gay employees to take time to speak at local school events or mentor gay undergraduate and graduate students with an interest in their profession.

Human Resources Programs

So far we have discussed the role of the HR department in somewhat general terms. There are specific programs, services, and forms of assistance that the human resources staff should implement.

Employee Communications

The human resources function must take care that all communications emanating from it to all employees stress diversity by way of both their content and choice of words. Organizations go to great lengths to use the correct words when referring to gender, race, ethnicity, and religion. Sexual orientation is no different. The word "spouse," for example, is still intrinsically tied to the concept of legal marriage. Since legal marriage is not (as this book is being written) an option for gays, the word "partner" is more inclusive and appropriate.

Beyond semantics, all communications from human resources should demonstrate that HR is aware that it represents and works for a diverse community. We recognize that nothing and no one can be all things to all people, and we urge human resources people to maintain a sense of humor in the face of the many objections and demands for "political correctness" that they will be subject to. In terms of communications, HR should simply give thought to all the possible constituencies within its workforce, create a masthead that includes them all, and monitor the workplace for any possible changes.

Resource Rooms or Referral Services

Human resources managers and all managers and supervisors, regardless of their own sexual orientations, can take the lead in outward demonstrations of support by making available a resource room or system of referral for anyone who has legitimate questions and concerns about these issues.

Resource room and referral services should be set up in such a way so that either can be accessed anonymously if an individual desires. Information about how to access these services could be posted on bulletins (electronic and otherwise), in company newsletters, on a human resources hot line, or by confidential appointment with appropriate HR personnel.

Such resources may be limited to existing Employee Assistance Plans (EAPs), or could also include listings of literature available regarding homosexuality, references to supportive clergy, statistical information about homosexuality including legal considerations, and names and phone numbers of national and local groups that offer support or information mechanisms. The organization can also use a consultant as an information resource. Consultants can provide a single information source, or can refer employees to groups, counselors, schools, and other organizations that have specific expertise in the employee's area of interest or concern.

Supplementary Programs

Managers might want to consider spearheading some of the following:

- A hot line to report all forms of harassment and discrimination including (but not necessarily limited to) sexual orientation.
- A system of accountability for a nonhostile work environment by division, work group, geographic location, facility, etc.
- Expansion of existing reward/award programs to include recognition of superior efforts to engender a safer, better working environment for all—with a specific emphasis on progress made in a unit toward sexual orientation.
- Encouragement toward gay workers to bring their partners to appropriate enterprisewide events, or to display (appropriately) items from

their personal lives in the same manner as their straight co-workers do.

- Incorporation in external communications about the company of information relative to policy on sexual orientation, the programs and resources the company offers to gay employees, and a statement of support for gay rights.

Education

It is impossible to overemphasize the importance of education programs focused on sexual orientation issues in the workplace. Once a program is in place, all management should be encouraged to attend and should be further encouraged to make the program widely available to their personnel. Please see Chapter 5 for a complete discussion of workplace education in the area of sexual orientation.

Mentoring

Over the last decade, mentoring has established itself as an effective and respected mechanism to leverage the strengths of individuals in the workplace. But within the last two or three years, mentoring has taken on a new meaning. Not only is it used to help people get a step *up* in the organization, it is being used to help people get a step *inside* the organization.

The concept of mentoring is very simple. A person who is already established, usually in a high management position, takes a specific individual (perhaps more than one) under his or her wing and personally monitors and contributes to that individual's advancement. When applied to diversity, however, mentoring takes on additional meaning.

Instead of one-to-one mentoring, organizations are exploring a system of *corporate mentoring* in which team-to-team replaces one-to-one guidance. The idea behind corporate mentoring is that it brings qualified individuals, regardless of race, gender, or orientation, into the executive level by extending the concept to whole groups instead of just individuals. This is a merit system rather than a predictive one. In a predictive mentoring system (one-to-one) certain assumptions are made about the person's ability. In corporate mentoring, there are no subjective predictions; there is only performance. And the responsibility for bringing people along is not left to one person with one set of standards or viewpoints, but rather is shared by a team of managers bringing to the table diverse standards and viewpoints.

We advocate this approach, and we advocate that human resources make sure that there is gay representation on both sides of the corporate mentoring model. If a gay mentor is not readily available (for whatever reason), then look outside your organization for a qualified civic leader, consultant, or professor to participate in the program. If gay protégés are also not readily in evidence, publicize the intent and desire for gay representation. We believe at least one person will make him or herself known to you, even if that person chooses to remain closeted at the start.

If the mentoring process is successful, then the closeted protégé will potentially be so empowered by the experience and by the willingness of the "out executive" to help him incorporate and succeed that he will become a walking advertisement for the program.

Coming-Out Coaches

While this term may be new and very much to the point when considering sexual orientation in the workplace, the concept behind it has been with us in an underground fashion for a few years. Human resources management could play a huge role in bringing it to light.

Coming-out coaches are people who have themselves come out at work, worked through various levels of difficulty engendered by their honesty, and now feel comfortable enough and ready to help others who are struggling with the same decisions.

These people are not advocates of coming out in terms of trying to talk people into it, nor are they qualified psychological counselors. They are just regular people who lend support simply by their willingness to attest to the fact that "I did it, and you can do it, too."

Recently the U.S. Department of Agriculture has lobbied for this strategy within its own operation. A specific recommendation made in their Ad-Hoc Committee report on Sexual Orientation in the Workplace called for "identifying individuals willing to be self-disclosed as contacts or mentors to gays unable or unwilling to risk disclosure, and to be available to the management team on sexual orientation issues including presentations to forest family meetings, new employee training, supervisor training, etc."

Human resources managers can help promote such an informal network in their own workplace, and help it grow by making it available to neighboring enterprises. Instigation takes the form of a bulletin or other announcement to the general employee population. It states that the organization would like to make coming-out coaches available to employees in need of someone other than management or licensed clinical counselors to talk to concerning their status as a gay person in that workplace. Armed with a list of people who are out and willing to share their experiences, HR can simply put two people together when one reaches out for help.

Coaching-type efforts are already part of the reason for (gay) employee groups to exist, and so help from human resources would reinforce in everyone's mind the fact that the organization is determined to do whatever it can to help all people feel safe and valued in the workplace.

Championing Employee Groups and Networks

Employee groups of any kind allow people with similar interests or characteristics to interact with others who are like them. In the case of a gay employee, the existence of such groups helps the individual simply feel that he or she is not alone. Feeling like "the only one" is a depressing condition common to many gays. HR managers can help gay employees start a support group (see accompanying box); more importantly, they can provide crucial organizational support.

Tips for Starting a Gay Employee Group

- Knowing what the organization will and will not allow is important. By all means, research the organization's position on gay issues and on employee groups in general. Your proposal for formation of a group should be in line with what's generally accepted at your workplace.

- Most potential members will hear about your group via word of mouth. To expand outreach, put notices in company newsletters, on bulletin boards (if allowed), and in publications of the local gay community. Use a post office box or phone number connected to an answering machine for RSVP purposes.

- Be sure to respect your participants' differing levels of comfort with having their orientation and/or membership known. And remember that not all your members will be gay; straight allies are an important constituency.

- Networking with other groups in your industry and in your community is a good idea, as are reach-out efforts to other employee groups at your organization.

- Frame your discussion in terms of total quality management, maximum productivity, respect for the individual, best effort, and so on. Look for and actively solicit senior management support of the group.

[Adapted from "A Guide to Starting an Employee Group" produced by Out at Work (or Not), Chicago.]

Human resources practitioners should champion gay employee groups or informal networks for several reasons. One is that formation of such a group gives an effective and responsible voice to the concerns of the gay employee population. If HR staff members don't know what to do to help their gay employees feel safer and able to be more productive, maybe it's because no gay person knows how to reach out and tell them, and they don't know how to ask. An employee group can be an extremely effective communication tool.

A second benefit of these groups reaches beyond the gay workers. Gay rights groups can lead to more productive dialogues about this difficult issue, and can help create a sense of community for potentially alienated workers. This strategy does not apply only to gays in the workplace; there are many straight people who have gay friends and family members they feel protective of or in conflict about. Their feelings can just as easily negatively impact their job performance.

Finally, employee groups provide a mechanism for management to stay in touch with the concerns of its gay employee population. Employee groups are (or can be) so important and effective for parties on both sides of the issue that a case study is devoted to them in Chapter 9.

It is necessary for the human resources department to provide the impetus for a gay employee group because even in those places where such groups are supported and sanctioned, the number of people willing to have their names openly associated with the group and the number who are actually active members or who monitor and occasionally participate in the group's activities are usually very different.

"I'd say we have several times as many people who are affiliated with our group in a shadowy sort of way than those who are openly members," maintained Intel's Liz Parrish, a founding member of their employee group. "We have gotten mention through the company newsletter in terms of articles written about us or letters sent in. But that's the same for everybody. In terms of electronic bulletin boards, they are run by administrators who use them for a variety of things, some of which are postings for other employee groups. But we have not been allowed access to this mechanism."

A company's human resources staff members can take it upon themselves to make sure the playing field is level in terms of corporate sponsorship and resource access. They can also help form an employee group safely in those places where the employees would like to reach out to each other and management but are afraid to. This is done using an intermediary.

We suggest that human resources management publicize a meeting time and place in which all people who would like to investigate forming or becoming a member of a gay employee group are invited. In order to protect confidentiality and each person's right to free and open expression, management should communicate that the meeting will be chaired by an outside party who carries the full authority to reprimand any people who show up for less than honorable purposes. In other words, people might not be afraid to gay bash if they think no one from management will be there to chastise and punish them. They will likely stay away if they know that the gathering has the full endorsement and support of management for the purposes of providing a support mechanism and communications conduit for its gay employees at which no disruption will be tolerated or go unpunished.

At the meeting, the intermediary simply records what transpires. He or she then brings the suggestions and concerns of the group back to management, who responds back to the group through the third party. This process continues until an employee group forms that is able and willing to discuss these matters without an outside intermediary; the intermediary is usually replaced by an internal employee who eventually steps forward voluntarily.

In other words, with a little creativity, it is possible to help people find each other and find an effective voice that will ultimately benefit the organization as a whole.

In those cases where confidentiality is a major concern or employee groups are not sanctioned as a rule, human resources can lobby for use of the organization's electronic bulletin boards and email to create a communicative support center for closeted and out gay employees at all levels. If that is not practical, a suggestion box will work in which the suggestions are made public by way of a newsletter or printed bulletin.

Lobbying for Equitable Benefits and Federal Nondiscrimination

This one is simple. If the organization has a policy of nondiscrimination that applies to sexual orientation and covers matters of employee benefits or compensation, then it is the responsibility and the duty of human resources management to lobby for these benefits for its gay employees. Likewise, if the company supports its gay employees, it can effectively demonstrate its commitment by insisting that the federal government make workplace nondiscrimination mandatory. Companies that have endorsed ENDA include Harley Davidson, Xerox, AT&T, Nabisco, Bethlehem Steel, and Merrill Lynch.

Union Strategies

Negotiating as part of a union or with a union can be different than dealing with a management-to-employee structure. For one thing, a lot less can simply be mandated by management; almost everything is negotiated.

If you are an officer or member of a union with direct responsibility or input into the human resources-type negotiations with management, there are some strategies that you too can keep in mind.

"When a union puts something on the table as part of negotiation, it first has to organize its own members around the idea that the issue at hand is one that the union should put on the table and fight for," explained Harneen Chernow of Boston SEIU Local 285. "For instance, when I was at Boston University and we were fighting for the inclusion of sexual orientation protection in our contract's nondiscrimination clause, a group of lesbian/gay union members first did a major campaign directed at our co-workers in the union to educate them about how this was a workers' rights issue and a civil rights issue. We wanted our co-workers, gay and straight, to take on this issue and fight for it in the same way they would any other benefit or change."

According to Chernow, there are a lot of strategies that unionized workers have developed for organizing their co-workers to support gay issues in the workplace. Union strategies for garnering support include forming gay caucuses, scheduling public forums for discussion and debate, developing steward-education programs so that each shop has a visible information resource, and taking advantage of the built-in networking capabilities inherent in some of the national unions.

"The fact that the AFL/CIO signed off on the provisions of ENDA is very significant for all union members," Chernow asserted. "There may be problems with ENDA, but it's a beginning and having labor's support is a big plus."

Finally, unions are primed to be an enormous growth arena for enlightenment and progress in the area of gay issues. Although some of the more industrial unions such as the UAW are admittedly more conservative, other unions are much more progressive, especially those in the public and service sector industries.

Union growth is taking place in the same workplace sectors where employment growth is occurring—for example, in the health care, information management, and municipal management industries. These are among the younger, more progressive industries, which are likely to support gay concerns.

"The two unions in this country that have probably done the most for their gay membership are the Services Employees International Union and the American Federation of State, County, and Municipal Employees," Chernow concluded. "These represent service and public sector workers, and these are two of the fastest-growing segments of our economy."

The Choice Is Yours: The Time Is Now

More evidence is available to suggest that the time is right (not easy, just right) for corporate support of gay issues. In November 1994, the independent firm

As more gay people come out, as more people acknowledge the gay people already in their lives and the new ones they meet, and as more enterprises take supportive positions, the wall of discrimination will crumble and eventually fall. When that time comes, organizations acting with trepidation now will be reassured that they did the right thing.

of Mellman Lazarus Lake, Inc., surveyed a random sample of 800 people who voted in midterm elections. Seventy percent of those surveyed said that gay people should not face unfair job discrimination of any kind, and 57 percent indicated support for the Employment Non-Discrimination Act.

As time goes on, companies can feel more comfortable making publicly positive statements concerning their support for equitable treatment of gays in the workplace because society is starting to come around. As more gay people come out, as more people acknowledge the gay people already in their lives and the new gay acquaintances they make, and as more enterprises take supportive positions, the wall of discrimination will crumble and eventually fall. When that time comes, organizations that now act with trepidation will be reassured that they did the right thing.

Starting today, you and your organization have an enormous opportunity to turn all of the challenges inherent in sexual orientation issues at work into win/win situations for everyone. Organizations are well advised to get ahead of the changes already in the works as they concern gay people. Employers can accentuate the positive by proactively disarming existing and potential conflicts through workplace education, where myth will be dispelled by fact. Employers can also exercise their enormous potential for positive influence on the behavior of the organization's members by working to understand and then communicate how acknowledgment of a person's sexual orientation can and does affect performance.

When the organization recognizes the validity of a person's values and understands that his or her attitudes are the result of those values, that organization can work to make sure that those values and attitudes are supported by the rest of the enterprise. As a result, everyone understands where everyone else is coming from, and more importantly, why the other person is coming from that place. This kind of understanding is crucial to fostering the kinds of workplace relationships that are the basis of teamwork and productivity.

While the organization is working through this process, as more and more people are exposed to the policies and programs that define the process, it will reap benefits in terms of greater productivity that is the direct result of almost universal increased job satisfaction. Granted there will be pockets of virulent resistance to change, and some people might leave. But those who stay will exhibit a higher degree of job involvement and organization commitment with less absenteeism and turnover.

No one said it would be easy, but we have no qualms in saying that it will be worthwhile.

Notes

1. James D. Woods, *The Corporate Closet: The Professional Lives of Gay Men in America* (New York: The Free Press, 1993).
2. Susan Spielman and Liz Winfeld, "Ins and Outs of Domestic Partner Benefits," educational seminar, 1994.
3. Kenneth Haseley, "Raising Awareness Precedes Changing Attitudes," *Public Relations Journal* (September 10, 1994).

4

Hiding and Coming Out: Personal and Workplace Productivity Issues

People do not work at their best if they work in fear. But prevalent homophobia and heterosexism in the workplace make it true that as of this writing, fear forces many homosexuals to hide their sexual orientation and stay in the closet. *All* the closeted employees we've interacted with admitted worrying daily about being found out, to the extent that it affects their performance every day. This is not good for the individual or for the organization.

According to a 1992 survey in *OutLook* magazine, 62 percent of gay women and men said that their orientation was always or often a source of stress on the job, and 27 percent said it influenced their choice of organization to work for.[1] According to a 1993 survey, 47 percent of gay men in professional settings try to avoid any mention of their personal lives at work, and 17 percent actively try to hide their sexual orientation. This hiding takes energy and time—energy and time that should be spent on the task at hand.

A principal goal of any organization should be to create a culture in which each employee has the opportunity to make a full contribution and to advance on the basis of performance. Hiding forces gay employees to lead a double life, to pretend that the things that motivate them to succeed on the job—their partner, their family, their home, their interests—don't exist. Organizations that continue to exclude segments of their workforce risk sending the message that some people are less valued, less important, and less welcome. These exclusionary practices are going to cost them dearly in the marketplace.

What If Gays Could Not Hide?

Consider this for a moment: What would everyone do if gays couldn't hide? Women and racial minorities, who are also historic victims of workplace discrimination, did not have the luxury of hiding even if they wanted to. If gays couldn't hide just as blacks and women could not hide, then all the questions surrounding them would come to a head that much faster.

If gays couldn't hide, companies could not pretend that they don't exist, as in the case of a world-renowned food manufacturer that employs over 40,000 people. When confronted by a gay woman on the upper management staff with demands for domestic partner benefits, a member of senior management responded that the company couldn't justify the benefits because she was the only gay person who worked there. We seriously doubt that the person who made this claim believed it himself. But the fact that gays can hide, and do hide, gave him license to not only say it, but to act in a discriminatory fashion accordingly.

Novell's director of employee group development, Andrea Sigetich, put it this way:

> If gay people could not hide, I think the issue would be much less of the hotbed of emotional controversy it is today. I think more homophobic people would find that gay people are just like straight people. Acceptance would not come overnight; it would be a process of acceptance like that experienced by women and other minorities. But it would happen. I think it would help things along if more gay people would come out.

Why More Gays Are Coming Out of the Closet

Being in the closet means censoring thoughts, words, and actions relative to one's sexual orientation for different audiences. A gay man may be in the closet to his family, but not to his co-workers—or to some of them. Perhaps a gay woman's brother knows the truth of her sexual orientation, but another brother, two sisters, her parents, and all the aunts, uncles, and cousins, save one that lives in Alaska, don't know. It can all be quite a handful to manage, and it should come as no surprise that more people are coming out. Michelangelo Signorile wrote:

> Most straight people don't understand the closet because they've never been in it. Because heterosexuality is the order of things,

"Most straight people don't understand the closet because they've never been in it. Because heterosexuality is the order of things, they say that gays who come out go too far, making an issue of their sexuality. And because straights have never experienced the closet, they think that coming out is the hardest thing. What they don't understand is that the real pain is in being *in the closet*, not coming out of it."

they say that gays who come out go too far, making an issue of their sexuality. And because straights have never experienced the closet, they think that coming out is the hardest thing. What they don't understand is that the real pain is in being *in the closet*, not coming out of it.[2]

As Jonathan Rauch wrote in *The Wall Street Journal*, "any [workplace or governmental] policy insisting that homosexuals lead secret lives is futile, inhumane, and unrealistic. Because fewer homosexuals are willing to hide, the old deal—gays pretending to be straight and straights pretending to believe them—is off."

The composition of the U.S. Congress and the 1994 elections notwithstanding, more and more gays are refusing to hide because hiding costs too much. It costs people their sense of self, their self-respect, their self-esteem. There are extremely courageous gay people who are literally putting their lives on the line in assembly plants in Detroit, in waste-removal plants in Mississippi, on workplace petitions in Iowa, by demanding equitable benefits in North Carolina, and by testifying for federal nondiscrimination protection in Washington, D.C. These people are risking their lives to save their lives, and more gays are joining them every day.

It's undeniably easier to be gay and out on either coast of the United States and in certain pockets of the Midwest, but that is starting to change. When looking for a job, more young people are asking themselves, "Will the new work environment be supportive of me as a member of a sexual minority?" Most universities have nondiscrimination policies inclusive of orientation, and many have domestic partner benefits. Today, more graduating students than ever are out of the closet, and they are not going back in. If they feel that a certain employer will force them back into the closet through subtle but exclusionary practices, they will likely go somewhere else to work.[3] The competition for skilled labor is much too intense for an organization to think it can make employees continue to play this game of hide-and-seek.

What Can Organizations Do?

An organization cannot and should not mandate that gay employees come out; that is a choice for each person to make. Rather, the organization can take the time to understand (1) what it means for a person to come out and (2) the process by which the organization itself comes out. In this section, we introduce a model that explains both individual and organizational coming out. We then discuss our model in light of the Riddle Scale, which is a sociological spectrum of possible feelings about and reactions to gay people. Armed with these insights, you can choose the strategies for promoting cooperation that are appropriate for your environment.

There are several models, developed primarily by psychologists and sociologists, that do an excellent job of generalizing a process that is very personal. Coming out, or being honest about anything in our lives, is an exceedingly private decision, and every person who's done it or who is contemplating it approaches the challenges in his or her own way. No one's way is more right than anyone else's way.

What these psychological and sociological models are good for is giving language to the process so that people can manipulate it as they see fit. For instance, gay people who are considering coming out can realize that what they are feeling is not isolated to them. Many have gone before; many will come after. And perhaps straight people can use the information to better understand how a gay colleague or family member is feeling and why.

Of the models we've read, we identify most with Vivienne Cass's "Homosexuality Identity Formation: A Theoretical Model," originally published in 1979 and explained by Brian McNaught in his book.[4] But we part company with them in the matter of scope: They limit the discussion to the process that the individual goes through; we believe there is also a process of *organizational* coming out that the enterprise goes through as it comes to terms with sexual orientation as a valid aspect of diversity.

The organization comes to accept that its gay employees who are able to be open enhance the productivity and profitability of the organization. And because the organization is nothing more than a collection of individuals, the process of the organization catching on to this concept is really no more than each individual within the organization accepting it and passing it along, sort of like a human domino theory. When the organization comes out, it becomes a more fulfilling environment for everyone concerned.

The Riddle Scale

The process of coming out that we describe here, both for individuals and organizations, borrows terms and ideas from the Riddle Scale of Homophobia.[5]

Psychologist Dorothy Riddle developed this scale in 1987, describing four negative and four positive levels of attitudes toward differentness in general and gays in particular. Notice that she lists both tolerance and acceptance on the negative side of the spectrum.

Negative Responses

- *Repulsion.* Gay men and lesbians are sick, crazy, immoral, and sinful, which justifies changing or eliminating them.
- *Pity.* Gay men and lesbians are somehow born that way and should be pitied. The goal is to help these poor people be as "normal" as possible.
- *Tolerance.* Homosexuality is just a phase of development that many people go through and most people grow out of. Thus, gays must be protected and tolerated like children.
- *Acceptance.* Heterosexuals need to make accommodations for gay and lesbian sexual identity. This attitude *does not acknowledge that anothers' identity is of the same value and importance as one's own.* An example is, "I don't even think of you as a gay person; you're just a person."

Positive Responses

- *Support.* Gay men and lesbians deserve legal and civil rights. Regardless of one's own comfort with homosexuality, people should treat others fairly.
- *Admiration.* Being gay or lesbian in this society takes strength. Openness to examining one's own homophobic attitudes.
- *Appreciation.* Diversity in people is a good thing, and gay men and lesbians are part of that diversity. Willingness to confront homophobia in oneself and others.
- *Nurturance.* Gay men and lesbians are indispensable in our society. Views them with genuine affection and delight. Acts as an advocate for gay men and lesbians.

Individual Coming Out

An individual who decides to come out may go through a series of phases, as follows, although this is not always the case.

Phase 1: Comparison

In the comparison phase, the person compares things she sees, hears, feels, and knows about herself with input concerning homosexuality and begins to make connections. The more this personalization of homosexuality happens, the more likely she is to begin to reassess her own sexuality. This period of reassessment is necessary because most people make the mistake early in their lives of believing that everyone is just like everyone else—which is, of course, nonsense. This nonsense becomes dangerous, however, when some begin to believe that certain people are better than others.

The comparison phase is a deeply introspective part of a person's life. During it, self-alienation can quickly become social alienation as the person first struggles to come to grips with what he is feeling and learning about himself and then tries to decide how he is going to deal with it in relation to everyone else in his life.

Some people never make it through either the self-alienation or the social alienation. It is not unusual for gays to try to devalue the reality about themselves and bury it in an attempt to be "normal," to live up to their family's expectations, to keep in line with their religious convictions, or for any number of self-deprecating reasons. Many gays get married and have children as a way to prove that they are just like everyone else. They can live their whole lives in this fashion but will always know that there is a part of themselves they are not acknowledging.

At work, people in the comparison phase who are trying to put it aside may be very resentful of those gay people who don't hide who they are, and they may be among the most vocal in their opposition to anything that tries to value homosexual relationships at the same level as heterosexual relationships. These people are undoubtedly under a lot of stress and can be among the most disruptive of employees.

Employers are well advised to understand that homophobia can come from homosexual and bisexual people as much as it can come from heterosexual people. Fostering an environment that encourages duplicity and secrecy is expensive. Hiding mechanisms that employees use include drugs and alcohol abuse, which require expensive treatment; absenteeism; tardiness;

conflict with others; and turnover. These things do nothing to enhance the bottom line.

Phase 2: Support

A successful transition out of phase 1 leads to a phase of support, which results from the migration from tolerance to acceptance to support. Tolerance and acceptance are not automatically good; tolerance or acceptance of something is just putting up with it. By implication, when you tolerate something, you would rather not have to deal with it. Worse, people do not make any effort to understand the things they tolerate, and they often accept things just because they are told to.

However, it's important for a gay person coming out to first be able to tolerate and then accept the fact that she is gay. Coming out is a process, and a refusal to at least tolerate a situation signals a refusal to enter into the process of resolving it one way or the other.

The point of the support phase is to move beyond tolerance and mere acceptance and ultimately become wholly supportive of one's sexuality. (A similar process occurs in becoming supportive of someone else's sexuality.) Once people are able to deal with sexual orientation as it really is, to go beyond the irrational fears and unsubstantiated myths, they can support whatever their own orientation happens to be. This is a crucial step in maintaining mental health and self-esteem. From here the person decides how he is going to make his place in the world.

Phase 3: Incorporation

In the last phase of individual coming out, mere support gives way to pride and a full-blown sense of incorporation in terms of understanding the ramifications of human sexuality and being able to make connections with the rest of the world because of it.

We use the word *incorporate* deliberately, to describe the process of bringing one set of characteristics in line with another. Many prefer the word *integrate*, meaning "to make into a whole by joining with something else."

Our difficulty with *integration* when applied to sexual orientation is the implication that people of other than heterosexual orientation must be in some way joined or related to heterosexuals in order to be whole. This is not the case at all. Both straights and gays are already whole and don't require the integration of another set of characteristics to make them so.

We believe that incorporation is a goal of coming out when it is defined as "the ability, fostered by understanding, to unite different characteristics." People who are united are better able to function together in the workplace or in any place. By coming out, gay people allow straight people to see, experience, and appreciate more of the characteristics they have in common and less of what differentiates them, which in truth isn't much at all.

People with a strong and positive sense of self are valuable employees. They are productive, forthright, clear-minded, and outspoken. It is at this point that others might accuse them of flaunting their sexuality, and the conflicts may begin in earnest. The employer must appreciate the journey that these people have made to get to the self-affirming place where they are. Such understanding will allow the enterprise to harness the individual's positive energy appropriately. Such understanding is the result of the organization coming out too.

Organizational Coming Out

Because organizations are simply a collection of individuals, organizational coming out is simply a process undergone, or not, by every individual who works there.

Phase 1: Acknowledgment

There are gay people in every kind of workplace. There are gay doctors, gay pilots, gay stockbrokers, gay lawyers, gay teachers, gay athletes, gay everybodies. In the acknowledgment phase, the organization states both verbally and in writing that it knows there are gay people in the world, as many as 10 percent of the world's population. In other words, it stops saying, "We don't have any issues of sexual orientation to deal with because there are no gays working here."

There are gay people in every kind of workplace. There are gay doctors, gay pilots, gay stockbrokers, gay lawyers, gay teachers, gay athletes, gay everybodies. In the acknowledgment phase, the organization states both verbally and in writing that it knows there are gay people in the world, as many as 10 percent of the world's population. In other words, it stops saying, "We don't have any issues of sexual orientation to deal with because there are no gays working here."

Organizational acknowledgment carries with it the same positive force as an individual's acknowledgment of his own orientation or of someone else's. It says, "I acknowledge your existence, and although I might not always agree with you or even like you, I will not pretend that I don't know you're here."

Phase 2: Accommodation

In the accommodation phase, the organization as a unit and all its individual cogs agree that specific provisions must be made to support their acknowledgment. So they will begin to do things like offering partner benefits to unmarried same-sex (and possibly opposite-sex) couples. They will use inclusive language in their communications, substituting the word *partner* for the word *spouse*. They will reprimand those who discriminate or harass their fellows, they will put gay members on appropriate task forces, and they will recognize gay employee groups (if other groups are so sanctioned). In short, they will back up their acknowledgment with concrete action whenever possible.

In this phase, the employer may have to be lobbied to be inclusive, but once asked, it will.

Phase 3: Incorporation

In the final phase of organizational coming out, the employer does not need to be asked anymore, and no one individual working there has to wonder at all what is expected of him as regards his behavior toward his gay co-workers.

Incorporation is the result of a completely internalized understanding of the fact that people are people with lots of differing characteristics, of which sexual orientation is but one. An incorporated organization, like an incorporated individual, is one that keeps its value judgments to an absolute minimum and strives to build in proactive correction systems for those times when negative judgments are made despite best efforts to avoid them.

Such organizations are marked by their progressive, proactive stances as reflected in everything they do. These organizations fully understand that an entity is only as healthy as each of its parts, and they will do everything they can to promote the well-being of every individual they take under their wing as an employee or customer.

Garrett Hicks of LEAGUE at the Walt Disney Company offered:

> Organizational coming out is sort of what parents may go through when one of their kids tells them that they are gay. In some ways, the hard part is over for the kid, and now the parent has to go through a process to be able to incorporate this information. In the

same way, I've noticed how Disney has slowly grappled with recognizing that they have gay men and women working here. Hopefully this company will get to the incorporation stage as Apple has done [see Chapter 1]. By refusing to back down in Texas, Apple demonstrated a real understanding not only of the needs of its gay employees, but of the need to live up to its stated principles. I hope Disney will get there too.

Coming Out Is a Process

Coming out is a process for both individuals and organizations, just as education is a process. A person's ability to come out is in direct correlation to her perception of her own level of competence and her perceived level of value and worth in the marketplace, and the same is true of a company. Coming out is bucking established trends no matter how you look at it. It's no accident that the majority of strategies offered to individuals and organizations that want to expedite their own coming-out process, or be supportive of such efforts in others, involve building coalitions and finding like-minded support mechanisms. This is not a risk-free proposition. As Kim Cromwell of Bank of Boston said:

> Coming out for the organization is a continuum, and we are all just learning what it looks like. There are stages for the corporation involving increased awareness of the issues, of its gay population and of its customer base, both gay and straight. We actively market to the gay community in Boston, and that represents yet another level of awareness for the Bank. By doing such advertising, we are sending messages not only to potential customers but also to potential employees.

The City of Miami is an excellent example of an entity's coming out in a positive way. An atmosphere of cooperation has allowed gays from the Northeast to be a creative force in the rejuvenation of a Miami Beach area that was once a crime-ridden sea of desolation populated with crack houses. Now it has a reputation for desirability.

Prior to renovation, the neighborhood at the southernmost tip of Miami known as South Beach was the run-down home of mostly elderly Jews and Cuban boat people. But that eclectic mix is held responsible for the vast improvement in the neighborhood. Basically, in a place where many people honestly considered themselves outsiders, it was not that hard to acknowledge, accommodate, and incorporate all differences—including, to a large extent, a gay population that migrated to the area searching for mere tolerance. Everybody in South Beach has gotten much more than that.

> If people did not believe in the boundless capacity for things to improve, for understanding to become more widespread, for positive change to occur eventually, and for people to be better tomorrow than they are today, no one would get up in the morning.

In 1992, the various groups in the area (including the Jews, Cubans and other Hispanics, gays, blacks, and whites), set about fixing it up, with the support and funding of the city's government. Three years later, South Beach is a model of incorporation where all feel safe, welcome, and valued. Property values are up 25 percent in three years, and Jews, gays, Hispanics, and all residents work together to keep both social and gentrification problems at bay.

The motto of the business guild in South Beach is "The Magic's in the Mix."

As we have said before, the decision to come out or not is intensely personal. It cannot be mandated; it can barely be easily suggested. However, homophobia would be greatly reduced if more people only knew how many of their friends, acquaintances, co-workers, and family members are gay. To the extent that every person in the world will be able to go through the entire process described here, there will be (1) no more closeted gay people, and (2) no more homophobia. These are lofty goals, to be sure, and difficult. But they are attainable. We are not naive, but if people did not believe in the indefatigable capacity for things to improve, for understanding to become more widespread, for positive change to occur eventually, and for people to be better tomorrow than they are today, no one would get up in the morning.

Notes

1. James D. Woods, *The Corporate Closet: The Professional Lives of Gay Men in America* (New York: The Free Press, 1993).
2. Michelangelo Signorile, *Queer in America: Sex, Media, and the Closets of Power* (New York: Random House, 1993).
3. John Kinyon, "Out on a Job Interview," *Gay Chicago Magazine*, May 12–22, 1994.
4. Brian McNaught, *Gay Issues in the Workplace* (New York: St. Martin's Press, 1993).
5. D. I. Riddle and B. Sang, "Psychotherapy With Lesbians," *Journal of Social Issues*, 34(3), 1978.

5

Designing and Delivering Sexual Orientation Education

Once an organization has decided to offer sexual orientation education, it is faced with another challenge just as difficult: designing and delivering the education program. This is new territory for most human resources and development professionals. Even as it becomes more familiar, it's sure to rank among the most controversial of programs for the foreseeable future. This chapter, in addition to addressing the issues surrounding such education in general, also provides a point-by-point description of effective education in this area.

Workplace Education in General

Corporate-sponsored education programs are rated higher for reliability than any other information source by adults. More than half of the adult employees surveyed would like more workplace education programs to deliver more information about what they consider to be difficult issues.[1] This statement might encourage organizations to rush right in and seize the educational day, but it is a double-edged sword. The same adults who say that they highly value information provided by their employer can also be quite critical about the intent and long-term effects of such education. Employees want more than just good information. They also want the spirit and the methodology to be beyond reproach.

Provide Education, Not Training

To plan for a program's intent and effectiveness, a company must first understand the difference between workplace education and workplace training. They are not the same, especially when the focus is sexual orientation. Education provides knowledge; training improves skills. Put another way, education provides information about the *what* or *why* of a topic; training deals with the *how*. When the objective is delivery of an effective program about a hypersensitive topic, understanding the difference between education and training (and making sure you are attempting one and not the other) is extremely important.

Applying strict training methodology to interpersonal relationships robs people of the quality that supposedly separates us from unsocialized animals in the first place: the ability to think for ourselves and determine our actions on the basis of our thoughts. Besides, changing minds about something as controversial as sexual orientation requires a herculean effort. By the time education has occurred, no one may have the strength left to do any training!

An effective workplace education program focused on sexual orientation attempts to educate people about concepts like the inherent nature of sexual orientation, the validity of same-sex based families, or the justifications for the equitable treatment of gays in the workplace and in all places. Acknowledging for the umpteenth time that it is workplace *behavior* and not *beliefs* that we want to influence, we insist that the only effective strategy is education. The best course is to educate, reinforce, and then hope that common sense and common decency kick in.

Banyan Systems Inc., a high-tech company in Westboro, Massachusetts, is exceedingly straightforward in its support of all employee diversities. Gay employees in particular benefit not only from Banyan's nondiscrimination policy, which expressly includes them, but also from Banyan's implementation of domestic partner benefits which are among the most comprehensive in the nation. At Banyan the emphasis is on helping employees understand that there are different types of people and that differences are good in the workplace. Having different styles is good, having different perspectives is good, having different types is good because each fosters different creative

---

Because it is workplace *behavior* and not *beliefs* that we want to influence, the only effective strategy is education. The best course is to educate, reinforce, and then hope that common sense and common decency kick in.

energies. Banyan does not key on training that deals with individual types; it keys on education to foster understanding so that people can more easily behave in ways that are beneficial to the company. Robin Schwartz, vice president of human resources, explained it this way:

> I personally believe that adults still learn, that education doesn't have to stop. I realize that what a person's been taught as a child affects how he or she behaves as an adult, but it isn't necessarily the last word. If a grossly homophobic person finds himself in a company like ours that is anything but, working here probably isn't going to swing him all the way to acceptance where gay people are concerned, but it will certainly point out, legitimize, and normalize that diversity for that person. When a person's company acknowledges something, it can have the effect of encouraging people to reevaluate where they stand. Maybe not, but it could. That's why, in my opinion, companies should do socially responsible things and tackle some of the tougher issues.

Effective workplace education that includes or focuses on sexual orientation is exactly the same process that children go through when they learn about the world and their behavior relative to it. Our parents (we hope!) expose us to different facets of life and different viewpoints, answer our questions, give us the tools for independent thought, and then hope for the best. This is decidedly different from a task-oriented lesson like toilet training. Toilet etiquette is an example where training could stand on its own merits. It is not mandatory for most that we understand the ins and outs of "human waste management" prior to or even after learning how to dispose of it properly. It's nice, it doesn't hurt, but it's not mandatory.

Perhaps the concept of acceptance is at the core here. Training is less about teaching people *why* they should do something and more about *how* they can do it. By implication, the ways in which we are trained to do things are likely to be what most consider socially acceptable for that activity. Education, on the other hand, is uncovering all the possibilities and letting each person decide how to act in relation to them. The hope is that people will behave appropriately from the employer's point of view.

Sexual Orientation Education Must Be Part of a Process

We started this chapter by saying that adults rate information they receive from the workplace as more reliable than from any other source. This is promising because employers therefore enjoy a potential to ensure that the time and money they spend on workplace education brings a positive return on investment; it is simultaneously dangerous because employers bear a responsibility to ensure that this does in fact occur. Chances are, an employer that tries to effect positive change in the workplace will get only one chance to do it effectively. First impressions are crucial.

When it comes to organizational programs or initiatives, employees take the cynical low road first. If employees believe that a program is the result of management bowing to some fad and that the initiatives are not completely supported by solid business reasons or personal conviction, the effort will fail. A strategy to overcome this is to consider not launching a program at all, but to sell a message that happens to have a program behind it. In other words, don't develop a finite initiative. Develop a process with never-ending possibilities.

Much has been written about the importance of workplace education as a process and not as an event. The logic behind this is that stimulating any significant changes over organizational landscapes takes time. In few other areas of diversity is this truer than diversity focused on sexual orientation. There are just more hurdles to jump where sex and sexual orientation are concerned. Clearing them requires that the following steps be taken and questions be answered.

Steps

Step 1:   Commitment to an open-ended, open-minded process of workplace education.

Step 2:   Utilization of a needs assessment tool to determine the tenor of the organization concerning gay people.

Step 3:   Implementation of an educational program that can fit the changeable requirements of an environment.

Step 4:   Constant follow-up and reinforcement of the diversity mission.

Questions

Question 1:   How does the organization ensure that the education won't do more harm than good?

Question 2:   Does the facilitator of sexual orientation education have to be gay?

Question 3:   Should sexual orientation education be mandatory?

The explanations of these steps, and the answers to these questions, form the building blocks for the point-by-point description of effective sexual orientation education in the workplace.

Step 1: Commitment

Commitment to an open-ended, open-minded process of workplace education is the first step. At Banyan, education is viewed as a mechanism to help people reach a behavioral plateau. The company is open to all different kinds of education that approach the issues from a variety of starting points. Banyan is expressing its educational philosophy in much the same way as it expresses its diversity philosophy: It takes all kinds to be successful.

Novell in Provo, Utah, is just beginning a full-fledged diversity management effort, starting by helping people explore their feelings and express themselves about identifiably different types of people. Sexual orientation as a differentiator is included but not weighted more or less than other kinds of diversity. Andrea Sigetich, Novell's director of employee group development, explained:

> In the video tool we're using, called *Diversity, A Winning Balance,* people are shown pictures of other people and are asked to note their impressions of them. Then all the subjects come back on the video and explain who they really are. This tool addresses all kinds of differences on a level playing field and allows the program's participants to explore their own feelings and possible misconceptions about people without it becoming overly emotional or making them feel defensive.

Novell's video tool is just a first step in what Sigetich believes will be a process of education at her corporation. Furthermore, she believes that education specific to sexual orientation and AIDS will be (and already is) necessary in her environment. Whatever mechanism Novell chooses, the organization is committed to an open-ended, open-minded process of education, having acknowledged that it is necessary for the continued welfare of any company.

Without this committed support from appropriate management, the process will not only fail, it will never get started. The experience of the diversity manager at a petroleum company who could speak to us only anonymously attests to this.

> I hope to address sexual orientation at work in 1995, but more organizations are still not willing to deal with this topic in public. Sexual orientation is that one piece of diversity that makes them say, "Well, I'm not going to discriminate against people because they are gay, but I'm not going to value the fact that they are gay either." We don't have a lot of latitude over what we do at our site.

I know we have gay people here who are suffering and that their suffering is having a negative impact on our bottom line, but when I told our headquarters group that we wanted to include gay issues, the response was extremely divided as to whether we could or should. All I know is, if I don't get support from our diversity management group, I won't be able to do anything.

Step 2: Assessment

Tweaking organizational thinking to accept education as part of a diversity process—and to include sexual orientation as part of that education—is most easily accomplished by doing a needs assessment. Some call it a cultural audit or cultural evaluation. Needs assessments have a solid-line relationship to a common management principle: No solution will be applied to any problem or potential problem until management is sure a problem exists.

In 1988 The Prudential noticed that many of its black employees were leaving the corporation. It directed a survey to that portion of its employee base and a large sampling of the rest of its personnel. Management discovered that a majority of respondents among blacks, women, Asians, and other minority groups felt that management was insensitive to diversity issues. The Prudential developed a process of diversity management, including education.

According to Charles Thomas, vice president of human resources, Prudential's diversity effort has gained status as a solid part of the corporate culture since its establishment in 1988. "People are no longer afraid to talk about differences or use the words *black* or *white* or *gay* or *lesbian* because management examined the core values of the company and installed a process to correct the deficient ones."[2]

Go back to the beginning of any honest diversity effort, and you'll find without exception that it started with an assessment of the environment. Whether the assessment is undertaken because human resources management takes the initiative, or whether it is an action forced on the organization by the activism of a group of employees (which is common in the case of sexual orientation), these assessments are vitally important to the development of a solid diversity effort. For gay people in the workplace, these assessments can be the first time management acknowledges their existence.

Gay people fall victim to many workplace catch-22s. One of them is that if they don't stand up, come out, and make their needs known, then those needs most likely won't be addressed. On the other hand, gay people's overall fear of being counted is the best indication that the organization has a problem in the first place. With so many gay people hiding at work, finding a large enough representative gay sampling can be difficult. We think that this difficulty is irrelevant and should not be an argument for not trying.

Our position is substantiated by three things. First, the point of collecting the information is to gauge the individual's impression of the environment relative to sexual orientation. A person's response is what matters. If a person has a pro-gay or anti-gay personal agenda, that will undoubtedly be reflected in his or her answers. The questions must direct themselves to finding the potential or real trouble spots about which the organization can do something.

Second, the intent of the assessment is to construct an educational program leading to rational thought and a possible change in behavior.

Last, the education itself should be part of a diversity management effort, not an initiative aimed at valuing diversity. They are not the same. Diversity management is intended to look at and improve corporate culture for the sake of the productivity and profitability of the entity. Valuing difference is directed at changing personal bias.[3] When it comes to sexual orientation education in the workplace, changing behavior is the key. If biases are changed, it's a bonus.

The questions that we use in our assessment tool help demonstrate to management that there are misconceptions about sexual orientation that have a detrimental effect on the business. Employees respond to such statements as:

- I have never been acquainted with a homosexual or bisexual person at work.
- If a person made his or her homosexual or bisexual orientation known to me, I would make every effort to disassociate from that individual at all times.
- Our customers will not do business with us if we have policies that are supportive of gays.
- Extending benefits to gays will bankrupt the company because of AIDS claims.
- Including sexual orientation in a company nondiscrimination policy gives special rights to gays.
- If a co-worker came out to me, I would not know what to do or say.
- I think that trust between co-workers is important.
- If someone came out to me, I would counsel that person to remain closeted in this environment.

The answers and comments collected from statements like these paint a detailed picture for management. From that, an educational strategy can be devised.

Step 3: Different Design Options

The ideal education program focused on sexual orientation is at least one day in length. However, we acknowledge that sexual orientation is a difficult topic to include in diversity education. Devoting an entire day and follow-up strategy to it is even more difficult. Therefore, a work-around strategy is a modular approach that allows an organization's human resources and development professionals to customize the content appropriately for their organization. A modular approach also makes it easy for internal staff to adapt the course content for particular management levels, constituencies, departments, or even geographical areas of their enterprise. When it comes to the current state of sexual orientation issues education in the United States in 1995, what is effective and appropriate in parts of the Northeast and West would be received very differently in the Midwest and the South. By the same token, what is appropriate for a management audience is not always the same message that the corporation wants to target to its manufacturing team. It's vitally important to the success of diversity education that development take such nuances into consideration.

Modular development and delivery also aid an organization's efforts to put a committed, open-ended, and open-minded face on its sexual orientation training. Regardless of how well the needs assessment prepares the organization and the facilitators, there are always new insights and unforeseen events that can instantaneously put a new spin on the whole process. Modularity allows such bumps and twists to be accounted for seamlessly. Modularity also allows for more content to be added over time as the organization becomes more comfortable with the subject matter.

Step 4: Reinforcement

Sexual orientation education reinforcement has three parts: accountability, program duration, and evaluation.

Accountability

Accountability is determined in two ways. First is whether or not education about sexual orientation in the workplace is perceived as fully integrated in the overall strategy of the organization. Second is whether or not the organization identifies a person who is held directly responsible for making sure that initiatives are enforced.[4]

Unfortunately, even in organizations that have diversity education initiatives in place, and even when their nondiscrimination policies extend to sexual orientation, two problems often occur. Either sexual orientation is not included as a curriculum topic, or it is listed as a topic but seldom actually covered.

If a company extends workplace protection to sexual orientation, then it must extend education to sexual orientation. Gay employees are not going to stand for talking the talk without walking the walk. They will hold the company accountable for its policies and expect that someone in management is making sure their issues are integrated into the fabric of the organization.

Liz Parrish, a member of Intel's company-recognized gay employee group, has a particular interest in corporate accountability:

> Sexual orientation is a listed part of our diversity curriculum, but it is seldom if ever actually delivered. There is no support for it in the education program right now. We expect that will change because our employee group can continue to bring that problem to the attention of the executive who's been charged with incorporating sexual orientation concerns into Intel's fabric. It's taken a while to get things going because she is the single lap into which everything falls, but at least we know who's accountable.

Program Duration

The second part of reinforcement is the duration of the program. This is a vitally important aspect of workplace education focused on any highly charged topic. Sexual orientation issues awareness could easily fall into the trap of management's "hot spot du jour," especially if the process is undertaken in reaction to an incident of gay-bashing or other blatant discrimination.

In a research project conducted by Drs. Rynes and Rosen using a sample of members from the Society for Human Resource Management as respondents, the following data were collected:

- Among topics receiving the least attention in diversity training* was how to help nontraditional employees fit in.
- Diversity training has an impact on the attitudes of attendees. Seventy-three percent believe the typical employee leaves diversity training with positive attitudes toward diversity; only 9 percent believe the typical employee enters the training with such positive attitudes.
- In long-term assessments, the largest group of respondents evaluated their own training as having either a neutral, negligible, or extremely ineffective long-term effect. The most prevalent reasons for this? The

* Their terminology.

training had no follow-up, management was not visible, and the training was available on only a limited basis.

A closer look at the length of the training programs that led to these less-than-enthusiastic results reveals that 46 percent of respondents were alluding to training of less than half a day; 26 percent were coming from a full-day model; 17 percent were talking about two-day training; 6 percent benefitted from three-day training; and 5 percent had training of four or more days upon which to base their comments.

Rynes and Rosen concluded that duration of training was one of the most significant predictors of overall success of a training program.[5] The experiences of AT&T serve to confirm this finding (see Chapter 9).

Evaluation

The third part of reinforcement and the other most significant predictor of the overall success of an education process is evaluation. We favor an evaluative strategy that occurs during and immediately after the education program by both the participants and the facilitators. People on both sides of the lectern should express their opinions about the effectiveness of the program.

Participants typically concern themselves with straightforward opinions about the deportment of the facilitator, the content of the course, what they got out of it, and what they're going to do (or not do) as a result of their participation. The facilitator's report back to management concerns itself with his impression of the group that arrived in the room at 8:00 A.M. in contrast to his impression of the group that left at 5:00 P.M.

The facilitator's impressions are used to recommend specific follow-up strategies that the organization can build into its ever-evolving educational process.

Three Questions

1. How does the organization ensure that the education effort won't do more harm than good?

We don't believe that education in and of itself ever poses a danger to anyone. But delivered by the wrong hands for the wrong reasons and without adequate preparation, education can be devastating to an organization.

One diversity director who requested anonymity learned this lesson well. A particular employee who just happened to be gay was also disliked by a number of his colleagues. Being gay was acknowledged as one of the reasons he was disliked, but it was not the only reason. Being gay was, however, the aspect of this individual targeted by those who did not like him. Their gay-bashing and harassment were blatantly discriminatory and obnoxious both to the employee and to management.

Acting in good faith, appropriate company representatives first spoke to each of the harassing employees individually and told them that their continued abuse of the individual for any reason would not be tolerated. Then management attempted to clear the air by sitting all the parties down and allowing all of them to express themselves. This turned out to be a big mistake. The director said:

> In trying to educate these employees in this situation, we actually made things worse because we allowed people to express themselves freely, and a lot of what they had to say was vehemently homophobic. We were not prepared to address their homophobia in any constructive way at that time, and the employee who was being harassed suffered further by finding out how pointed and hateful the attitudes of his co-workers were about him.

Whether or not sexual orientation education can do more harm than good is also a function of who's facilitating it. Diversity education is a growth area. More professional educators are entering the field because U.S. employers increasingly want to provide these programs.

2. Does the facilitator of sexual orientation education have to be gay?

The short answer to this question is "No." The longer answer is "It wouldn't hurt." The best answer is "Yes."

The results of this education will be better if the person delivering it is openly other than heterosexual. We are well aware that facilitators dealing with race issues are neither all black nor all white, and that excellent educators dealing in other difficult issues like sexual harassment come in both genders. Although we agree that it is inappropriate for an organization to solicit either contractors or employees on the basis of sexual orientation, we believe that if a well-qualified, affirmed gay facilitator is available, he or she should be used.

The willingness of even one person to stand up and make his or her orientation known so that all the participants can confront their doubts, fears, ambiguities, and stereotypes speaks volumes. In particular, the willingness of a professional educator to stand up and make such an affirmation is incredibly effective in diffusing irrational hatred against gays.

If it is neither possible nor practical for the facilitator to be an openly gay person, then external resources exist to fill in part of the gap. These are described in greater detail later in the resources section of this chapter.

3. Should sexual orientation education be mandatory?

One of the characteristics of workplace education considered by Rynes and Rosen in their study was whether or not programs are mandatory for all personnel.[6] Their findings, statistical and anecdotal, led them to believe that any education initiatives undertaken at an organization should be mandatory for all.

We believe that when it comes to both sexual orientation education and HIV/AIDS education, there are several strong arguments for and against mandatory attendance. On the one hand, such education should be mandatory because if it is, people who want to avail themselves of it for whatever reason can do so without fear of stigma. Nobody is singled out because everybody goes. Second, if the education is mandatory, then individuals whose existing biases would not allow them to go to such a presentation voluntarily will at least be led to the water even if they choose not to drink.

On the other hand, making either course mandatory might be construed as trying to shove a position down employees' throats, and this would be extremely counterproductive. These programs are not mandatory either at AT&T, where sexual orientation education is prominent, or at Polaroid, a pioneer in HIV/AIDS education. (See Chapter 9 for case studies on both.) AT&T and Polaroid have found that interest in these programs is so high, the programs themselves are so well done, and the feedback from both is so positive, that they don't have to be mandatory. Each sells itself to the extent that there are waiting lists for each scheduled session.

Our opinion is that these programs should be mandatory for senior and line-management personnel, and voluntary (although strongly encouraged) for all others.

The most important thing to remember about sexual orientation education is that it must be fact-based. Both emotions and opinions must be set aside by the facilitator if that person hopes to be effective.

Our Modular Program for Sexual Orientation Education

(This section is derived entirely from Common Ground's model for workplace sexual orientation education.*)

The most important thing to remember about sexual orientation education is that it must be fact-based. Both emotions and opinions must be set aside by the facilitator if that person hopes to be effective. This is not easy, but it's not impossible either. By sticking to known facts, logical conclusions, nonconfrontational exercises, and verifiable anecdotes, it is possible to present an unbiased, effective program.

The best orientation education program is exceedingly comprehensive and most likely long. Because this is not always possible, we offer a modular approach in which the content is broken down into logical sequences and sections.

Module 1: Just the Facts
Module 2: Language Tools and Empathy
Module 3: The Heart of the Matter
Module 4: Strategies for Progress

Each module travels specific avenues of inquiry. Each part builds upon the one immediately preceding it.

Module 1: Just the Facts

The first module begins with an introduction.

Introduction

We call our own "Gay Issues for the Organization—The Bottom Line" an "edusession" to reflect the emphasis we put on education. It begins the same way as this book began, with the analogy of sexual orientation to left-

---

* The modularity of the content is ours, as are facets of the program such as the detailed analogy of orientation and handedness, individual and organizational coming out, and homosexuality in relation to the "traditional" family. Like most of the other sexual orientation educators that we know, we are more concerned that organizations adopt effective sexual orientation programs and less with whose model they choose. Frankly, many of the content points run together and are so similar that it is impossible to tell who came up with what strategy first. However, the authors would like to specifically acknowledge Brian McNaught, the Boston Speaker's Bureau, and the Campaign Against Homophobia.

handedness. The reasons we start this way are because the analogy is humorous and interesting, and because it immediately forces the audience to confront the most basic of misconceptions about gay people: that a non-heterosexual orientation makes people so bizarre or deficient that they deserve to be discriminated against or live in fear for their lives because of it.

Not only does this analogy do a good job of letting the participants know exactly where we are coming from, it also serves as an icebreaker. There is usually a lot of tension in the room at the beginning of a program dealing with human sexuality. The analogy allows some of that nervous energy to be released.

Premises

Next come the premises upon which the sessions are based.

Sexual orientation is genetic. It is not a choice any more than skin color, eye color, or handedness are choices. Religious affiliation, political registration, and whom to root for in the Super Bowl are choices. Sexual orientation is not.

The facilitator can forestall any argument on this point by explaining that he will attempt to offer proof for this position, but that he acknowledges it remains a question for which no one has a completely satisfactory or verifiable answer. Tell the audience that all the differing opinions on this subject are respected and could be discussed off-line. Ask only that if they disagree, they suspend their disagreement on this important point temporarily and see whether they can make room in their minds for new information.

We borrow a "Let's Make a Deal" strategy from McNaught in which he sets up a scene where a person is faced with two doors. The door on the left is labeled "heterosexuality," and it's full of dances and dating and familial support and big fancy weddings. The door on the right is labeled "homosexuality," and it promises isolation, alienation, fear, and a lot of energy wasted sneaking around and hiding your life from your family and friends. What a choice!

In a more serious vein, the facilitator can point out that a lot of people grow up with misinformation or no information at all about a lot of subjects. Homosexuality (or any sexuality for that matter) tends to be one of them. According to a Gallup poll in 1990, only 15 percent of Americans feel they had good sex education at home, and only 10 percent believe they had good sex education in high school. That is an enormous deficit to try to overcome. Many people feel fear, anxiety, stress, or out-and-out repulsion discussing these things, but we insist that if people can't or don't talk about them, they can't ever really figure out how they truly feel about them.

The organization wants to provide a safe, productive working environment for everyone. Coming into the program, one of the biggest issues for people (usually straight people) is about why sexuality has anything to do with the workplace at all. Until the facilitator takes a good look at heterosexism in the second module, this is a real sticking point for participants.

To ensure they are not distracted by this particular issue, he can offer some published, verifiable anecdotes. Among them is the documented proof that many gay people receive death threats through telephone messages and electronic mail with alarming regularity in homophobic environments.

Even companies that have a policy of nondiscrimination that includes sexual orientation are not immune. At Lotus Development, one of the most progressive and diverse companies in the country, management was surprised that fewer people than they anticipated signed up for domestic partner benefits. An informal survey brought to light the fact that of those gay and lesbian employees who qualified for and had a need for the benefits but didn't elect them, the prevalent reason was that they still did not feel safe. They did not feel safe from violence or from the possibility of their careers being irrevocably damaged. The only way to change a situation like that is through education.

In every workplace, there are gay people and straight people who care about gay family members and friends. Gay people are not the only ones with concerns about sexual orientation at work or in their lives. Incidences of homophobia and their resultant damage to the psyche or morale of the workforce are not only a gay employee problem. Straight people, sometimes referred to as straight allies, have questions and concerns too. In many cases these people have gay family members and friends to whom they would like to reach out but don't know how. Education in the workplace can help them understand reality for the gay people in their lives and how they might want to react because of this understanding.

Heterosexism and homophobia are present in the edusession. They are manifested in negative comments, jokes, or assumptions of heterosexuality. Try to get participants to understand that these kinds of utterances make people uncomfortable and that nothing will be accomplished if all participants do not feel comfortable in expressing themselves. People should try to monitor what they say to ensure that it is both honest and constructive. Certain figures of speech or outbursts are inappropriate; a simply stated opinion without derogatory language is fine.

Homophobia and heterosexism both have a negative impact on a person's ability to be productive and happy in the workplace. Being happy where we work is very important to all of us, or it should be because we all spend an awful lot of time at our jobs. Blatant displays of either homophobia or heterosexism make people uncomfortable.

The following analogy is a good example. A person might want to express her belief that homosexuality is wrong for whatever reason. That person should think for a minute what a negative effect it might have on teamwork if she also claimed that divorce, adultery, and abortion are also sacrilegious and that all practitioners of those things go straight to hell. Take it a step further and try to think about loudly stating that coveting another's possessions and lying are both condemned acts. Pretty soon everyone is going to feel alienated to some extent because few of us are entirely innocent of what others might consider sin.

Homophobic behavior results from misinformation, fear, and a lack of exposure to gay people. Education reduces the chance that people will engage in or tolerate homophobic behavior. It is our experience that when people learn more, they become less afraid and eventually stop their homophobic behavior. Education might also encourage a change of mind, but not always. The point is that people are entitled to their opinions, and education does not equal endorsement.

The sexuality of the participants is irrelevant to the program. Participants are never asked to either declare or affirm their orientation. Whether any do so during the course of a discussion is entirely up to them.

Human Sexuality

This content is not intended as a lesson in biology or human psychosexuality. It is intended to give all workshop participants a common base of language and understanding about terms whose misrepresentation often lies at the heart of destructive behavior.

- Biological sex is the gender, male or female, with which we are born. With some rare exceptions, people are either male or female.
- Gender identity means whether we perceive ourselves as male or female. According to experts in the field of child development, gender identity is set between eighteen months to three years of age. This is true for all people, regardless of their sexual orientation.[7]
- Gender role is what our culture expects of us because of our biological sex. For example, in many European countries, it is common for people to hold hands, especially women with other women. It is also normal to see friendly and affectionate physical contact between men. In the United States, such behavior is assumed to indicate a homosexual relationship. In fact, when Bill Clinton and Al Gore were elected president and vice-president respectively, much was made of their tendency to hug rather than to simply shake hands. Gender role is a cultural thing.
- Narrow concepts of appropriate gender roles in the United States can cause havoc in the workplace. If a woman wants to move up the corporate ladder, she is often viewed with suspicion because that kind of drive and ambition is not considered an appropriate part of the female

role. In many cases, these women are accused of being gay—of wanting to be men, to be more precise—when in fact they are not and do not. Even if she is gay, this still does not mean that she wants to be a man. Gender role has nothing to do with sexual orientation or vice versa.

- Sexual orientation is what dictates a person's sexual attraction to others. A person's orientation is set sometime between birth and age three. Most young men are completely aware of their sexual orientation by age 13. For young women, the average age of awareness is between 15 and 17.[8]

Pinpointing the distinction between gender role and sexual orientation is very important. A good example is ballet dancer Mikhail Barishnikov. If a man is a ballet dancer, many people automatically assume that he is also gay, yet Barishnikov is decidedly and publicly heterosexual. Another example is Olympic champion Greg Louganis. If a man is an Olympic athlete, many people automatically assume that he must be straight, yet Louganis is decidedly and publicly gay. When participants come to understand through facts and anecdotes that sexual orientation does not mean that gay men want to be women or gay women want to be men, the first light has a chance to go on.

The Numbers

The human sexuality section of module 1 closes with an in-depth look at the numbers of gay people. We, like many of our education compatriots, find it hard to understand why numbers matter, but they seem to. Our position is that discrimination against one person is no more defensible than discrimination against one thousand people.

An overview of the available research concerning the number of gay people is well worth the effort. The facilitator should included details of the work done by Kinsey in 1948 and 1953 and again by the Kinsey Institute in 1994; studies by Janus in 1993; Guttmacher in 1994, and some of the results of a survey reported in the book *Sex in America*, also in 1994. More information about all these is available in Chapter 8 of this book.

Many people believe that there are also environmental factors involved in the development of sexual orientation, but no one knows for sure just what they are. Gay people and straight people come from the same family dynamics. Both authors of this book have brothers, and both brothers are straight. Further, homosexuality has existed in societies throughout history and in cultures throughout the world. With our Western civilization mindset, it is difficult to understand other cultures and the practices involved in them. In one study, 64 percent of 190 cultures showed homosexuality to be normal and socially acceptable for members of the community. It has also been proved that homosexuality exists in every species of animal.[9]

> If the highest-end estimates of the occurrence of homosexuality in humans are true, that number being 10 percent, then 21 million Americans are gay, lesbian, or bisexual. If the lower estimates are right, then the number would be 7.5 million. Either way, it's a lot of people. But even if it were just one, would discrimination against that person be right?

If the highest-end estimates of the occurrence of homosexuality in humans are true, that number being 10 percent, then 21 million Americans are gay, lesbian, or bisexual. If the lower estimates are right, then the number would be 7.5 million. Either way, it's a lot of people. But even if it were just one, would discrimination against that person be right?

Module 2: Language Tools and Empathy

A big part of people's problems concerning gays in the workplace has to do with lack of honest exposure to gays, combined with the lack of opportunity to express themselves about homosexuality. An important focus of the education is on affording the participants the opportunity for both. Try to get them talking about what they already know or think, and give them language to explore their ideas further.

There are several good methods to get people talking in sexual orientation education. In the beginning, the important thing is not what they talk about, just that they feel comfortable enough to talk about *any* aspect of the matter. Use exercises that allow people to express themselves without feeling defensive. This is accomplished by not having them discuss exactly how *they* feel or what *they* think as individuals (unless they want to), but rather by letting them talk about what they think other people think, or what their work environment is like.

One such exercise is called the continuum choice, in which people are given a range of answers to choose from to questions or situations concerning gay people in their work environment. The questions and situations presented desensitize the exercise by letting people talk about their environment or other people's perceptions and not necessarily their own.

An example of a continuum-choice question is: "How do you think senior management would honestly respond to seeing a group of people march down the main street of this city with a banner identifying themselves as gay employees of this organization? Do you think they would be very angry, angry, somewhat accepting, or very accepting?"

This exercise never fails to get a dialogue going. The facilitator monitors the conversation to make sure that neither a debate nor an argument gets started. Monitoring carefully allows the facilitator to make note of opinions based on misinformation. A good facilitator will come back to those particular misconceptions later in the program and specifically correct them.

Another exercise is called continuum of community, in which the participants are asked to identify a situation in their lives in which they felt very accepted and one in which they felt completely unaccepted. The point is to get people to identify with and express feelings of fear, alienation, or loneliness that made them feel powerless. It also helps them examine how truly empowering it is to be fully embraced by any group with which you are involved, such as a work group. Naturally, the facilitator tells the first pair of anecdotes.

Still another strategy is using read-arounds. The facilitator prepares index cards in advance of the class, each of which contains a paragraph or two about some facet of the main topic. The cards might contain statistics, coming-out stories, poll results, scientific theories, or anything that gets the people in the room to listen to themselves and each other's voices express something about sexual orientation. Once they've found their voice, the facilitator can start to give them information and specific language tools to figure out what they really want to say.

Specific Language

Chapter 2 offers lengthy definitions of both homophobia and heterosexism. Coming out individually and organizationally are described in Chapter 4. All of that information is imparted to the participants at this point in the edusession in order to encourage them to apply their newly acquired expression skills to a narrower focus.

The simplest example is to mention to the class that the ordinary act of putting a spouse's picture on one's desk is heterosexist. It is harmless and by no means should straight people be prohibited from doing it, but it is an exclusionary act because gay people do not have the same freedom. Because heterosexuality is the behavioral standard, no sexual stigma is attached to the act of putting a heterosexual family picture on a desk. But gay people who put out pictures of their families are accused of "flaunting their lifestyle."

Another example of heterosexism is when the words *wife* or *husband* appear on a company memo. The same is true when the boss asks Mike, who is unmarried, whether he will take a position at another office across the country, since he obviously doesn't have a wife and family to keep him in town. For sexual orientation educators, these are clearly demonstrations of heterosexism. For a majority of people, however, they are revolutionary.

In terms of homophobia, point out that when jokes are told at the expense of gay people, seemingly all in fun, a disservice has been done to them. It doesn't take long for people to make the mental leap to being the foil of a joke about Jews, or blacks, or Poles, or anyone else.

What this part of the edusession is trying to accomplish is making a connection in the minds of the participants between discrimination against gays and every other kind of discrimination. Try to get people to relate personally to discrimination against gays so that they can no longer think of it as (1) a socially acceptable prejudice or (2) a distant bias that has nothing to do with them because they don't know any gays.

In one useful exercise for this purpose, participants are given a sheet that describes several scenarios. One is a gay woman who had been honest about her sexual orientation with her family, but whose family will not acknowledge her life or her partner. They don't reject her; they simply ignore her. Another is about a black man who is stopped at least five times a week by police in his neighborhood while walking home from work. Still another is about a young woman who is getting too much personal attention from her male supervisor. Another is a single father who has to balance caring for his sick daughter with the demands of his job.

The possible examples that can be raised are endless, but the point is always the same. Discrimination is always oppressive. Everyone has been victimized by discrimination at some point in life, and no one ever likes it.

Such techniques allow the participants to combine their new understanding of homophobia, heterosexism, and discrimination with some examples to which they can already relate. At this point perhaps the second little light clicks on. When someone approaches you at the end of a session and simply says that he is not going to let his kids use the word *faggot* anymore, you will feel that you accomplished something that day.

The Guided Fantasy

This tool is used by most sexual orientation educators because it is simple and effective. The guided fantasy, of which there are several variations, is a story that the facilitator tells to the class in which the whole world is turned around. Instead of straights being in the majority, gays are. Gays hold the power and set the standards for every activity from birth to death. This is not about suggesting that gay people take over the world. It's about helping people experience a world in which, if they were straight, everything that came naturally to them would be declared sick, illegal, disgusting, or all three.

The fantasy is at its most effective when it describes events that are common in all lives, like the songs we sing, our first dates at a school dance, living in a college dorm, sharing our first apartment with a partner, going out to movies or bars, having to take care of our loved one in an emergency.

The guided fantasy is a powerful tool that allows the participants to reflect upon what they've learned to this point. It sets the stage for breaking through other, more personal barriers in the third module.

Module 3: The Heart of the Matter

Up to this point in the edusession, things are purposely kept very safe for the participants. They have neither had to confront their own biases nor had to express them if they did not choose to. Until module 3, gay issues in the workplace are held up for consideration, but could be held at arm's length. More personal involvement is demanded in this module.

Myths, Misconceptions, and Mistakes

The first part of module 3 requires that the participants identify the myths and fears they harbor about gays. It also demands that they identify the words that they use to refer to gays and the questions they have about gay people.

It's either comforting or frightening that the things you'll hear at this point in the program are always pretty much the same. Rarely does anyone manage to come up with a new, different, or plausible expression of homophobia; rarely does anyone ask a question not heard before. Fortunately, anything that's asked can be answered if you remember certain basic truths:

- Gays are everywhere.
- Sexual orientation is not sexual behavior. People are not wholly defined by either their sexual orientation or their sexual behavior.
- Homophobia is hatred and fear based on ignorance of the facts.
- The people you are working with want to learn and must be treated with respect.
- Debate is fruitless. You will not reach everyone, so you must be prepared to agree to disagree.
- People are entitled to their opinions. It's their *behavior* you should be interested in affecting.

What facilitators will usually hear are that the words associated with gays are: homosexual, he/she, AC/DC, fag, dyke, lezzie, punk, poof, bulldyke, or queer. According to people who might indulge in these words, gays are further characterized by limp wrists in men and manliness in women. The only professions for gay men are hairdresser, dancer, interior designer, and air steward; truck driver and physical education teacher are popular occupations for gay women. Common characteristics of gay people are that they are promiscuous, AIDS-infected, child molesters, and transvestites who would prefer to be transsexuals also.

Each of these words, questions, and misconceptions must be addressed one by one. Offer definitions for the words, give employment statistics for the occupations, and explain facts about human sexual behavior in depth.

For many people, this is both the best and the most difficult part of the entire program. It's the best because it directly confronts negative stereotypes that they've carried for years. Many have found the burden to be extremely tiresome. Running these education programs convinces us beyond a shadow of a doubt that although people are capable of great cruelty, most are also very uncomfortable with discriminatory thoughts and feelings and would like information to mitigate them. They don't really want a justification for continued animosity towards gays. They want reasons to feel commonality with gay people in order to reach some sort of understanding everyone can live with.

Confronting stereotypes and deciding that they might not be valid is not an easy task, but nothing worth doing ever is. Some people who avail themselves of this education have said that it's some of the best work they've ever done and they're proud of it.

You need only look at any other civil or human rights movements to see that sooner or later, people understand that our similarities as human beings consistently outweigh differences reflected by our sexuality, our race, our ethnicity, or our religious convictions. If you offer a plausible definition, explanation, or rebuttal for every semantic or mythologic weapon used against gays, you constantly reinforce the similarities of gay people to all other people. As you remember, *homophobia* literally means "fear of sameness," but fear of difference is the problem. When people grasp that, they stop being homophobic because they can't fear differences that don't exist.

What's the Bottom Line Here?

At this point in the program, it's possible to lighten things up a little and get people talking about what it is gays really want from their workplace. There are any number of lists that different facilitators use; we prefer to keep ours short. As laid out in Chapter 1, gay people expect their workplaces to provide equitable benefits, a safe work environment, and both internal and external support. In order to explain not only these requirements but their validity, the edusession looks at each one at a time.

Equitable benefits, for the purposes of this edusession, are defined as medical, dental, and pension, along with some examples of "soft" benefits (see Chapter 6). This part offers simply an example to back up the statement that sometimes gay people need and deserve these benefits for the same reasons straight people might. The next and last parts of this module offer both (1) a very detailed story about the facilitator's own experience as a gay woman in this society and (2) an equally detailed look at the realities of family and law in late-twentieth-century America (see Chapters 1 and 8).

Our example is a true one, and we tell the participants it is true. Ellen leaves her full-time position to start her own company. In doing so, she loses all her employer-provided benefits. When her COBRA medical coverage runs out (monthly cost $168), she is faced with a choice of either no medical insurance or basic medical insurance (no dental) at a cost of over $3,500 per year.

Ellen is in a very committed relationship with Dianne and has been for more than three years. If she and Dianne could marry or in some way legalize their relationship, Ellen would automatically get access to Dianne's insurance through her employer at no charge. As it is, Ellen does not have this option, so she and Dianne petition Dianne's employer to offer the benefits. Although Ellen must now pay tax on a portion of the premium for this benefit, which costs her about $800 per year, it is a lot less than $3,500 for basic insurance and a lot better than no insurance at all. Then we tell the participants that the names "Ellen" and "Dianne" are pseudonyms and that we are the women in question. Common Ground got its start helping organizations implement domestic partner benefits as a creative solution to a problem that we faced ourselves.

When this anecdote is related, people are able to put a face on a recognizable, not uncommon, situation. It is not hard for most to understand that when faced with a problem, people will look for a creative solution. That's what domestic partnership benefits are: a creative solution.

The next requirement, a safe working environment, explains the necessity for and dynamics of a nondiscrimination policy that expressly includes sexual orientation. It also offers more examples of heterosexism, homophobia, and AIDS-phobia, a further justification for edusessions like this one, and a discussion about the importance of all members of the workplace community feeling as though they are a completely accepted part of it.

The last requirement of gays from their employer, public support both internal and external, concerns itself with ways to substantiate the nondiscrimination policy and strategies to establish and maintain lines of communication. (See Chapters 3 and 9.)

A Personal Story

After all the facts are offered and discussed, after all the statistics are dissected and all the definitions are understood, the best strategy for achieving common ground is a true story. If only one thing were possible in a fifteen-minute sound-bite, it should be the personal recollection of a lesbian, gay, bisexual, or transgendered person.

The stories told by every speaker are all different, and they are all the

> Real change occurs when people begin to act on what they accept as the truth. In this society, we are conditioned to believe that real changes are made by someone "out there"— by the government, by laws, by powerful people. We are taught that our actions cannot and do not affect the world. It is time that we begin to take ourselves seriously enough to believe that our personal changes in attitude, the resulting changes in our behavior, and our joining together to push for changes in our communities are indeed how real change happens. And if we as individuals can change, we know that the people around us can too.

same. Some speak of suicide attempts, some speak of being disowned, some speak of running away. Most speak of losing an important person to ignorance. Most tell about loneliness and alienation and fear. Most speak of the terror of coming out each and every time they have to do it.

This is the most difficult part of this edusession for the facilitator because it is not a performance; it is a release. It is not just part of a curriculum; it is part of the person's life. It is the best reason for making sure that the facilitator of this education is a gay person too, or for going to great lengths if you have to in order to secure a gay person who will speak to the group and tell his or her story.

Module 4: Strategies for Progress

Real change occurs when people begin to act on what they accept as the truth. In this society, we are conditioned to believe that real changes are made by someone "out there"— by the government, by laws, by powerful people. We are taught that our actions cannot and do not affect the world. It is time that we begin to take ourselves seriously enough to believe that our personal changes in attitude, the resulting changes in our behavior, and our joining together to push for changes in our communities are indeed how real change happens. And if we as individuals can change, we know that the people around us can too.

Follow the advice of whoever first said that you can lead a horse to water, but you can't make him drink. We believe that the most effective strategies are the ones that people arrive at themselves...even if you steer them a little.

McNaught describes the actual things that people can do to combat discrimination against gays in the workplace as either "reactive" or "proactive." Examples of reactive strategies are using humor to derail a conversation in which gays are being victimized; refusing to laugh at anti-gay humor; educating colleagues about AIDS, heterosexism, and homophobia; citing company policy about nondiscrimination; confronting an offensive person with the possible damaging effects of his or her behavior; leaving a place where discriminatory behavior is indulged; reporting such behavior appropriately; and personalizing the issue by saying "I know gay people, and I am offended by this conversation."

Proactive strategies include attending an edusession like the one we're describing, displaying gay-friendly literature in your office, talking positively to colleagues about the issues, using inclusive language, making sure there is a nondiscrimination policy that includes sexual orientation, lobbying for domestic partner benefits, and supporting gay employee groups.

Steering participants toward these strategies is achievable in several ways. For example, use role plays that allow members of the class to act out a highly believable scenario. Then ask participants to discuss their reactions to the statements and actions of the actors playing the parts.

Another mechanism is narratives read to the class, each one ending in a question designed to get the participants to formulate possible answers.

A favorite of ours is the "What do you feel/what do you know" model that we adapted from the Campaign to End Homophobia. Sometime at the beginning of the edusession, we hand out a sheet of paper to each person entitled "What do you feel, what do you know about gays?" This tool presents continuum choice (strongly agree to strongly disagree) statements like:

- Gay and lesbian people can usually be identified by certain mannerisms or physical characteristics.
- Being gay is a choice.
- If I found out that a family member or friend was gay, I would disassociate myself from that person.
- I'm against anything that offers special rights to homosexuals.

First you ask the people to respond to the questions and then put the sheet aside. At the end of the class, you give them each the same sheet and ask them to fill it out again without looking at their first set of responses. More often than not, their perceptions have changed, and they feel more able to free-associate strategies they can use to make the environment more productive, profitable, and satisfactory for everyone. They also feel that they want to.

All or Nothing?

If it's not possible to offer the entire day's edusession, or to incorporate all this information into a lengthy process of diversity education for all employees, then the following content points take precedence:

- Human sexuality.
- Definitions of homosexuality and heterosexism.
- Correcting myths and misconceptions about gays.
- Personal recollection of a gay speaker.
- Strategies for improvement of the company environment.

Resources for Curriculum Development and Delivery

One school of thought teaches that external consultants are more objective, are more comfortable in front of your employee audience when it comes to delicate subject matter, and are therefore more effective. If this is true, then it would be hard to find a subject matter to which such a rule would be better applied than sexual orientation in the workplace. If your internal training and development staff is comfortable with including sexual orientation in its diversity management initiatives, an outside consultant might be sought to help develop the program content but not necessarily to deliver the program.

We encourage human resources professionals not just to hire a consulting company for such a delicate subject, but to hire a person whom they can meet and talk to, with whom they can develop a solid working relationship. Their education will not be served by trying to depersonalize the most personal of subjects. In those environments where a great many people require or request this education, it may be possible and extremely effective for the organization to modify a "train-the-trainer" scheme, which we like to call "educate-the-educators" for sexual orientation training.

It is possible to teach competent educational staff the facts. It is even possible to help them arm themselves with anecdotes and personal experiences that are directly relevant to the subject, whether or not they are gay themselves. However, they can't tell the personal recollections unless they've lived through them. So an educate-the-educator approach must be augmented with some outside or inside assistance.

If your company has a gay employee group, chances are you will have to look no further. If it does not and you are close to a major city, you can reach out to the local Gay Speaker's Bureau or P-FLAG (Parents and Friends of Lesbians and Gays) organization or contact in that city. Even if the city is far away, call these groups.

The two national gay advocacy organizations are also excellent resources for data, references, and help with workforce initiatives. Both the Human Rights Campaign Fund (HRCF) and the National Gay and Lesbian Task Force (NGLTF) have staff focused on workplace issues. Both organizations are located in Washington, D.C., with nationwide memberships and representatives who are able to help.

In some states, the local school system, college, or university will be an excellent resource for outside speakers. Massachusetts is the only state that expressly offers nondiscrimination protection to its gay youth, but many individual school districts or schools across the nation are supportive of their gay students. Call yours to find out whether it's one of them. If so, there are students and/or faculty there who can help you themselves or refer you appropriately.

Notes

1. "AIDS Education in the Workplace: What Employees Think," *Report of a Study by the New York Business Group on Health, Inc.* (New York: New York Business Group on Health, Inc., 1990).
2. Shari Caudron, "Training Can Damage Diversity Efforts," *Personnel Journal* (April 1993).
3. Shari Caudron, "Valuing Difference Not the Same as Managing Diversity," *Personnel Journal* (April 1993).
4. Sara Rynes and Benson Rosen, "Profiting From Other's Experience: A Diversity Training Checklist," *HR Magazine* (October 1994).
5. Sara Rynes and Benson Rosen, "What Makes Diversity Work," *HR Magazine* (October 1994).
6. Ibid.
7. Brian McNaught, *Gay Issues in the Workplace* (New York: St. Martin's Press, 1993).
8. Alfred C. Kinsey et al., *Sexual Behavior in the Human Male and Sexual Behavior in the Human Female* (Philadelphia: W.B. Saunders, 1948 and 1953).
9. Taylor Cox, *Cultural Diversity in Organizations: Theory, Research and Practice* (San Francisco: Berrit-Koehler, 1993).

6

The Ins and Outs of Domestic Partner Benefits

As the twentieth century comes to a conclusion, more employers can expect some constituency within their organization, probably their gay constituency, to ask for benefits for domestic partners. Domestic partner or just "partner" is fast becoming the most popular way for gay people to describe their relationship to their lover or significant other because words like *spouse* are too intrinsically tied to the legally recognized relationship of marriage. Equitable benefit plans are one of the most important things to a gay employee population because they represent both a recognition of gay relationships and the concept of equal pay for equal work.

This chapter presents a comprehensive discussion of domestic partner benefits for the business reader. In it we include:

- A history of benefits in general and domestic partner benefits in particular.
- Possible motivations for the implementation of partner benefits.
- A description of the types of benefits involved.
- The cost to both the organization and its employees of implementing domestic partner benefits.
- The tax ramifications of benefits.
- Options for benefits implementation both from a procedural standpoint and a dollars-and-sense perspective.
- How to determine who is a domestic partner and prove such a partnership.

- The pros and cons of offering benefits to opposite-sex couples as well as same-sex couples.
- The current state of the insurance industry concerning partner medical benefits.
- Retirement plan issues.
- Strategies for the successful implementation of domestic partner benefits.

Why Are There Employer-Provided Benefits at All?

Our generation tends to think of employer-provided benefits as a birthright. They aren't, of course, but they may be the closest most people ever get. Benefits as a form of workplace compensation started in the 1940s, when companies who wanted to pay certain employees more were prohibited by law from doing so by way of simple pay increases. So instead of giving the cash directly to the employee, the employer paid for certain products and services like insurance or housing on the employee's behalf. For those laborers traditionally holding the shorter end of the compensatory stick, workplace benefits derived in part from President Franklin D. Roosevelt's New Deal as a way to subsidize both businesses and employees during and immediately after the Depression.

Since the 1940s, workplace benefits have continued to constitute an integral part of compensation. Even during the boom (no pun intended) years of World War II through the development of the suburbs in the 1950s and 1960s, benefits from the workplace were taken for granted. Employers found new and different ways to package benefits, both for the good of employees and to enhance the attractiveness of their workplace over that of their competitors. Therefore, the idea of benefits constituting a competitive advantage is not a new one. Organizations have been trying to outdo one another in this fashion for decades.

The economic and symbolic importance of workplace benefits is undeniable. The U.S. Chamber of Commerce released a study in 1992 stating that between 37 percent and 40 percent of employee compensation is in benefits. And as also stated earlier, 67 percent of respondents to an Employee Benefit Research survey in 1994 said they would not give up their employer-provided benefits even in lieu of a higher cash salary. Ironically, the principle that led in part to the creation of such benefits fifty-odd years ago—namely, giving employees benefits in lieu of additional cash salary—is the same one that won't allow employers to back away from this expense now.

Make no mistake, benefits do constitute an expense that employers are looking for ways to mitigate. Between 1983 and 1991, the employer cost of health-related benefits increased from 7 percent of payroll to just over 10 percent of payroll. Employers in all sectors are making more of an effort to push some of the costs of benefits back onto the employees through sharing of premium costs, raised deductible limits, exclusion of some preexisting conditions, or reducing benefits coverage overall. But even though individuals are asked to carry a greater portion of the fiscal load, workplace benefits are not going to disappear anytime soon. Therefore, all employees are going to demand their fair share.

Who Receives Benefits?

Most organizations' decisions about the benefits they offer and the people to whom they offer them are determined either by need or by merit. However, since most employers offer some form of workplace benefits to all who work there, we think that three other factors are more significant when determining who is going to be able to take advantage of whatever benefits are offered. One is the construct of the family, one is the enterprise's interpretation of its legal responsibility, and one is an interpretation of the entity's own nondiscrimination policy.

The Family as Benefit Determinant

Chapter 1 offers a detailed discussion of the reality of the family within the boundaries of its relevance to workplace benefits. To summarize, the majority of benefits are awarded to workers who come from traditional family backgrounds. The traditional family is no longer in the majority, so the majority of workers run the risk of being shortchanged by family-oriented benefits.

Historically the construct of the family was hardwired to a needs-based justification for benefits. Employers simply rationalized that an employee with a "family" (which traditionally meant a man with a nonworking wife and children) had a greater need for employer-provided benefits like medical insurance or relocation assistance. Instead of trying to refigure entire salary models, which are based on merit, employers subsidize those making less money with benefits. However, with the constantly changing dynamics of what constitutes a family, the once clear lines between who needs what become increasingly cloudy.

Many organizations that have opted for domestic partner benefits believe what Sybase expressed very well in its public announcement of adopting the benefits. Part of the Sybase statement read, "Many of our employees are members of households of people who are committed to and financially responsible for each other. While many of these households are traditional families, many others are less traditional but just as significant to the individuals involved."

Interpretation of Law as Benefit Determinant

The law and justice are not the same thing, but the terms are frequently used interchangeably. Justice is what does or does not result from the law. While there are few direct legal precedents for domestic partner benefits, there are ample precedents of justice.

In the 1989 New York Court of Appeals case *Braschi* v. *Stahl Associates,* which concerned rent control laws, the court found itself in the position of having to redefine *family* in order to make a ruling:

> We conclude that the term *family* should not be rigidly restricted to those people who have formalized their relationship by obtaining, for instance, a marriage certificate or an adoption order. The intended protection against sudden conviction should not rest on fictitious legal distinctions or genetic history, but instead should find itself in the reality of family life. Only one quarter or less of all U.S. families are composed of two parents with children.

In 1991 an Ohio appellate court ruled that lesbian and gay domestic partners must be included in the interpretation of the state's domestic violence laws that protect those "who live as spouses or otherwise cohabitate."

In 1994 a man named Henry Kirkpatrick won a posthumous battle with the board of a New York cooperative to legally inherit the apartment he had shared with his partner, who predeceased him. As a result of this settlement between the New York City Human Rights Commission and the Sutton Place South Cooperative, the Council of New York Cooperatives' lawyer said he would forever after "advise any co-op to treat a domestic partner of any one of its shareholders in exactly the same manner as it would treat a legal spouse."

Both as matters of justice and law, an employer is obligated to provide equal pay for equal work to its employees. By providing benefits to the families of married employees and denying the same to families of unmarried employees, the employer is violating that obligation and discriminating according to the marital status and sexual orientation of its employees. Likewise, many cities and states prohibit discrimination on the basis of marital status and/or sexual orientation. By refusing to provide the same benefits to unmarried employees as it provides to married employees, the employer may be violating any number of those laws. As noted in Chapter 1, the disparity between what a legally married couple versus a domestic partner is entitled to was at the core of a decision in Vermont to extend benefits to all state employees.

In 1984 there was an interesting case in California that might one day be cited as a precedent to force domestic partner benefits. The court decided that domestic partners can receive unemployment benefits if they can prove that they left a job for compelling reasons, such as preservation of a family relationship established with a partner and a child. The lack of a legally recognized marriage was found not to prevent a claimant from establishing that compelling familial obligation.[1]

Each case, though not directly related to extending benefits to the partners of employees, establishes precedents for cases that will be filed specifically to make such benefits possible. As reported in the epilogue of a U.S. government report called *Sexual Orientation: An Issue of Workplace Diversity*, "…while movement in these areas (benefits among them) to a multicultural workforce won't come easily or overnight, change is inevitable."[2]

Nondiscrimination Policies as Benefit Determinant

Some organizational nondiscrimination policies or codes of conduct contain the words *sexual orientation*. Some say *sexual preference* or *lifestyle*, both of which are poor choices and should be changed to *sexual orientation*. In cases where the latter language appears, logic dictates that families founded on same-sex unions would be entitled to whatever benefits or perquisites their heterosexual peers were getting. Employers can expect that if their nondiscrimination policy does extend to sexual orientation or any term interpretable in that way, they will be asked to extend whatever benefits they offer to those families who need and qualify for them. Furthermore, if a policy says that such nondiscrimination will be evident in matters of compensation, numbers of benefits, or company-provided services (to name a few of the semantic possibilities), the company will be called to put its money where those words are.

Where domestic partner benefits have been implemented or are under consideration, it is nearly always because a company has decided to adhere to the letter and spirit of its nondiscrimination policy, or because it has just implemented a new one. Infrequent is the instance where the company decides to revamp its policy or add sexual orientation language to it without being compelled, but perhaps that will change too.

For the time being, gay employees don't mind asking.

When the employee asks, the exercise that takes place next can be as simple as the organization saying something to the effect of "You're right. It does say we won't discriminate, and we might very well be engaging in discriminatory behavior right now that we should fix!" Or it may be a long, drawn-out, and emotionally difficult task for people on all sides of the issue.

At Banyan Systems it was literally as easy as pointing to the nondiscrimination policy. That's all it took to get the organization to consider implementing partner benefits. At most other places it takes longer, and this time could be better spent. Arguing about a policy that is in black and white is a waste of time, energy, and money. If your nondiscrimination policy includes issues of compensation, benefits, or equal pay for equal work—and if it also includes *sexual orientation, sexual preference,* or *lifestyle*—your organization would be better served if you took a proactive look at who is benefiting from your benefit programs instead of waiting to be asked and then arguing about whether such benefits are really called for.

At the University of New Mexico, a lot of energy went into reaching the only logical conclusion. The University's Equal Opportunity and Equal Education statement "...forbids unlawful discrimination on the basis of race, color, religion, national origin, physical or mental handicap, age, sex, sexual preference, ancestry, or medical condition, in recruiting, hiring, training, promotion, and all other terms and conditions of employment. All personnel policies, such as compensation, benefits, transfers, layoffs, terminations, returns from layoffs, University-sponsored education, tuition assistance..." It's a long statement.

Although the university was not in violation of any New Mexico or federal laws, the Equal Opportunities Program office found that the school was violating its own policy because it was not in fact offering equal pay for equal work. Benefits, the office said, comprise a large portion of an employee's compensation package. When one employee is eligible for fewer benefits than another because he or she is not permitted to marry and the difference is not made up in wages, that employee is being paid less for the same work.

The History of Domestic Partner Benefits

The first implementation of domestic partner benefits was in 1982 as the result of union contract negotiations between District 65 of the Distributive Workers of America and the *Village Voice* in New York. Many people think upon hearing this news that it makes perfect sense that the *Voice* would have been first. After all, the *Village Voice* is well known for its liberal, left-wing politics, and it's located in New York. But in fact it was the union that brought these benefits to the bargaining table that year, not the publication.

In 1983 the American Psychological Association Insurance Trust began providing these benefits, followed by the cities of West Hollywood and Berkeley in California in 1985, and Ben & Jerry's Ice Cream Company in 1989. The City of San Francisco opted for domestic partner registration in 1989 and augmented that policy with benefits in 1991. Montefiore Medical Center also implemented benefits in 1991. Several colleges and universities implemented some form of partner benefits during the year 1992 to 1993. Lotus Development Corporation became the first public company to offer domestic partner benefits to its employees in 1991. Lotus is generally credited with breaking through the significant barrier represented by industry—public and private—to these benefits. Without question, the high-tech industry, the entertainment industry, and perhaps to the surprise of many, law firms are leading the charge in domestic partner benefits.

As this book was completed in early 1995, corporations, institutions of higher education, unions, and municipal governments were adding some form of domestic partner benefits at the rate of one to three per week. Many more than that were being petitioned to do so. As of December 1, 1994, there were 42 American cities and states, 96 private-sector companies, and 68 colleges and universities that offer some or all benefits. This may not be a deluge, but it is a trend that is gaining momentum. Fewer than five organizations of any kind could boast domestic partner benefits as recently as 1990.

At least one of Canada's six major banks, Toronto Dominion, offers benefits. El Al offers benefits in Israel, as does Digital Equipment Corporation in Belgium. Efforts to implement benefits are under consideration in public and private industry in Australia and in trade unions in the United Kingdom. In several other European countries, benefits are offered to same-sex partners as part of extremely progressive social policies regarding the validity of same-sex unions. This is dealt with in greater detail later in this chapter.

Benefits: Hard and Soft

Workplace-provided benefits are frequently thought of in relation to the workplace sector—public, private, or campus—in which they are offered. The types of workplace perquisites in each of these sectors can differ slightly, but the environment for the benefits continues to matter only in terms of the hoops that an individual or group must go through in order to see to their implementation. The benefits themselves, and most issues related to them, are basically the same.

The two classifications of benefits are hard benefits, which carry a direct out-of-pocket expense to the organization, and soft benefits, which also cost money but less directly.

Hard Benefits

Hard benefits are the cost-intensive ones, including medical and dental benefits and the payment of some pension benefits.

As a rule of thumb, any employee benefit that the enterprise offers as a matter of policy to its employees can be offered to their partners and their families as the enterprise defines those people. All employers, even those under the watchful eye of a state government or a board of regents, have a great deal of latitude in choosing their definitions. The only exception to this is life insurance. As of the end of 1994, it is a matter of state law across the United States that an unmarried or nonlegal dependent cannot be party to group life insurance plans employers offer unless the employee pays the entire premium. In some cases, paying this premium might be worth it to the employee.

Soft Benefits

Which soft benefits are available may differ substantially depending on the workplace sector. In the private sector, such benefits may include but are not limited to adoption benefits, bereavement and family leave policies as per the 1993 Family Leave Act, employee assistance programs, parenting leave, use of health and fitness programs, relocation policy, and sick leave.

In the public sector, examples of soft benefits are access to school records, bereavement and family leave, parenting leave, registration of partnership, use of recreational areas, sick leave, visitation in hospitals and prisons, and tax benefits for companies in the cities that recognize domestic partners.

On campus, bereavement and sick leave, child care, faculty/staff privileges, family leave, student/faculty housing, home purchase loan (so classified because it is a loan), university ID issuance, class auditing privileges, and tuition waiver are possible examples.

Miscellaneous Benefits

Some other items that don't fall strictly into the hard or soft benefits categories, such as short-term mental health services through a company employee assistance plan, are already available to anyone in the employee's household as the *employee* defines his or her own household and are not subject to an employer definition of domestic partner or an affidavit of any kind.

How Much Do Domestic Partner Benefits Cost the Organization?

The first thing to understand about domestic partner benefits is that you are not introducing new benefits; you are simply extending existing benefits. This is not a new program with new cost factors to consider. It is the same pro-

> The first thing to understand about domestic partner bene-
> fits is that you are not introducing new benefits; you are sim-
> ply extending existing benefits. This is not a new program
> with new cost factors to consider. It is the same program of
> benefits you offer now, only now you make them available to
> more people. And frankly, as proved by all statistics, it's not
> that many more.

gram of benefits you offer now, only now you make them available to more people. And frankly, as proved by all available statistics, it's not that many more.

There are three questions that most often arise during any discussion of domestic partner benefits:

1. How many people will actually elect the benefits?
2. How much will it cost the issuing organization?
3. What are the tax ramifications?

For those readers in a hurry to implement the benefits, the answers are:

1. Not many.
2. Not much.
3. There aren't any for the organization, but there are for the employee who elects the benefit.

For the rest of you, here are the details.

Enrollment Realities

The first thing that determines how much a plan will cost is how many employees will adopt it. Average enrollment in any organization offering these benefits remains at less than 1 percent of the total employee population. The company can control enrollment to a certain extent by offering the benefits only to same-sex couples. Whether or not an employer should make domestic partner benefits available to only same-sex couples or to both same- and opposite-sex couples is a big issue for most organizations, and it will be discussed in greater detail later in this chapter. One of the reasons it is such an issue is that it is directly related to the cost of offering both hard and soft partner benefits. Quite simply, if the organization makes the benefits available to all unmarried partners regardless of sexual orientation, the benefits will cost more because more people—specifically, more straight people—will elect them.

> In 1994 Stanford University announced that the cost of its insurance plans, including those for domestic partner benefits, had actually gone *down* because of its superior bargaining position with insurance providers.

- In the city of Berkeley, ninety-seven opposite-sex partners and nineteen same-sex partners elected benefits.
- In Santa Cruz, three-quarters of those adopting domestic partner benefits have opposite-sex partners.
- In San Francisco, 50 percent of those adopting benefits have opposite-sex partners.
- In Seattle, 2.3 percent of 10,000 municipal employees adopted the benefits. Estimates are that opposite-sex couples outnumber same-sex couples at least 2:1.
- Ben and Jerry's employs 300 people. Fifteen opted for benefits, of whom one has a same-sex partner.

When hard benefits are offered to same-sex couples only, the average cost increase to the organization is 0.3 percent. If offered to opposite-sex couples too, the increase is 1 to 3.4 percent.* In Apple's 1992 analysis of the cost ramifications of implementing domestic partner benefits, twelve of sixteen organizations reported no resulting changes in premiums. In 1994 Stanford University announced that the cost of its insurance plans, including those for domestic partner benefits, had actually gone *down* because of its superior bargaining position with insurance providers.

Why Is the Percentage of Same-Sex Partners Enrolling So Low?

The question remains, why do heterosexual couples elect the benefits in such greater numbers than homosexual couples if both are allowed to? The most obvious reason, of course, is that there are simply more heterosexuals in the world. There are other reasons, however.

---

* These cost increase percentages were first reported by Apple Corporation in 1992 after it conducted a survey of organizations with partner benefits up to that time. There is absolutely no evidence to suggest that these percentages are not as true today as they were in 1992. Our own analysis of more than thirty plans shows an average 1 percent increase in cost. In fact, *The Wall Street Journal* has, on more than one occasion, flatly stated that same-sex partner benefits are cheaper for the organization than benefits for traditional families are. More statistics are available.

Unemployed Partners Qualify More Easily

In many heterosexual relationships, married or not, one partner performs the more traditional role of housewife/house husband and child caretaker. That makes it easier for the employee's partner to qualify for partner benefits because the partner's employment status is a big part of the qualification process. (Qualifying for partner benefits is reviewed shortly.)

Negative Tax Consequences

In gay relationships two things are common. First, both adult partners usually work and therefore have their own benefits through their own employers. Because of the tax ramifications of domestic partner benefits, even if one partner's plan is much better than the other's is, it might cost more in the long run to adopt it.

Fewer Children

Second, gay relationships tend to involve fewer children, and childbirth remains the most costly of all insurance expenses. This trend is definitely starting to change, and it will no doubt have some effect on the cost of domestic partner benefits in the future. To mitigate that, we are hopeful that benefits for all families, regardless of orientation, will also be much further advanced by the year 2000.

Fear of Revealing Orientation

In some other cases, gay people don't enroll in domestic partner benefits plans even if they need and qualify for them because they remain fearful of being "outed" (having their orientation revealed) as a consequence of signing up for the benefits. Even though benefits election is a confidential process, a person must still in most cases file an affidavit with the company's human resources department, which may in turn share that information with an insurance company. The risks of disclosure are slight, but they are painfully significant and frightening for people who have to work in homophobic environments.

Adverse Selection Issues

Contrary to warnings and predictions made by insurance companies and other concerned parties since the mid-1980s, extending coverage to domestic partners has not resulted in increased costs due to adverse selection. In no instance where a surcharge was demanded by an insurance carrier or HMO at the start of same-sex partner plans was the surcharge on premium left still in existence two years later. Since mid-1993, no surcharges have been assessed on partner plans, regardless of the orientation of the participants. Experience to date emphatically indicates that employers are at no more risk when adding domestic partners than when adding spouses.

By including straight couples in domestic partner medical plans, the employer is guaranteeing that any cost increases will be greater than if they offer the benefits only to gay couples. This is true not only because of the enrollment ramifications as explained above, but because of the types of claims that straight people make on their insurance plans more than gay people do (or have to this point in time).

Specifically, as mentioned earlier, medical expenses related to childbirth continue to be the most significant hit to any organization's benefits budget. And when a birth is problematic, expenses rise exponentially.

Childbirth aside, many organizations continue to resist domestic partner benefits because they fear that a disproportionate number of AIDS-related claims will arise from covering same-sex partners. This particular roadblock is disturbing, narrow-minded, and dangerous.

It's disturbing because it supports the homophobic viewpoint that AIDS is solely a gay disease, that all domestic partners are gay, and therefore that issuing benefits to employees' partners will absolutely result in increased costs due to AIDS claims.

It's narrow-minded because it forgets that lesbians are gay too and remain in the lowest risk group for HIV-related disorders.

It's dangerous because gay men are the best educated about AIDS and have been changing their sexual behavior patterns for over a decade. The incidence of HIV-related disease is currently increasing more in the heterosexual population, and in the young heterosexual population faster than in any other segment of the world's society.

Even though not one provider of domestic partner health benefits has reported a significant number (most have experienced none) of HIV- or AIDS-related insurance claims from the same- or opposite-sex partner of an employee, AIDS-phobia runs rampant. Leaving behind the social ramifications of this phobia for a moment and remembering that benefits are a dollars-and-cents issue, it is worthwhile to examine the cost of AIDS in relationship to other possible claims.

1. Heart disease: $50K to $100K (in *two-week period* following a heart attack or stroke).
2. Cancer: $30K to $120K.
3. Premature birth: $70K to $1M (birth to one year).

4. Alzheimer's disease passed AIDS on the list in 1994 in terms of expense.
5. AIDS: $85K to $100K. However, the Spring 1994 issue of *Inquiry*, a journal put out by Blue Cross/Blue Shield, revealed a maximum cost of $32,000 per HIV-infected employee and an average of $17,000 total and included health insurance, disability, hiring, training, life insurance, and pensions.

Frankly, employers should be pursuing two programs aggressively if all they want to do is save money in the long run:

1. They should be educating their workforces about HIV, AIDS, and other sexually transmitted diseases. If the current trend continues, many more people are going to become infected. These will be heterosexuals who, thanks to homophobia and insidious ignorance, think they are immune.
2. They should be helping all their female employees take advantage of all available precautionary measures against breast cancer. Yearly mammograms, Pap smears, and blood screenings are much less expensive than treating uterine and breast cancers.

In a study released by the University of Iowa just prior to enacting domestic partner benefits for faculty and staff, the costs of these benefits for the employer and the employee were predicted to fall into two main categories. One small cost to the employer, in this case the University, would be the additional charge paid to Blue Cross/Blue Shield of Iowa to administer the contracts for domestic partners. Another cost consideration would be the potential increase in premiums for the group from any adverse claims experience from HIV-related disease. Iowa estimated their cost increase in a range of 3.8 percent to 7.2 percent. The actual increase from 1992 to 1993 was 0.2 percent.

When domestic partner benefits were first proposed in New York City in 1993, their estimated cost was $40 million to $75 million. The actual cost to the end of 1994 is $4 million, well below the $1.1 billion the city pays out in contracts for married employees.

The Cost of Benefits Related to Taxes

The question of how the IRS views employer contributions to health benefits coverage for domestic partners is a major area of concern. It turns out that employers should be less concerned than the employees electing the coverage. For employers it is more of an administrative detail than a cost concern.

The Tax Picture for Employers

Most employers are treating their premium contribution to the domestic partner's coverage as a compensation expense under Code Section 162, attributable to the employment of the employee. In other words, they treat it just as they treat premium contributions for legal spouses. Employers are also taking these premium contributions as tax deductions by classifying them as an "ordinary and necessary business expense," again just as they treat spousal premiums. The IRS has not made a sweeping decision about the deductibility of these premiums, but it did issue at least one private letter ruling (PLR 9034048). The party in question sought clarification on this question and was told that contributions to partner benefits could be treated like spousal and legal dependent contributions.

On November 10, 1994, the IRS issued another PLR to the Writers' Guild Industry Health Fund, a multiemployer health plan that enjoys tax-exempt status. In this PLR, the Writers' Guild was told that it would not lose its tax-exempt status if the amount it spent on nonqualifying coverage (that is, for people who do not qualify as legal dependents) did not surpass a "de minimis," or allowable, amount. The amount estimated by the Health Fund was 3.4 percent of the total cost of the benefits paid. Because there is no actual published "de minimis" amount, one can only assume that 3.4 percent does not exceed it.

The import of this ruling is that there are over ten million workers covered by multiemployer plans similar to that of the Writers' Guild. Therefore, fear of loss of tax-exempt status should no longer be a deterrent. However, we must caution that in the case of either (1) a for-profit enterprise that is deducting the cost of partner premiums as a common and ordinary business expense, or (2) those who are concerned about also maintaining their tax-exempt status, private letter rulings never constitute a precedent, and a tax attorney should always be consulted.

The Tax Picture for Employees

The tax picture for employees who elect coverage for their partners is not as favorable. According to PLR 9034048 and at least two others issued since 1991, employees must pay tax on the fair market value of the benefits they elect for their partners. Fair market value will be explained in a moment.

Employer-provided health benefits for domestic partners or nonspouse cohabitants of an employee are excludable from imputed (taxable) income only if the recipient of the benefit is a legal spouse or legal dependent. For federal tax purposes, the determination of legal spouse status is based on state marital laws. What constitutes a dependent is determined by state and local laws as well as by the definition of a dependent under Section 152 of the IRS Code. If the recipient of the benefits is a legal spouse or dependent, the fair market value of the employer-provided benefits is considered tax-qualified and is therefore excludable under Code Sections 105 and 106. If the domestic partner is not a legal spouse or cannot qualify as a dependent under Section 152, the fair market value of the employer-provided benefits will be taxable.

A quick read of Tax Code Section 152 demonstrates that it is extremely difficult to be an adult who qualifies as the dependent of another adult. Also, no state currently recognizes homosexual marriages or in any way grants legal spouse status to same-sex partners. Therefore, most if not all gay employees who receive benefits for their partners are technically required to pay taxes on those benefits.

Some common-law marriage statutes may give legal-spouse status to heterosexual partners in the states where they are recognized. However, preadoptive children do not qualify as dependents until they are fully legally adopted.

The IRS recognizes that these rules cause different tax treatments in different states because common-law marriage and adoption rules are different or nonexistent. The IRS explains its position by saying that it "illustrates the deference Congress has demonstrated for state laws in this area and its attempts to ensure that, in the application of federal law, taxpayers will be treated in their intimate and personal relationships as the states in which they reside treat them."

Furthermore, in those cases where the employer-provided health care coverage is offered through a flexible benefits plan in which employees contribute to the cost of dependent coverage, coverage for domestic partners is allowed. The current catch is that although legally married employees can pay premiums for their spouses with before-tax dollars, employees covering their partners must do so with after-tax dollars. Therefore, the same benefits when granted to partners are more expensive for the employee not only because they are taxed, but because of how those taxes can legally be paid.

What Is the Fair Market Value?

The amount of a benefit that is taxable (imputed) is called its fair market value. In those organizations offering domestic partner benefits as of the time this book is written, most are determining this taxable number by doing a calculation of the full unsubsidized individual rate for insurance, less the remainder of subtracting the employee's individual rate from the employee's family rate. In other words, the fair market value is the amount of premium paid by the employer toward the partner's coverage minus whatever the employee contributes for that coverage.

A recurring problem with this *premium model* is that first, in those cases where a partner is being added to what is already a "family" policy where *family* is not specifically defined as employee-plus-one or employee-plus-two-or-more, it is almost impossible to determine what portion of the premium the employee must pay with after-tax dollars. Second, it is likewise difficult to determine what portion of the employer contribution is imputable. Our research shows that in many cases where the premium model to determine fair market value is being used, the employee is paying too much with after-tax dollars and is assessed too much for imputed income.

The other model for determining fair market value is what we call the *actuarial model*. Some companies determine the fair market value by figuring out the exact dollar value of every kind of policy that they offer from every service provider based on actuarial claims experience. This method is common in fully self-insured plans where no premiums, per se, are involved.

In the actuarial model, the values are determined typically for employee only, employee-plus-one, employee-plus-children, and employee-plus-family. This last category serves well those instances where a partner and/or partner's dependents are added to an already-existing family plan. In this model, unlike in the premium model, it is possible for a value to be determined that can then be relatively fairly—if not always completely fairly—divided by those people on the employee's plan who are legal partners or dependents and those who are not. Once this division is made, the employer can more accurately determine what portion of the premium must be paid by the employee with after-tax dollars, and what portion of its contribution to the partner/dependent coverage is imputable. Usually this will be the difference between the actuarial value of the employee-only cost and that of the employee-plus-one cost. Appendix I provides numerical examples to explain the dollar and tax ramifications of partner benefits based on these two models.

Our Conclusion?

We have reached three conclusions where the cost of domestic partner benefits are concerned:

1. Domestic partner benefits are neither complicated nor expensive for the employer.
2. These benefits cannot be elected lightly by employees and can represent a significant expense to them, not to their employer.
3. Domestic partner benefits represent an honest effort on the part of an employer to level out the compensatory playing field for all employees. But partner benefits are still not equal pay for equal work.

Options for the Organization to Mitigate Cost

The organization can also consider alternatives available in the methods for both implementing and paying for domestic partner benefits:

- It can decide not to offer all the same benefits to partners as it does to legal spouses.
- It can opt not to include dependent children of partners in the benefits plans.
- It can offer to split premiums with the employees, or it can offer cash incentives to offset cost and/or taxes for the employees.
- It can, as the University of Minnesota, the University of Iowa, Gardiner Supply in Vermont, Xerox, and others have done, simply give the employees cash in lieu of coverage as a way to offset the cost of their getting coverage for their partners.
- The employer also has the option of just helping the employees coordinate this coverage through the company plan without actually contributing any monetary or administrative support at all.
- Still a relatively new strategy is the cafeteria plan or benefits credits scenario with which some organizations are experimenting. In this strategy, a smorgasbord of benefits is laid out, and everyone is given the same number of credits to spend on what they and their families need. One employee might opt to insure a partner, whereas another might opt for elder care. One might be more concerned with child care; another might want to spend more credits on 401(k) matching contributions. This seems to be a very workable idea, but again it is not entirely equitable for unmarried partners of either orientation because of the before-tax dollars/after-tax dollars payment requirements.

Phasing In

In the mid-1980s and early in this decade, it was not unusual for employers to take one of these halfway measures as a first step in implementing partner benefits. It is much less common now, however. If an organization is going to implement the benefits today, it will typically offer them under the same conditions as it offers all other benefits to all other employees. It is still common, however, for organizations to experiment by offering some of the soft benefits before offering the hard benefits to same-sex partners of employees.

We call this a "phasing in" of benefits. Organizations adopted a phasing-in approach in order to stick their toes into the water to see whether they would get scalded. Some still do it because phasing these benefits in is literally the only way they can gain any equitable benefits for their gay employees.

Phasing in will become less valid shortly for two reasons. First, more than two hundred and seventy organizations have domestic partner benefits already, and they are generating enough statistical and anecdotal evidence for new organizations to predict accurately what implementation costs and what employee reactions are to be expected. Second, gay employees are going to be less patient as more organizations give these benefits to their employees.

The Less Tangible Cost of Domestic Partner Benefits

Domestic partner benefits are far from a perfect solution to create equity in the workplace where benefits and compensation are concerned, but they are better than nothing for the time being. A discussion about the conceivable impact of the legalization of gay relationships in this country and the status of such movements worldwide is included later in this chapter. For now, employers and employees must deal with what is, not what will be.

Employers fear possible negative repercussions from implementing partner benefits that include same-sex couples. Apple's experience in Texas (see Chapter 1) is a good example of what could happen, although it rarely does.

Several corporations and universities have told us, always off the record, that they are concerned by what the negative ramifications will be if they elect these benefits for the same-sex partners of their employees. Communications companies are watching AT&T closely, for instance. AT&T can boast very progressive policies and support efforts for its gay employee group (LEAGUE) and gay population, but it hasn't implemented partner benefits yet. Representatives on both sides of the issue at AT&T continue to express concern about the possible negative impact on business if the company makes that move. Domestic partner benefits may be the only area where US West, Sprint, and MCI are not tripping over themselves to beat out AT&T! All have publicly expressed their concerns about what might happen if they offer domestic partner benefits.*

---

* All these organizations, and many others, are actively investigating domestic partner benefits at the time this book is being written.

In the banking industry, the worry is that longer-standing, more conservative customers would strenuously object to such plans. Walt Disney Corporation is trying to figure out what the adoption of such benefits would do to its "family-oriented" image, even though the corporation is very supportive of its gay employees (see case studies in Chapter 9).

ASK Computers had the benefits and then lost them when it was acquired by Computer Associates (CA). CA's CEO commented that the company will have only "regular benefits for regular people." Organizations like the Bank of America still hesitate to consider domestic partner benefits because of an indirectly related experience. When the Bank of America publicly refused to give any more financial support to the Boy Scouts of America because the Boy Scouts strictly prohibit gay scout leaders or members, the Bank endured a lot of negative publicity. On the other hand, companies like Levi Strauss, Microsoft, and Apple (all of which have partner benefits) also condemned the Boy Scouts' policy and did not suffer unduly because of it.

In Austin, Texas, in 1993, the city council voted to implement domestic partner benefits. Later in 1993, the benefits were rescinded in a questionably written referendum. The whole issue sparked quite a debate, but smack in the middle of it, American Micro Devices of Austin quietly granted these benefits to the same-sex partners of its employees in Texas and California. The company reports no severe ill effects of this decision.

The University of New Mexico's initial decision to implement domestic partner benefits for same-sex couples did lead to some problems. People who disagreed with the benefits' implementation argued that by limiting the benefits to same-sex couples, the university was giving gays special rights. However, New Mexico does not offer civil protection to its gay citizens, nor does it recognize same-sex unions as legal.

The University of New Mexico chose not to argue the point of "special rights" with its detractors; it simply disarmed them by extending the benefits to opposite-sex couples as well as same-sex couples. The university (and others that have gone this route) are to be commended for accepting the burden of additional monetary cost by so extending the benefits. Gays are not asking for special rights; they are asking for equal treatment under the existing laws. They are asking their employers to help them implement policies in the workplace that they believe will trickle out through the rest of society and help adjust laws to be more reflective of the construct of the family as it exists in reality, not as it exists in mythology.

More than once, organizations have expressed to Common Ground that they don't want to take a leadership position on the implementation of domestic partner benefits. Our reply to them is that they should not worry about it. There are over two hundred organizations that can claim a leadership role; everyone else is hereby invited to take up support positions.

Some Relevant Questions and Answers

Are domestic partner benefits legal?

Domestic partner benefits, including medical, dental, COBRA, FMLA, pension, and all "soft" benefits are entirely legal. However, it is not legal to include a domestic partner in a company-provided group life insurance plan unless the employee pays the entire premium. In some cases, employers have offered life insurance by simply paying the partner's premium for the employee.

Legally, a domestic partner can be defined in any way that the organization chooses to define him or her, and that person (and in some cases his or her legal dependents) can be party to benefits that the company chooses to extend. Any monetary contribution made by the employer for the partner constitutes imputed (taxable) income to the employee.

If we offer benefits to partners, will there be less available for traditional families?

Gay families, the partnerships and unions entered into by two adults who happen to be gay, the children they bring to the relationship or produce, their values, interdependence, and commitment are exactly the same as those entered into by heterosexuals who enjoy societal, legal, and religious recognition through church- and state-sanctioned marriage. The fact that the law does not make provisions for gay families is not relevant, at least not to those families. Interracial marriage was at one time illegal too.

As detailed in Chapter 1, the dynamics of the family are already grossly different from those that were predominant when our existing laws were written. The kinds of nontraditional groups that businesses must account for in their benefits plans include but are not limited to families founded on a same-sex union. There are also single-parent families, foster situations, handicapped people who live together for support and assistance, and extended families, to name a few.

This last type, extended families, warrants attention. Since 1992, in refusing domestic partner benefits to gay employees' partners, more than one organization has tried to use the argument that if they give benefits to partners, then they'll also have to give benefits to parents, grandparents, aunts, uncles, nieces, and nephews. A man is obligated to aid and support his wife and children; a woman is obligated to aid and support her husband and children. Neither is *obligated* (although both may *feel* obligated) to support their parents, grandparents, aunts, and other relatives.

When two people, gay or straight, with or without children, enter into a committed relationship involving mutual dependence and responsibility in every way that a married couple does, they face the same responsibility to take care of their partner and their children as their straight, married counterparts. Therefore, if the organization feels no compunction to offer benefits to a married employee's parents, aunts, uncles, what have you, it need not feel any to offer it to the extended family members of any employees just because it recognizes the validity of a committed partnership.

How do you determine who is a domestic partner?

Another of the principal worries for organizations thinking of implementing partner benefits is how to determine who constitutes a domestic partner, and what sort of proof of such partnership can and should it require.

Each organization can define a domestic partner in whatever way it sees fit. The most common definitions are:

- A relationship resembling a family or household with close cooperation between the parties, each having specified responsibilities.
- A committed, nonplatonic, family-type relationship of two unrelated partners.
- Two unrelated individuals who share the necessities of life, live together, and have an emotional and financial commitment to each other.
- Two individuals who have an intimate and committed relationship and are jointly responsible for basic living expenses.

Other words used for domestic partner include *cohabitant, significant other, spousal equivalent, nontraditional dependent,* and *live-in companion.*[3]

Columbia University defines partners as "two individuals of the same gender who live together in a long-term relationship of infinite duration, with an exclusive mutual commitment similar to that of marriage, in which the Partners agree to be financially responsible for each other's welfare and share financial obligations."

Columbia also clearly delineates the requirements it decided upon for two people to substantiate a domestic partnership:

- To be of the same sex and not married.
- To have lived together for at least six months and intend to do so indefinitely.
- To meet the age and mental competency requirements for marriage in the state of New York.
- Not to be related by blood to a degree of closeness that would prohibit legal marriage in the state of legal residence.
- To be jointly responsible for each other's common welfare and to share financial obligations, as demonstrated by three of the following:
  — A domestic partner agreement where registration applies.
  — A joint mortgage or lease, designation of the partner as beneficiary of life insurance and/or retirement benefits.
  — Designation of partner as primary beneficiary of a will.
  — Assignment of durable property or health care power of attorney to the partner.
  — Joint ownership of a car, bank account, or credit account.

Both Columbia's definition of a partnership and its requirements for proof are representative of the norm. However, Columbia offers partner benefits only to same-sex couples. In those instances where benefits were to be offered to opposite-sex couples as well, the requirement "to be of the same sex and not married" would obviously be changed or deleted altogether.

Definition and requirement statements can be more or less stringent than Columbia's policy, which is pretty much middle-of-the-road. For instance, Stanford University requires a legal document be signed in which the partners assume mutual responsibility for each other's debts. According to attorneys we asked, this particular document actually causes domestic partners to have more responsibility for each other financially than legally married couples might. You can annul the financial responsibilities in a marriage and yet remain married.

In almost all cases of partnership termination, the employee is required to notify the company in writing. In some cases, the employee must file a second affidavit of termination signed by both parties. It is also not unusual for an employee who terminates a domestic partnership to have to wait six months or a year before enrolling a new partner. By contrast, if you're married and get divorced, you can get remarried the day your divorce papers come in, and your new spouse can be covered on the spot. Any way you look at it, proving and terminating a domestic partnership is always more difficult than musical marriages can be for heterosexuals (if they choose to behave that way). This is another instance in which efforts to level the playing field are still a bit tipsy.

How does the organization protect itself from fraudulent partner claims?

Some organizations worry that gay people signing up for these benefits will just sign up any friend of theirs who is HIV-infected and who doesn't have insurance. In order to protect themselves from fraudulent claims, almost every organization offering domestic partner benefits requires that an affidavit be filed attesting to the veracity of the partnership and all documented proof submitted to substantiate it.

In contrast to this, most organizations do not even ask an employee who claims to be married to submit a copy of the marriage certificate.

Gay employees (and, we would imagine, straight unmarried employees) do not sign these affidavits lightly. In signing an affidavit, the employee knows that doing so fraudulently could result in a loss of employment. Furthermore, the tax ramifications of accepting benefits on behalf of another person are substantial and verifiable.

From 1982 through 1994, there have been no reported incidences of fraud in the filing of an affidavit of domestic partnership. However, there have been plenty of cases of fraud among heterosexuals falsely claiming to be legally married.

The fact is that companies that are worried about fraud would be just as well served to ask for marriage or common-law marriage certificates, but few actually do. And that goes for the insurance providers too. Recent research by organizations interested in the implementation of benefits shows that companies and municipalities have actually saved more money uncovering insurance fraud in existing plans prior to implementing domestic partner benefits than they have spent on those benefits after fraudulent participants were removed from the plans.

Should benefits go to same-sex couples only?

The next big question that confronts a company considering domestic partner benefits is whether these benefits should be offered to same-sex couples only, or to opposite-sex couples too. There are two schools of thought on this question.

The first holds that because straight people always have the option of getting married, there is no need to offer them benefits outside of the state of matrimony. Interestingly, when three employees at Lotus approached the company about offering these benefits in 1989, they did so with the idea that they would be for everyone. It was the company's decision to offer them only to gay employees, who do not have the option of legal marriage.

The second school of thought says that if you are offering domestic partner benefits in support of a nondiscrimination policy that extends to sexual orientation, then you are obligated to offer the benefits to both gays and straights. The reason is that if your organization chooses not to discriminate on the basis of orientation, it should not discriminate against straight people who, for whatever reason, choose not to legally marry.

There is actually a third point of view. Some people argue that many things in our society, workplace benefits among them, should not be tied to a person's marital status at all. And as we've said before, if a state or an employer prohibits discrimination based on marital status, but things are being withheld from people on the basis of their marital status, there could be grounds for lawsuits.

What if we can't offer benefits because we are downsizing or trying to return to profitability?

All longitudinal data collected since 1989 prove beyond a doubt that adding same-sex partners to a benefits plan results in a total cost increase to the employer of less than one percent. Second, there are no administrative monsters or taxation beasts (for the employer) that must be beaten down in order to implement the benefits. Third, most insurers will work with the employer to implement the benefits. Fourth, the employer could choose to offer all soft benefits first and add the hard ones later. And fifth, neither downsizing nor a return to profitability justify discrimination against one employee constituency over another, especially if the organization has a policy of nondiscrimination based on sexual orientation.

Won't the national health-care debate solve all of these benefits issues?

No. First, even if it would, and it doesn't currently come close, it would not do anything to address those benefits classified as "soft."

All 239 pages of the Clinton Health Plan when originally unveiled were silent on domestic partner benefits. The document does not even define the word spouse, leaving most to believe that traditional spouses and dependents were and are all the current administration is thinking about.

If the United States adopts a system of universal health care, then everyone would be entitled to coverage. This does nothing to solve the matter of who is going to pay for this coverage. Under the Clinton plan as written, a noninsured, self-employed, or unemployed domestic partner of an employee would have to pay 100 percent of his or her pre-

> In those cases where the employer insists that it cannot af-
> ford to add same-sex domestic partners "at this time," it
> should be asked whether it is going to direct all its currently
> single partners not to marry, or tell all its married employ-
> ees not to have children, until the economic difficulties are
> surmounted.

mium, whereas the spouse of another employee working for the same
company would be covered to 80 percent by the employer. The proposal
as drafted also says that the employer can pay up to 100 percent of the
cost of individual or family coverage, but is silent on whether it can pay
the cost of family coverage that would include a partner. It's also silent
on what the tax implications would be.

In other words, the ongoing national health-care debate does not
even consider the problems that implementation of domestic partner
benefits seeks to correct: equal pay for equal work and fair access to
employer-provided benefits.

What if same-sex unions become legal?

It is not, in our opinion, unreasonable to assume that legalized homosexual relationships will exist, at least in some of the United States,
by the turn of the century. There are already many places in the United
States where same-sex couples can register their relationships. Although
these registrations are primarily symbolic and carry little legal weight,
they are still significant because at least they exist.

In December of 1994, the American Medical Association overturned
a long-standing policy of supporting efforts to change a person's sexual
orientation. The paper it released said in part, "Homosexuals may have
some unique mental health concerns related to negative social attitudes
regarding homosexuality, but most of the emotional disturbance homosexuals may feel about their orientation is due more to a sense of alienation in an unaccepting environment. For this reason, aversion therapy
is no longer recommended."

This change in policy and practice by the AMA is significant and over-
due. Gradually, some of the institutions of our society are starting to understand that orientation is inherent and does not warrant discrimination of any kind. It is only logical to assume that things will continue to
progress to the point where orientation will no longer be a factor in the
legalization of relationships.

The word marriage, however, poses semantic difficulties because of its religious connotations. We believe that the unions of gay people will be legal for a long time before they are ever called marriages. For the purposes of the rest of this discussion, we'll refer to gay marriages as "same-sex unions."

At the end of 1994, the Icelandic Parliament, Alltinget, submitted a report to the Icelandic government in which it recommended that Iceland prepare a partnership law after the models established in Denmark, Norway, and Sweden, where gay people in committed relationships enjoy many of the same societal benefits and privileges as straight people do. However, Iceland is considering taking the idea even further by suggesting that its partnership law be in all ways equal to heterosexual marriage, including church marriage privileges and the right to adopt children. In mid-1995, the Netherlands legalized same-sex unions on par with heterosexual marriages.

As of the end of 1994 in the United States, the most significant movements in American history for and against the legalization of same-sex unions are taking very definite shape. In Hawaii, where three same-sex couples first sued the state for marriage licenses in 1993, the governor subsequently appointed a commission to study the question and make a recommendation before the end of 1995. Meanwhile, the Hawaiian courts ruled in 1994 to approve same-sex unions unless the state could show a compelling state interest against them. Legislative attempts to block such unions by law in Hawaii have failed to date.

In the balance of the United States, movements are under way in some states like Wisconsin, Massachusetts, and New Jersey to extend legal reciprocation of legal same-sex unions performed in Hawaii in exactly the same way as all heterosexual marriages are reciprocated in all fifty states; that is, approved Hawaiian same-sex unions would be recognized even though such unions cannot be legally performed in those states themselves at that time. Such reciprocity would be a stepping-stone toward legalization in those states.

We believe that Hawaii's constitutional law dictates that same-sex unions will be legalized there. Furthermore, U.S. constitutional law substantiates the reciprocity of all marriages, regardless of the sex of the participants. (This is true because no one ever thought to put heterosexist language into the Constitution!) We believe that if same-sex unions are legal in Hawaii by 1996, they will be reciprocated in at least three to six other states by the year 2000. Last, we believe that the United States Supreme Court will eventually rule on the reciprocity between states of such unions.

Having said all this, domestic partner benefits provided by employers will continue to be an issue until such time as the U.S. Supreme Court rules on the legality of same-sex unions. Because this event is at least six years away, gay people will push as hard as possible to have their employers implement benefits in order to be able to prove to the court that gay relationships are valid and have been recognized as such (at least in terms of benefits) by employers since 1982.

Ironically, it's also possible that opponents of the legalization of same-sex unions will find themselves working just as hard for partner benefits as a way to forestall the full and legal recognition of same-sex relationships. They may gamble that winning the short-term battle will distract gays from losing the long-term war. Gay people will probably take the small victories for a while, but sooner or later, the question will have to be answered once and for all in its entirety. Business has a great financial and moral stake in the resolution of this question.

The Insurance Industry

The insurance industry is also playing a significant role in the implementation of domestic partner benefits.

What Can Insurers Do?

In 1985 when the city of West Hollywood went looking for an insurer to cover its domestic partner medical benefits, it was turned down by no fewer than sixteen companies. If the city had to go through the process today, those sixteen companies and more would be lined up to write the policy.

When an organization tells its employees that it won't offer domestic partner benefits, it will often try to blame their insurer. The employer will say that it would like to offer partner benefits, but the insurance company said it won't or can't write the claim. A disturbing number of these rejections are not true, and as time goes on such statements are even less likely to be true.

There is nothing in any state's laws in the United States that precludes any insurer from offering domestic partner benefits to the partners of their employees as the employer defines those people. However, in some states, typically states with greater population densities such as those in the Northeast and on the West Coast, the state insurance department regulations can stand in the way of such plans being offered by standard insurers.

In New York, for example, a plan to cover the partners of the New York City Teachers' Union and Prison Guards' Union was delayed for over two years until the New York State Insurance Department decided that "financial interdependency" qualified to satisfy the "dependent" mandate in the state insurance code. However, in New Jersey, the same disagreement about the definition of "dependent" is keeping standard insurers in that state from being able to offer partner plans. And in Pennsylvania, the Insurance Department is maintaining (as of November 1994) that by applying to offer domestic partner benefits to same-sex couples only, the insurer (in this case, Independence Blue Shield) is in violation of the Unfair Insurance Practices Act that prohibits discrimination based on marital status or sex. In other words, the Pennsylvania insurance department is saying that unless opposite-sex partners are included too, the plans are discriminatory. We expect that by the time this book is published, the situations in New Jersey and Pennsylvania will have been resolved, as all such administrative/bureaucratic barriers have been in other states concerning partner benefits.

Some state insurance departments have no regulations whatsoever about partner benefits, so employers in each state have to check. Chances are, your insurer already knows the answer to this question on a state-by-state basis. Even in those states where current regulations seem to block partner insurance plans, there are ways around them.

When Sarnoff, a company in New Jersey, wanted to offer partner benefits, it went around the blockade at the New Jersey insurance department by getting permission for the benefits through the insurance department in New Mexico where its parent company, SRI, is licensed. The ACLU Gay/Lesbian Project is considering legal options to make all the insurance departments in all fifty states play by the same rules.

The main point is that there is currently nothing illegal about partner benefits in any state. At the end of 1994 a group in Oregon was trying for the third time to pass a law (in 1996) that would prohibit such benefits, but it failed in 1992 and 1994. Even in those states where the insurance department continues to complicate things for standard insurers that wish to write these plans for their clients, health maintenance organizations (HMOs), preferred provider organizations (PPOs), and self-insured plans that don't fall under the auspices of the state insurance department do not have a problem and currently have a competitive advantage.

What Do Insurers Want to Do?

Most standard insurers—companies like CNA, Prudential, Aetna, Travelers, and New York Life—don't heavily advertise their willingness to write partner policies, but not one of them will turn away such a request from a client company either.

The change in policy toward domestic partner benefits by most insurers since 1992 is dramatic (see case studies, Chapter 9). In summary, what most would not do two or three years ago, most will do now. The reason for the change is simple: competition. The insurance industry as a whole acknowledged two things, both regarding fears of an increase in adverse selection (read AIDS-phobia). First, insurers recognized that they already cover people who could be HIV-positive. Second, an increase in these claims has not materialized in the domestic partner population.

What an insurer wants to do concerning partner coverage has more to do with its marketing strategy than anything else. In terms of marketing, partner coverage is the same as any other classification of coverage offered by a standard insurer.

A larger company gears itself toward groups of 500 or more; mid-range companies look at groups of 100 to 500 people. Some other companies specialize in the small groups of fewer than 100. Until 1994 it was probably true that very small groups of fifty or fewer people would have best results getting domestic partner coverage with HMOs, more of which extend partner benefits along with bonus services like chiropractic and adult vision care in order to remain competitive. Rare is the HMO that asks for a surcharge on partner premiums any more.

Blue Cross/Blue Shield organizations are also excellent choices for extremely small groups of thirty or fewer. But unfortunately, their efforts to write these policies can still be held up in some states by the state insurance department, as is currently the case in Pennsylvania (December 1994).

On the other hand, more of the standard insurers like Prudential, Aetna, and Travelers have lowered or are lowering the threshold on the number of people they will accept as a small group to thirty or thirty-five. This is bound to make the market for partner policies more competitive and is also bound to encourage insurers like Blue Cross/Blue Shield to fight insurance departments in states like Pennsylvania as a matter of economic survival.

What Should the Organization Do Regarding Insurance?

Companies that want to offer domestic partner benefits must decide whether they should buy standard insurance, whether they should self-insure and to what level, what amount of stop-loss insurance they should buy and from whom, and who should administer their plan.

Organizations with fewer than 500 employees typically purchase insured types of policies from standard insurers or HMOs. In other words, the company buys a fixed set of benefits for a fixed rate, similar to homeowners' or car insurance policies.

Once beyond the 500-employee marker, it is more common for companies to self-insure. In a self-insured plan, all claims that employees file are paid through a banking arrangement between the company, the insurer, and the care provider. When the insurance company doing the administration pays the claim, the bank is notified and the insurance company is reimbursed. The insurance company is paid an administration fee.

Not only can the organization enjoy more autonomy in its coverage if it self-insures, it's also usually cheaper to self-insure. Insurance premiums to an outside insurer are made up of anticipated claims, plus expenses, plus some margin of profit for the insurance company. That margin can be 10 to 15 percent, which is a lot of money in most cases. Ten percent on a 5,000-life case that may be valued at $30 million is $3 million. Three million dollars is a lot of money to save.

For entities with over 5,000 employees, the risk is so spread out that a pure self-insurance plan will usually generate enough money to cover all claims. However, in the range of 500 to 5,000 employees, some sort of additional protection for the employer is warranted. This is called stop-loss protection. Maximum liability limits under most medical plans today are set at $1 million per lifetime. But on a very fast-moving claim like the birth of a premature child, you can exceed $1 million very quickly. Therefore, most companies covering fewer than 5,000 lives want some additional protection of corporate assets and buy stop-loss insurance. For example, Company X can say it will take care of all claims up to $75K per insured, but after that, it wants insurance to cover the rest.

Stop-loss insurance is the reason why even some self-insured plans can fall under the auspices of a standard insurer, which can in turn fall prey to the policies of a given state's insurance department. But it is also why insurance departments in many states will be encouraged to loosen up on the regulatory reins a little bit. If a client company cannot get the insurance it wants from its insurer, it will go to another one that can provide it somehow. More organizations, sometimes in the form of coalitions, are demanding that their insurers make provisions for partners, and more insurers are doing just that.

Pensions, COBRA, and FMLA

Three other areas in which companies can take a proactive stance toward equity to their gay employees are company-paid pension plans and benefits under COBRA and FMLA.

Pension Plans

You can name in your will whomever you choose as executor and primary beneficiary of all your assets. You can choose any other party to hold your power of attorney (durable or otherwise); to inherit your stock or proceeds from a private pension plan like a SEP, IRA, or KEOGH; or to be the beneficiary of any and all insurance policies you hold. You can also choose a partner or any other person, by virtue of health-care proxy in those states where such documents are available, as the one to decide what would happen to you should you become physically or mentally incapacitated.

But in cases where a pension plan is wholly paid by the company, gay domestic partners—and in fact anyone who is not a legal spouse—can be denied payment upon the death of the employee. This is true at any organization that chooses to make legal spouses the only eligible beneficiaries of a company-funded pension plan. In 1994 Hewlett-Packard changed its retirement payout so that only legal spouses could collect. Such decisions are perfectly legal, as set in the precedent of a case between AT&T in New Jersey and Ms. Rovira, the surviving lesbian partner of a deceased AT&T employee (Rovira v. AT&T, 760 F SUPP 376, Southern District New York, 1991).

Ms. Rovira lived with an AT&T employee, Ms. Forlini, for twelve years. The couple shared child-rearing responsibilities for Ms. Rovira's children from a previous marriage. Because Ms. Rovira did not receive benefits after Ms. Forlini's death, she sued AT&T on the grounds that this denial violated ERISA (Employee Retirement Income Security Act) because it violated promises made under the plan and the company's policy not to discriminate on the basis of sexual orientation. Ms. Rovira lost her case, with the court ruling that the ERISA provisions were entirely separate and distinct from any corporate policy regarding discrimination, and because ERISA payouts are commonly tied to blood and legal relationships and have nearly always been denied lesbian and gay or other alternative family members.

As of November 1994, an employee who tries to sue for domestic partner benefits to be extended to a same-sex partner or to a nonlegal spouse will probably lose; the same is true of pension benefits held in a private pension fund. This is because ERISA supersedes any other regulations or internal company policies on the subject. This explains why there haven't been too many direct legal challenges, and why most legal eagles are thinking about suing on the basis of nondiscrimination laws or marital status statutes.

COBRA Benefits

Technically, only legal spouses and dependents are "qualifying beneficiaries" under COBRA (the Consolidated Omnibus Budget Reconciliation Act of 1985). However, there is nothing to stop an employer or an insurer from offering COBRA or COBRA-like plans to the partners of employees. Most companies, universities, unions, and municipalities that offer domestic partner benefits also offer COBRA arrangements identical to those available to married couples.

Where retirement benefits are concerned, most companies are treating coverage in retirement for partners exactly as they are treating the COBRA issue. However, they are not obligated to do so.

FMLA Benefits

FMLA (the Family and Medical Leave Act of 1993) is similar to COBRA in that the law requires covered employers to provide up to twelve weeks of leave to eligible employees for certain reasons affecting the employee and members of his or her immediate family. The leave is unpaid, but all benefits must be maintained. While the act does not specify partners in *immediate family*, it doesn't negate them either, and the choice again is up to the employer.

Winning and Implementing Domestic Partner Benefits

The first step toward implementing domestic partner benefits is to win upper management's approval of the concept and then of the actual plan. Getting these people on board is the only way to ensure the proposal's success.

Whether it is one highly interested senior manager or an entire task force, management's support will depend on being provided with the answers to two basic questions:

1. How much is this going to cost?
2. Exactly why should we do this?

Whether you or someone you hire broaches this idea to management, arguments and data about those two things should figure prominently.

All arguments made must be based in fact, not on emotion. The concept of fairness is an appropriate subtle theme, but arguments related to profitability, competitive and market advantages, and productivity will get the proposal much further. The presenter(s) must be absolutely up to date on all cost figures, statistics, and relevant equations. Senior managers will not seriously consider any proposal that leaves them with a lot of action items; you must leave them with only decision points.

Consultants

It is at this juncture that many organizations find it more efficient and effective to turn to a consultant. It's efficient because a consultant specializing in domestic partner benefits will have all the pertinent information at hand and can therefore save management a lot of time. It's effective because use of a consultant removes emotion from the equation.

Anytime an organization is considering a progressive step like the implementation of domestic partner benefits, it is making a very significant statement about the organization as a whole. The decision of whether or not to implement the benefits will have ramifications for the enterprise both internally and externally. Internally, the organization is sending a clear message to all its personnel about how it views equitable treatment, and externally, the organization is making a statement to society as a whole about its values and how it intends to conduct itself within the bigger picture.

Whether a consultant is utilized or a task force of concerned personnel and management comes together to influence policy, the very first step is to make sure that the company's nondiscrimination policy expressly includes sexual orientation. That is the foundation upon which any rational argument for the implementation of the benefits—in whatever form—must be built.

People will argue that it is easier to win these benefits in the "more liberal" areas of the United States, such as the Northeast and the West Coast, and it is undeniable that most of the companies who have these types of programs are in those places. But it is equally undeniable that, as mentioned earlier in this chapter, American Micro Devices in Austin, Texas, awarded these benefits to its employees in the same week that the city of Austin itself repealed its own domestic partner benefits plan. (This reversal is under appeal.) It is also undeniable that the University of Minnesota and the city of Minneapolis were and are leaders in the fight for equal treatment; that Principal Mutual in Iowa offers these benefits to its employees; and that the state of Wisconsin enforces some of the most equitable statutes in the United States, including those that protect on the basis of sexual orientation. The point is, if people stick to facts and logic and utilize the services of a consultant with these tools, they stand an excellent chance of winning the benefits regardless of their geographic location.

Any single employee can be the impetus to start this ball rolling. Any single employee can reach out to others in order to establish a task force, or can approach the human resources department and ask for help. The amount of personal involvement is a matter of individual preference. It is true that a certain amount of courage is involved, but persistence and reaching out to resources both inside and outside the company are the real keys to success.

What to Include in the Proposal

Relevant management should be presented with facts and figures that address the proposed benefits, including (in the following order):

1. A definition of domestic partner benefits.
2. A justification for their implementation at your organization.
3. The meaning of a nondiscrimination policy that expressly includes sexual orientation.
4. Requirements for qualification as a domestic partner.
5. A recommendation of which benefits currently offered to legal spouses and/or dependents would be extended to partners and/or their dependents.
6. Examples of the projected cost of the benefits to the company.
7. Examples of the projected cost of the benefits to the employees who elect them.
8. An explanation and example of the tax ramifications to all parties.
9. Explanation of how the implementation of these benefits would affect the enterprise.
10. Information about the position of the insurance industry in general, and your insurers in particular, in regard to these benefits.
11. A detailed plan to handle registration for and administration of these benefits.
12. A detailed plan for the communication of the benefit plan to all employees and to the outside world.

Accountability as a Weapon Against Homophobia

In this chapter and in this book we've provided supporting documentation for the twelve items on this list. They are based in fact, they are verifiable, and they are statistically correct. Most of all, they are logical.

Armed with all this, a person might be led to believe that there is no way a businessperson looking at all the evidence could decide against implementing domestic partner benefits. However, blatant homophobia can stand in the way of even a reasonable investigation and remains the biggest roadblock. Homophobia is a real problem that can be defeated. The key to its defeat is accountability.

In late 1994 we were approached by faculty at a medium-size university in the Midwest to help them win domestic partner benefits at their institution. This group of concerned faculty first approached the president of the school and asked him to consider the benefits. The president referred the matter to his vice president of finance, who in turn directed his assistant vice president of business affairs to study the question and make a recommendation.

The assistant vice president was given this directive in about September of 1994; by Christmas, he had not yet started and informed us that he did not know when he would. He thought he might be able to make a recommendation by July of 1995. In the meantime, he acknowledged that the concerned faculty members were providing him with enough information to investigate the matter fully without even having to leave his office. They were, with our help, doing the job for him.

Still, he felt it would take half a year to make a recommendation but declined to say why. Then, in a surprising bit of candor, he told us that although he knew of several other schools in his state that were actively pursuing domestic partner benefits or had implemented them, he doubted seriously that his institution would follow suit. He would not say why.

We asked him how he could make this determination when he had not even begun the process of investigation, and he declined to answer. This, coupled with his very clear statement that he had no intention of keeping the faculty group involved or apprised of the issue, made it clear to us that we were dealing with a person whose individual views about domestic partners and their benefits would preclude him from doing his job.

Passing judgment on him or trying to convince him to change his point of view was fruitless. He freely demonstrated his willingness to act unprofessionally; efforts to change his behavior for the sake of his employer would be pointless. So the only thing to do was to go around him to the point of accountability. That person is his boss, the vice president of finance.

When dealing with homophobia as the principal block to the implementation of domestic partner benefits, those involved must be prepared to seek out every possible avenue—inside and outside the organization—to find an accountable person who is willing to look at the facts. Do not let blatant homophobia stand in the way. Homophobia is an emotional thing; domestic partner benefits are business.

Communication and Education

Once a benefits plan is agreed upon, and while all the final logistical arrangements are being made, a great deal of attention is necessary to determine how the plan will be communicated to employees and, in fact, to the world. There may be resistance to domestic partner benefits, especially if the enterprise chooses to offer them to gay couples only. Straight, unmarried-but-no-less-committed couples are going to have a hard time with that.

Be prepared to provide some level of education to the entire employee base that covers not only the benefits themselves, but all the underlying issues behind the benefits' implementation.

The importance of company-wide education at this juncture cannot be overemphasized. Many of the objections to domestic partner benefits for same-sex couples are based upon ignorance about those relationships and about gay people in general.

Every company considering benefits should also consider the extent to which its employee education program covers these difficult and sensitive subjects. In developing written or verbal communication plans about any new benefits, the company must consider the extent to which the general employee population has been informed about the nature and reason for the changes.

If a company does not offer diversity training of any kind, it should implement this training. If its diversity training has steered away from issues related to sexual orientation and AIDS education because of the difficulties inherent in those subjects, it must find the courage to include them. It is difficult, if not impossible, to communicate effectively with parties who are ignorant of the facts.

Companies should provide straightforward and simple documentation about the plan. Many companies experience great success in introducing these benefits in conjunction with the overhaul or retooling of their entire benefits packages, thereby creating a need for all members of the organization to reenlist or reevaluate their choices at the same time. This gives the company the opportunity to position and explain the domestic partner benefits as just one more option in a benefits plan that is well thought out and well constructed. Wherever possible, it is appropriate to hold a meeting or series of meetings to have the benefits explained by the appropriate personnel rather than just by memo.

Representatives from senior management should be present at each meeting, thereby silently (or not) lending their visible support to all the programs. Senior management sets the tone from the very beginning through the very end. Its involvement is crucial to the success of the endeavor.

Finally, implementors of the policy must make sure that there is a streamlined, efficient, and accessible mechanism in place for people to ask questions, voice comments, and discuss concerns (anonymously if necessary). This includes human resources personnel managers and social service providers, who should be given adequate information and training to discuss, answer, and address employee questions and concerns.

Notes

1. Loralie Van Sluys, "Domestic Partner Benefits Study" (Chicago: Hewitt Associates, 1991).
2. Submitted by the Ad-Hoc Committee of the Regional Civil Rights Committee prepared for the United States Department of Agriculture.
3. Van Sluys.

7

HIV/AIDS: Workplace Policies and Education

AIDS is not solely a "gay disease." However, this incorrect perception necessitates a chapter about it and HIV infection in this book. To be HIV-positive or to have AIDS is devastating enough in and of itself. The role these conditions play in contributing to the homophobia of those who are uninformed about them, or who refuse to help educate their employees or their constituencies through proactive programs and policies, is undeniable. Therefore, while acknowledging the risk of furthering the misconception that HIV and AIDS are "gay" things, we felt it more important to include this chapter so that more people will understand that neither is solely the burden of gay people, and that employers owe it to all their employees to be well informed and proactive in addressing these issues in their workplaces.

The Reality of the Situation

As of February 1, 1995, Acquired Immune Deficiency Syndrome (AIDS) is the number one cause of death in the United States for people between ages 25 and 44.[1] As of that same date, one in every 250 Americans is infected with human immunodeficiency virus (HIV-positive) or affected by AIDS-related disease(s). One in every 100 workers is so affected.[2] Three of every 100 workers are caretakers of someone with HIV or AIDS. Two hundred people per day become infected with HIV.[3]

According to the 1994 American Management Association survey on HIV- and AIDS-related policies, the number of organizations that have had to deal with cases of infection increased over 64 percent from 1991 to 1994.

But the same survey found that only about 50 percent of these organizations have any policies in place to deal with HIV- or AIDS-afflicted people effectively. Only 32 percent have any AIDS awareness programs, and only 19 percent provide supervisory training. These statistics, we believe, are attributable to AIDS-phobia and homophobia.

These survey results led the American Management Association to conclude, as dozens of other agencies have, that experience is driving policy; that companies tend to be reactive instead of proactive in their treatment of HIV and AIDS; that an incidence of HIV infection or AIDS is what leads firms to create new policies or reenact old ones instead of planning for what seems more and more to be a statistical certainty; and that HIV infection or AIDS will occur in every workplace sooner or later.[4] Employers must understand that sooner is now and later is irrelevant.

The same survey also concluded that companies are more active in AIDS identification and treatment than they are in AIDS prevention. Although efforts to be compassionate after the fact are commendable, more workplaces (and society in general) would benefit from (1) proactive AIDS policies in the workplace to foster awareness, and from (2) education initiatives to keep more people from getting sick, or to help improve conditions for those who already are sick or who are caring for family members or friends so afflicted.

HIV/AIDS-Specific Policy

In this chapter, we are going to look at two important parts of the conversation concerning HIV/AIDS in the workplace. The first section is about why an organization should specifically draft and implement a workplace policy for HIV and AIDS. This includes an overview of employers' and employees' legal rights, resources, and responsibilities relative to HIV/AIDS, and relevant cost issues. The second section concerns itself with why education programs must be initiated prior to the onset of an HIV/AIDS case in the workplace, and what that education should include. This second section also outlines an effective HIV/AIDS curriculum.

The Policies Themselves

Organizations that have documented, posted policies concerning organizational behavior specific to HIV and AIDS take either what is called a life-threatening illness approach or an HIV/AIDS-specific approach to that policy. (Full examples of both kinds are offered in Appendix II.)

In the first, the HIV/AIDS policy is part of the continuum of all life-threatening illness or disabilities. These policies usually state that HIV/AIDS will be handled as are all other serious illnesses—that is, sensibly, compassionately, and without discrimination. In the second, HIV and AIDS are specifically addressed as major health issues with potential impact on the workplace. In addition to the policy statement itself, this type often contains an educational component stating that HIV/AIDS is not transmitted through casual contact, and that employees with HIV/AIDS are not a health risk to their co-workers.

Some companies that do have written documentation regarding HIV and AIDS don't have a policy at all. Rather, they use something called *Responding to AIDS: Ten Principles for the Workplace,* which was developed by the Citizens Commission on AIDS of New York City and Northern New Jersey.[5] These ten principles cover the rights of infected individuals, the legal responsibilities of employers, the need to be cognizant of the medical facts, the importance of vocal leadership and support by management, the need for education, the requirement of confidentiality, and issues related to both screening and employee responsibilities—those infected and those not infected. Specifically, the principles are:

1. People with AIDS or HIV infection are entitled to the same rights and opportunities as people with other serious or life-threatening illnesses.
2. Employment policy must, at a minimum, comply with federal, state, and local laws and regulations.
3. Employment policies should be based on the scientific and epidemiological evidence that people with AIDS or HIV infection do not pose a risk of transmission of the virus to co-workers through ordinary workplace contact.
4. The highest levels of management and union leadership should unequivocally endorse nondiscriminatory employment policies and educational programs about AIDS.
5. Employers and unions should communicate their support of these policies to workers in simple, clear, and unambiguous terms.
6. Employers should provide employees with sensitive, accurate, and up-to-date education about risk reduction in their personal lives.
7. Employers have a duty to protect the confidentiality of employees' medical information.
8. To prevent work disruption and rejection by co-workers of employees with AIDS or HIV infection, employers and unions should undertake education for all employees before such an incident occurs, and as needed thereafter.
9. Employers should not require HIV screening as part of preemployment or general workplace physical examinations.

10. In those special occupational settings where there may be a potential risk of exposure to HIV (for example, in health care, where workers may be exposed to blood or blood products), employers should provide specific, ongoing education and training, as well as the necessary equipment, to reinforce appropriate infection control procedures and ensure that they are implemented.

Laws That May Drive Policy

Whether the organization adopts the life-threatening illness approach, the HIV/AIDS-specific approach, or the *Ten Principles*, it will likely make its decision based on its understanding of its legal rights and responsibilities regarding HIV/AIDS in the workplace. The pertinent parts of a legal discussion are the Federal Rehabilitation Act (FRA), the 1990 Americans with Disabilities Act (ADA), the Occupational Safety and Health Act (OSHA), and applicable state and local laws.

The basic tenet behind all of these is that employees with disabilities, which HIV and AIDS are considered to be, are protected by law from discrimination in employment, housing, public accommodations, and other parts of life.

Federal Rehabilitation Act (FRA)

This act prohibits discrimination against handicapped people in all programs or agencies that receive federal funds and in all federal agencies. This law has continually been interpreted in the courts to include people who are HIV-positive or AIDS-affected.

Americans with Disabilities Act (ADA)

ADA, which was enacted in 1990 and which completed its phasing-in process in 1994, holds employers liable for discrimination against an employee with HIV/AIDS or one who is perceived to be infected. Such discrimination is classified as firing, refusing to hire, or failing to make reasonable accommodations that allow that employee to continue work if the employer's decisions are based on the individual's HIV/AIDS status. Businesses may also not deny the equal enjoyment of goods and services to people who are affected or who are perceived to be affected.

The specific requirements under ADA are extensive and can be quite taxing. It behooves the organization to go to great lengths to ensure compliance. For example, in terms of hiring, employers can legally ask certain questions of prospective employees but not others. Legal questions include:

- Can you perform this job with or without reasonable accommodation?
- Can you meet the attendance requirements of this job?
- How many days of leave did you take last year?
- Do you have the required licenses to perform this job?

Illegal questions include:

- Do you need reasonable accommodation to perform this job?
- Do you have a disability that would interfere with your ability to perform the job?
- How many days were you sick last year?
- Have you ever filed for workers compensation?[6]

Knowing the difference between what you may and may not ask a job candidate in an interview can either save or cost the organization a great deal of money. Intent is irrelevant in discrimination cases, even when the employer acts in good faith. The test for discrimination is based on the plaintiff's ability to demonstrate that treatment by the employer adversely affected her or him. Examples of such adverse affects can be failure to hire, termination without cause, failure to promote, or failure to make available the same opportunities as others in similar situations have received.[7]

Occupational Safety and Health Act (OSHA)

Parts of OSHA apply to HIV and AIDS in the workplace. One OSHA stipulation is that an employer must provide a safe working environment for all, and that workers cannot be discharged for complaining about what they perceive to be an unsafe environment. Some people have tried to use this stipulation as an argument to support firing HIV-positive employees or those suspected of being HIV-positive. But because there is no proof that simply working with an infected person puts anyone at risk, this argument has never successfully been used to remove people from their jobs.

The other relevant part of OSHA has to do with the responsibilities of an infected employee. Although infected employees cannot be forced to disclose their status, and they have a right to demand confidentiality of whomever they do tell, they also have an obligation to take reasonable precautions to protect the safety and well-being of their fellow employees, and to follow whatever policies and guidelines the employer has mandated for HIV-positive and AIDS-affected people. This part of OSHA is one of the best reasons for an employer to have a well-thought-out and comprehensive AIDS policy proactively in place. By law, employees are responsible for harm that they cause to their co-workers under the "fellow servants" rule. Under this rule, an HIV-positive employee could be liable if he or she willfully exposes co-workers to bodily fluids or caused them to suffer bodily harm. If such a case were to occur, it could directly involve the employer if it can be shown that the employer knew or should have known that the employee was capable of transmitting a potentially dangerous condition, but the employer had failed to establish policies and procedures that might have prevented such transmission.[8]

State and Local Laws

As of the end of 1994, thirty-three states have antidiscrimination legislation related to HIV/AIDS that cover the workplaces in those states, and some local communities also have regulations of their own. In Philadelphia, for instance, all employers of more than three people are required to provide AIDS education to their employees. We encourage all employers to contact their state's attorney general to find out the rules and regulations in their jurisdictions.

Specific Considerations That May Drive Workplace Policy

ADA, OSHA, FRA, and other relevant acts, rules, and laws make specific mention of several items important to the workplace. Among them are voluntary disclosure and confidentiality, reasonable accommodations, workers compensation, testing, and insurance. We will examine each of these in greater detail.

Voluntary Disclosure and Confidentiality

Employees can never be compelled to disclose their HIV or AIDS status for any reason. Those who bear the burden of a positive diagnosis for either condition are going to be extremely concerned about many things. They will be worried about losing their jobs, losing their insurance, and the reactions of their co-workers, for example. Employers should make every effort to communicate to their entire workforce how the organization will treat people who choose to—or who have to—disclose their status.

Employees who voluntarily disclose their condition have every right to expect the full cooperation of the organization as per its policies on working with such affected employees, and they have every right to confidentiality under the law and the rules of that organization.

If you are a manager, supervisor, administration member, or any other person in an organization who is privy to information about another person's status and someone else inquires about it, you should point out immediately that you are not at liberty to discuss another person's health status. We also encourage you to take the opportunity to reinforce the message that no employee has any reason to fear casual contact with any other employee.

You should also not try to influence a person's decision to disclose his or her status to co-workers. Simply be supportive of whatever decision that employee makes. Further, all employees who disclose a positive HIV or AIDS status should be encouraged to seek out appropriate counseling inside or outside the organization.

Exceptions. There are organizations and occupations in which confidentiality is, for the greater good, treated with different rules. People who are HIV-positive or AIDS-infected may pose a danger to emergency and law enforcement personnel, health-care workers, laboratory technicians, morticians, or others who are routinely exposed to other people's blood or bodily fluids.[9]

Because of this there are confidentiality statutes that allow disclosure under special circumstances. It is incumbent upon all workers to know and understand the confidentiality statutes under which they operate, and for those rules to be clearly delineated for everyone.

Reasonable Accommodations

Reasonable accommodations are steps taken by employers to allow people with disabilities to apply for work, become new employees, or remain at work as long as reasonably possible. Reasonable accommodations may include but are not limited to the following: providing flexible hours, changing from full-time to part-time work status, allowing employees to work at home (if practical), job sharing, providing physical apparatus to help physically challenged employees, allowing extended absences and tardiness, and transferring people to different jobs. Job transfers may be made only to accommodate a person's disability.

The type of reasonable accommodations made available for persons with HIV or AIDS should be no different from those extended to persons with other disabilities. Nor should employees be discriminated against in the form of having to accept accommodations that they don't want or feel are inappropriate. For instance, if a woman is a college professor who is HIV-positive and who gives a lot of lectures, it would be inappropriate and illegal for her school to lessen her exposure to the student body by assigning her classes to someone else and giving her more of a research-oriented position against her will.

The jury is still decidedly out on what is "reasonable," however. In a Texas case, an HIV-positive surgical technician was reassigned to other work and sued his employer. He lost because the court found that while the possibility of his transmitting the virus was small, it was not so small as to be inconceivable. But in Minnesota, a dentist tried to transfer an HIV-positive person who was taking the AIDS therapy drug AZT to a university facility with special isolation treatment rooms. The patient sued for mental anguish and suffering, and won.[10] Employers are encouraged to research carefully any actions they may want to take, and to keep lines of communication open with the affected individual. What is reasonable to one party may not be to another, but perhaps compromises can be reached.

Workers Compensation

If a person's infection can be traced to an identifiable incident or injury, the infection is considered in most places to be an accident and is therefore eligible for compensation. If it was acquired through a less dramatic contact, it is typically considered a disease and is not eligible.

Since 1986 there have been case law precedents established in many states for whether different kinds of HIV and AIDS-related workers compensation claims are eligible for compensation. This is very much a state-to-state matter, so organizations and individuals are encouraged to seek informed counsel.

Testing

Voluntary testing for HIV falls outside of the boundaries for this book's discussion about HIV and AIDS in the workplace. However, most workplace HIV/AIDS educators do discuss people's testing options in their sessions, and general information about testing is contained in Appendix II.

In almost all cases, mandatory testing of new applicants or of existing employees is prohibited by human rights laws governing the entire United States. A responsible employer will, in our opinion, educate its workforce about people in high-risk categories for these conditions and make testing easily available for those who choose it.

Insurance

AIDS is comparable to other serious, chronic diseases and should not be treated any differently by employers. AIDS has not, to date, adversely affected the insurance program or premium structure of any organization to a lesser or greater extent than other conditions have. This may change as more people become infected.

As for the cost of insurance, it is true that employers offering hospitalization and medical coverage to employees can expect to pay a portion of the cost of caring for people with AIDS. However, as we pointed out in Chapter 6, the average cost of treating an AIDS patient is less than that of treating those with heart disease, cancer, Alzheimer's disease, or certain birth-related traumas.

Insurance is another area in which employers can be proactive about how they approach the HIV/AIDS problem. According to the National Leadership Coalition on AIDS, employers should:

- Be aware of laws mandating extension of benefits for employees leaving employment and for their dependents. The most important of these mandates is COBRA.
- Understand the health and disability benefits offered by their insurance contract, including preexisting-conditions clauses.
- Determine whether additional benefits appropriate for people with chronic illnesses might be cost-beneficial. Such benefits are substitutes for expensive hospital stays and include home care, hospice care, nursing home care, and prescription services.
- Look into the possibility of using cost containment strategies like case management, which provide the appropriate level of care at the right time.

The Cost of Inaction

There is a popular saying in the AIDS action community that "silence equals death and action equals life." For business, this saying could be "inaction equals expense." The most obvious cost of doing nothing about the potential spread of HIV and/or AIDS infection within a given employee population is the literal loss of human resources. The loss of a valued employee also means the loss of years of job experience, on-the-job training, and institutional memory that is an inherent part of all employees. Losing employees translates into higher costs for recruiting, screening, hiring, and training new employees. Other cost considerations are that:

- AIDS is responsible for more workplace lawsuits in its short but deadly fifteen-year history than any other condition in U.S. business history.[11] Attention to HIV and AIDS issues can help organizations avoid lawsuits and litigation involving charges of noncompliance and discrimination.
- AIDS education programs are extremely cost-effective, and there are many qualified resources. Such education programs are certainly less expensive than dealing with workplace disruptions from co-workers of an infected employee (or one who is suspected of being infected).

> The most obvious cost of doing nothing about the potential spread of HIV and/or AIDS infection within a given employee population is the literal loss of human resources.

- The reduced productivity of employees with AIDS, and of employees who may be caregivers to someone with AIDS, can often be managed by reasonable accommodations that don't infringe on the organization's integrity, productivity, or profitability.
- The cost of HIV and AIDS is being mitigated by new and improved treatments. There is certainly a cost associated with these treatments, but they often pay for themselves many times over by allowing people who are HIV-positive or AIDS-afflicted to live longer, function better, and contribute on the job for much longer than they could have even five years ago.[12]

This is a business book, and it is designed to provide insights, explanations, and strategies for people involved in all types of commerce who are trying to be productive and profitable. The health and well-being of your organization is no less a bottom-line consideration than the condition of your physical plant or the margin in the price of your products and services. If you do not have an HIV/AIDS policy, strategy, and education program, we implore you to start one. Inaction will cost you, and us all, dearly.

HIV/AIDS Education

There can be laws, statutes, and policies, but without education, none of them will be effective. AIDS education should be one part of a comprehensive strategy of workplace education that features other difficult subjects like sexual orientation, race relations, male/female sexual harassment, gender conflicts of a nonsexual nature, issues related to physical disabilities, and even ageism. "American business keeps away from three forbidden topics: death, sex, and drugs," said Dr. John F. Bunker, a health-care consultant with the Wyatt Company. "AIDS potentially involves all three, so companies have been very slow to deal with it."[13] It's ironic to us that the same things that sell the most books and movies are considered off-limits in situations where frank appraisal of them might really do the world some good.

We recommend that organizations find the courage to embrace AIDS education proactively in their environments. The benefits of taking this recommendation are threefold:

1. Most importantly, it will disseminate information that will save lives.
2. It will allow people to begin to gingerly explore things that they have not felt comfortable delving into before, and will give them an excellent excuse to do so.
3. It will correct the misconception that AIDS is a gay disease while communicating that straight people with a false sense of security are currently at the greatest risk.

Often the spread of a disease is stopped before its causes or origins are known. Cholera is a good example. After a severe outbreak of cholera in London in 1832, John Snow was able to halt its spread by means of a careful epidemiologic, or causal, study that demonstrated the importance of hygiene in stopping the disease. This was years before the germ theory of disease was proposed, and before the discovery of the cholera bacillus. Similar patterns of cessation before reason repeated themselves with Legionnaires' disease and with toxic shock syndrome. Through education, HIV/AIDS can be similarly slowed or stopped before a cure is found.

What HIV/AIDS Education Should Include

Effective AIDS education is available at little or no cost, in programs ranging from a half an hour to six hours. As an example, Common Ground's program was designed using our perception of the best and most relevant parts of education offered by the American Red Cross, the U.S. Surgeon General's Office, the National Leadership Coalition on AIDS, the Center for Disease Control AIDS Clearinghouse, the AIDS Action Committee of Boston, the Gay Men's Health Crisis, AIDS Education from the Environmental Protection Agency, and the New York Business Group on Health.

It was not hard to draw a solid program from these myriad resources because so much of quality HIV/AIDS education contains the same components. A very representative sample includes:

Module 1: HIV/AIDS as Workplace Concerns

- Why HIV/AIDS and STD information is appropriate and important in the workplace.
- Definitions and characteristics of HIV/AIDS and STD's.
- HIV/AIDS: theories of origination and nomenclatures.
- Center for Disease Control classifications of AIDS.
- Non-STD or -HIV causes of comparable symptoms.

Module 2: History and Precautions

- How HIV and AIDS are and are not transmitted.
- AIDS is not a gay disease.
- Who's at risk?
- Precautions and precautionary prevention.

Module 3: What to Do

- Testing, treatments, and related conditions.
- The best you can do for yourself and for others.
- Therapies and vaccines to date and in progress.
- Other diseases reappearing in conjunction with HIV/AIDS.

Module 4: AIDS in the Workplace

- Why employers should be concerned.
- The legalities of HIV and AIDS.
- How HIV and AIDS affect the bottom line.
- Steps to take to avoid problems related to HIV/AIDS in the workplace.
- The rights and responsibilities of all employees, infected and unin-fected.
- Workplace policies and education.

The first part of this chapter covered most of the content of module 4, so the balance will cover some crucial parts of the other three modules. They are why HIV/AIDS information is appropriate and important in the workplace, theory of origin, what HIV and AIDS are, how HIV and AIDS are and are not transmitted, and who's at risk. We also examine resistance factors to education and options for program development.

Why HIV/AIDS Information Is Appropriate in the Workplace

Some people take the position that education about AIDS is worthwhile but does not belong in the workplace. Here are two important reasons why it does belong there.

Your Employees Want This Information

Earlier in this book, we reported the finding of the New York Business Group on Health (NYBGH) that employees want more information about dif-ficult subjects from their employers, and that they rate employer-provided education as more valuable than education from any other source. The NYBGH also reported, specific to AIDS education, that employees believe workplace AIDS education to be extremely valuable. The perceived value of such programs increased significantly where the education was comprehensive, where it was given on company time, and where it was compulsory so that employees did not have to feel self-conscious about their interest.[14]

People who are HIV-positive or AIDS patients are afraid, but people who are not infected are afraid too. The fears of infected people are extremely understandable since they concern life and death. These illnesses are life-threatening, and there is no easy comfort for that. But people who are afraid of working with HIV-positive or AIDS-infected people, or who are afraid of doing business with a company known to employ such people, have fears that can be corrected with factual information. Most good, informative, and highly effective HIV/AIDS education can be delivered in two hours or less. Our experience is that most sessions take about three hours because people have many good questions.

An Important Misconception Must Be Corrected

Although HIV and AIDS can be and are occasionally transmitted through the nonsexual exchange of human blood (as in transfusions) or bodily fluids (such as perinatal fluids), they are primarily sexually transmitted. It's not a problem that most people think of HIV as sexually transmitted. The problem is that these conditions are thought of primarily as *homosexually* transmitted. AIDS is not solely a gay disease. Not all gay men have AIDS or are HIV-positive, and not all the people in the world who suffer from either affliction are homosexual. In fact, gay women have always been and continue to be in the lowest risk group for HIV or AIDS infection. This is not to say that gay women are immune. No one is immune; that is the point. An important message of workplace HIV/AIDS education is that diseases do not discriminate on the basis of sexual orientation, race, creed, or anything else.

AIDS is not solely a gay disease. Not all gay men have AIDS or are HIV-positive, and not all the people in the world who suffer from either affliction are homosexual. An important message of workplace HIV/AIDS education is that diseases do not discriminate on the basis of sexual orientation, race, creed, or anything else.

The misconception that HIV and AIDS are gay diseases sometimes provokes the violent harassment of openly or perceived-to-be gay people. If people continue to believe that HIV infection and AIDS are the problem of gays only, then their false sense of security is going to lead to an even more devastating spread of these conditions than doctors are already predicting. Sixty percent of the 200-plus new HIV cases per day are women and minors who contracted the virus through heterosexual activity.[15] By the same token, if young gay men and women think that the scare is over, they will likewise find themselves dead center in a second wave of infection. The only way to stop the cycle of harassment and epidemic is through education. It is increased, intense workplace awareness and education that we are advocating here.

Theories of the Origin of AIDS

AIDS can be said to have three histories. The discovery of the virus and its identification as HIV-related is one history, the fight to stop its spread is another, and the fight to cure it will be yet another. Samples of blood frozen for decades in Africa reveal evidence of AIDS antibodies, and vast numbers of Africans in countries in the midsection of the continent are infected now. In fact, it is hypothesized that huge numbers of Africans have been infected and have been dying of AIDS for as long, if not longer, as the disease has been known in North America.

One theory among AIDS experts as to its beginnings is that an ancestor of the AIDS virus actually started in rural areas of Africa in primate animals like monkeys, and spread to man when these animals were slaughtered for food. The urbanization of Africa brought infected men or women into the cities, where sexual contact *between heterosexuals* fueled the spread of the virus.[16]

In the late Randy Shilt's book *And the Band Played On*, detailing the beginning of the epidemic in North America, he named a gay flight steward as Patient Zero. Patient Zero worked for Air Canada and traveled all over the world. He had many sexual partners. The sexual habits of many gay men until the 1980s, the bathhouses, the amyl nitrate (or poppers) helped spread the epidemic, but soon other people were added to the mix. Through drug abuse and prostitution, it quickly made the transition from the homosexual population to the bisexual and heterosexual populations. Many people believe that because victims of AIDS in its early history were not mainstream members of society, government was extremely lax about taking action anything to stop it. This caused the epidemic to spread like wildfire through the gay community, and eventually to all kinds of people in the world.

Exactly What Are HIV and AIDS?

AIDS is an acronym for "acquired immune deficiency syndrome," a condition that leaves the body unable to fight illnesses that a healthy immune system might overcome. It is *acquired*, that is, not inherited, but rather associated with the environment and with behavior. *Immune* refers to the body's natural system of defense, while *deficiency* implies that the system is not functioning normally. *Syndrome* means a group of particular signs and symptoms that occur together and indicate an illness.

The Federal Centers for Disease Control (CDC) first began monitoring AIDS in 1981. The number of cases was small and little was known. In 1994 the number of cases is inconceivably large and still not enough is known.

AIDS patients are susceptible to diseases called opportunistic infections. These are illnesses caused by organisms commonly found in the environment and harmful mostly to individuals whose immune systems are deficient. It's ironic that people with AIDS have more to fear from nonafflicted individuals in the workplace than vice versa. A person with a healthy immune system can easily ward off the small viruses and bacteria that can cause death in an AIDS patient. By being around sick people with healthy immune systems, HIV and AIDS sufferers put themselves at risk.

AIDS is believed to be caused by a virus belonging to the retrovirus family. Retroviruses are viruses made up of genetic material called RNA, or ribonucleic acid, rather than the more common DNA, or deoxyribonucleic acid, found in living things. In the United States this virus is called "human T-lymphotrophic virus type III" or HTLV-III. It is also sometimes called AIDS-associated retro virus, or ARV, and in Europe it is called the lymphadenopathy-associate virus, or LAV. The most common name is now HTLV-III/LAV, and its current scientific designation is HIV, or human immunodeficiency virus. There is import in the inclusion of reference to the lymph system in the retrovirus's name. One of the more serious opportunistic conditions of HIV infection are lymphomas or cancers spread by the lymph system, which is quite an effective superhighway in the human body.

HIV infects a specific class of white blood cells called helper T-cells. These cells have a very important regulatory function in the immune system. The disruption of this function lies at the heart of the immunodeficiency that characterizes AIDS. HIV also causes direct damage to other types of cells that it infects, particularly certain types of brain cells.

Sometimes there is confusion about the relationship between HIV and AIDS; the terms are often used interchangeably, but it is very incorrect to do so. It's important to realize that the consequences of HIV infection can be very mild, very severe, or somewhere between those two extremes.

There are approximately 750,000 to 1.4 million Americans thought to be HIV-positive, a majority of whom don't know it. The Center for Disease Control estimates that about 50 percent of HIV-positive people will develop AIDS by the ten-year point of their infection. By the end of 1994, there were 440,000 reported cases of AIDS in the United States, and 250,000 people dead as a result of it.[17]

How HIV and AIDS Are and Are Not Transmitted

HIV is known to be transmitted through contact of infected sexual discharges with mucous membranes, injection of infected blood or blood products, and perinatal transfusion, which is the transfer of fluids from mother to fetus during pregnancy.

The virus cannot pass through undamaged skin, the lining of the respiratory tract, or the mucous membranes lining the digestive tract. HIV apparently can enter the body through the mucous membranes that line the vagina, rectum, and possibly also the mouth. Viral entry is particularly easy if these membranes are damaged even slightly.

HIV has been isolated in high levels from blood and semen, but only in low levels from vaginal and cervical secretions, breast milk, urine, saliva, and tears. It probably exists in other bodily fluids, secretions, and excretions, but epidemiologic evidence implicates only blood, semen, breast milk, and vaginal and cervical secretions as agents of transmission. Materials that could theoretically carry the virus in small amounts—such as saliva sprayed in a cough or sneeze, or left on a drinking glass—have not been implicated as the cause of any case of AIDS, probably because the virus is a delicate organism that will not live long without the right nutrients and environmental conditions. HIV can be inactivated immediately with a 10 percent solution of household bleach; it requires moist, warm conditions to survive.[18]

HIV/AIDS is not spread through casual nonsexual contact. You can't get it if you share a cubicle, a phone, or a computer with an HIV-positive person. In one study of hundreds of people who lived in the same house as someone with AIDS, there was no evidence that the virus could be spread by close nonsexual contact such as hugging, kissing, or sharing kitchen or bathroom facilities. In another study of a European boarding school attended both by healthy children and by many children who were hemophiliac and infected with the HIV virus, none of the healthy children in the school showed evidence of infection despite very close contact with their schoolmates. Researchers also studied ninety children raised in homes with AIDS patients. At the start of the study, none of these children were infected, nor were they infected at the end. All these studies, and more, absolutely support the fact that AIDS is not spread through close physical contact except when body fluids are exchanged. Nor is AIDS spread by the bites of insects such as ticks or mosquitoes.

Furthermore, HIV is not spread by vaccines, although vaccination does challenge the immune system, and certain vaccines could make AIDS flare up in a person who is already infected. When a vaccination contains a live virus, there is always the danger that the person will develop the disease that the vaccine is intended to prevent. However, there is no vaccine for AIDS now, and certainly not one that contains HIV. And giving blood does not put the donor at risk.

It is important to note that the AIDS virus has been located in frozen semen used for artificial inseminations, and it can be present in fluids discharged from the penis before actual ejaculation. It is also important to note that not every contact with infected semen results in the spread of AIDS. Studies show that some people have been able to escape infection despite direct contact with such semen, but the research also shows that your risk of infection goes up every time you tempt fate in this fashion.

Who's at Greatest Risk of HIV or AIDS Infection?

Almost everyone is at risk. Persons are at the greatest risk if they have had unprotected vaginal, anal, or oral sex with a person whom they know to be HIV-positive, or a person who injects drugs intravenously. You are at risk if you have ever shared needles with someone who is infected, or have had sex with someone who shared needles. You are at risk if you have had multiple sex partners, or if you have had sex with a total stranger. If you have used needles or syringes that were used by anyone before you or if you have ever given or received sex for money or drugs, you are at risk. You are also at risk if you or any of your sex partners received treatment for hemophilia between 1978 and 1985, or if you or they had an organ transplant or blood transfusion between those years.

It cannot be stressed enough that as long as people, especially straight adults, continue to bury their heads in the sand when it comes to sexually transmitted disease, particularly HIV, then people are going to become infected in even more unimaginable numbers. Women and young people are particularly vulnerable, but they are also the ones who seem to be resisting the message most.

In April of 1994, according to a study by Yale University, 45.8 percent of 172 students polled at Manchester High School in New Hampshire said they would have been at least moderately likely to engage in unsafe sex. After viewing an episode of *Life Goes On* that featured an AIDS theme, only 24.4 percent said that they would still be likely to have unprotected sex. Imagine the improvement that focused and direct education would have.

American women as well are in a state of denial about their risk of getting one of the 13 million cases of sexually transmitted diseases spread in the United States every year, diseases other than AIDS. In fact, one of the most dangerous, syphilis, is at its highest level in forty years. According to a survey also done in early 1994 by the Campaign for Women's Health, some 84 percent of 1,000 women polled said they didn't believe they would contract an STD. In fact, women contract STD's more easily than men do, experience more severe complications, and often go undiagnosed until permanent damage is done. As a result, more than 1 million get pelvic inflammatory disease, become infertile, or develop life-threatening ectopic pregnancies. In the Campaign for Women's Health survey, 72 percent of women under twenty-five, 78 percent of women who have had many sexual partners, and 85 percent of women whose partners have had many sexual relationships do not fear contracting an STD, yet these are the women—the people—most at risk. Women say they know a lot about HIV and AIDS, but nothing about the other STD's that can be prevented in much the same way AIDS can.

Without increased education, AIDs, HIV, and all STD's are going to continue to spread. Knowledge increases protection. Women who learn that they are at greater risk and who learned about precautions were more likely to discuss sexual histories with new partners, to ask their partner to use a condom, or to discuss these matters with their doctors. Education is the key.

Overcoming Resistance

The numbers bear repeating. There is no cure for AIDS in sight. There is no vaccine expected for general testing in the population before 1998 or the year 2000. One in every 250 Americans is HIV-positive. Two hundred people are infected daily. There are over 6,000 cases of full-blown AIDS among children. In 1992, heterosexual sex became the leading transmission route of HIV in women. More young men, gay and straight, are starting to show signs of a second epidemic in the age group of 16 to 25. In 1993, about thirty-five of every 100,000 young adults died from AIDS. The same year, about thirty-two of 100,000 died from accidents. AIDS is the leading killer of young adults in seventy-nine U.S. cities including Springfield, Illinois; Omaha, Nebraska; Tulsa, Oklahoma; and Raleigh, North Carolina. In the Northeast, HIV infection is increasing among heterosexuals and IV drug abusers while stabilizing among gay men. In the South, most new cases are among gay men. In the Midwest, there is a spread among both homosexuals and heterosexuals. In the West, incidences of HIV among gay men are steadily decreasing. "The one clear message," according to Dr. Harold W. Jaffee of the CDC, "is that in all areas, there is increasing evidence of a heterosexual AIDS epidemic in this country."

AIDS is now the leading killer of all people ages twenty-five to forty-four. This age range represents over 50 percent of the nation's workforce. The rate of infection is increasing most among the same people predicted to dominate the workforce by the year 2000.[19] From 1990 to 1994, the number of reported AIDS cases in women attributable to heterosexual contact increased more than 40 percent.[20] There are a number of sexually transmitted diseases in the world. All of them are unpleasant; one or two of them aside from AIDS can be fatal if neglected; none of them carry the negative stigma of AIDS or a positive HIV status. We believe this stigma and the resulting resistance to deal with the conditions exist for two reasons. One, because once fully developed, AIDS is almost always fatal. Two, HIV and AIDS gained a threshold in North America among the perceived outcasts of this society: gays, drug addicts, and prostitutes of all sexual orientations. While AIDS was undeniably prevalent in the gay male population through the 1980s in the United States, it is not a gay disease, nor did gay men in North America "invent" it.

When the National Leadership Coalition on AIDS asked working Americans how their employers would treat a person who is HIV-positive, 78 percent said that person *would* be treated just like any other person with a serious disability or illness. Even more, 89 percent, said that an HIV-positive person *should* be treated like any other afflicted employee.

Then the Coalition asked the same people whether their co-workers would feel comfortable working with someone who was HIV-positive. Over two-thirds said they *would not*; a quarter said they *should not*. One-third said that at the first sign of such disability, the afflicted person would be dismissed or put on disability; a quarter said the person should be dismissed.[21]

It's easy to see from this study that people know what they should believe, but what they do believe is quite different. The truth seems to be that if you find a way to let people express opinions perceived to be socially unacceptable as someone else's and not their own, you are more likely to find out how they really feel.

It is no longer appropriate, as if it ever were, to allow the stigma surrounding HIV and AIDS to block action to fight their propagation. At the 1994 International AIDS Conference in Yokohama, Japan, dozens of statements were made about overcoming the stigma surrounding HIV and AIDS. Specifically, it was agreed that problems such as sexual orientation and gender inequality, cultural barriers to open discussion of sexuality, and discrimination against HIV-positive or AIDS-afflicted people must be addressed. Furthermore, if these problems are addressed, people who are already infected can seek out appropriate treatment both from their workplace and from the medical community. Today people risk spreading the conditions because stigma compels them to hide the fact that they have one or the other.

In early 1994 President Clinton mandated that all federal employees would receive education about HIV and AIDS. Health experts are adamant that all employers get over their resistance to such education and implement it. As of the middle of 1994, more than two-thirds of companies with 2,500 or more employees and nearly one in every twelve companies with fewer than 500 workers have had to deal with an employee who is HIV-positive or AIDS-afflicted.[22]

"More and more, people know somebody they work with who has AIDS or HIV," Wyatt's Dr. Bunker said. "But for reasons of fear, homophobia, and stigmatization, companies have not responded properly."[23] It's way past time for employers to roll up their sleeves and get involved through workforce policies, education, and programs to slow down the spread of HIV and AIDS.

Using Consultants and Educate-the-Educator Strategies

Both consultants and educate-the-educator strategies are highly effective and appropriate for AIDS-awareness education.

Because of the sensitive nature of the subject matter, consultants can be among your most effective resource for delivering straightforward, unbiased, fact-laden education about the nature of HIV and AIDS in the workplace and in society. With a little help from internal development staff, a responsible and knowledgeable consultant can customize a curriculum model to meet the specific needs of any given environment. Consultants with experience delivering this education to a wide variety of audiences—management, supervisory, or staff—will have the ability to tailor the presentation appropriately for those audiences. Further, a consultant who is familiar with other issues, such as sexual orientation in the workplace, will be able to handle a wide range of resistance and inquiries effectively.

On the other hand, using a consultant to train an entire, geographically diverse and numerically large workforce is not always the most time- or cost-effective strategy. In these cases using a consultant to educate the educators might be better.

HIV- and AIDS-awareness education are the dissemination of fact and the correction of misconceptions. Therefore, any well-schooled, proficient workplace educator can do a terrific job given the right tools and curriculum. Organizations should consider an aggressive program of educating their educators, management, and supervisory staff to become allies and change agents in the fight against HIV, AIDS, and ignorance in the workplace.

We strongly recommend that all organizations begin the process of workplace education devoted to some of these more difficult subjects with a full-blown program of AIDS education for their human resources, development, senior management, administration, and management personnel. We further recommend that individuals from all of these parts of the organization be chosen to continue the process of educating the educator for AIDS-awareness education, and that they and the balance of personnel also take part in sexual orientation training in the workplace. It is crucial that education about HIV, AIDS, and sexual orientation should finally be made available to *all* employees, whether through a consultant or through managers trained by one.

The more people the organization arms with information to fight the spread of HIV, AIDS, and AIDS-phobia at work, the better off everyone will be. This cannot help having a positive impact on the bottom line as well.

Notes

1. The Center for Disease Control, "Morbidity and Mortality Weekly Report," February 3, 1995.
2. Ibid.
3. Pamela M. Walsh, "Growing AIDS Epidemic Becomes More Diverse," *Boston Globe*, February 7, 1995.
4. Eric Rolfe Greenberg, "1994 AMA Survey on HIV- and AIDS-Related Policies," American Management Association (New York, 1994).
5. National Leadership Coalition on AIDS, "Sample Policies" (Washington, D.C., 1992).
6. Larry Reynolds, "ADA Is Still Confusing After All These Years," *HR Focus*, November 1994.
7. "HIV/AIDS in the Workplace—Q&A," New York Business Group on Health and National Leadership Coalition on AIDS (New York and Washington, D.C., 1993).
8. Ibid.
9. Ibid.
10. Bordwin, Milton, "AIDS: The Disease for Which You Call Your Lawyer," American Management Association (New York, January 1995).
11. New York Business Group on Health, "HIV/AIDS and the Workplace: What Employers Need to Know and Do!" (New York, 1992).
12. Rick Williams, "When a Co-Worker is Living With AIDS: A Guide for the Workplace," New England Consortium for AIDS Education (Massachusetts, 1994).
13. John M. DiConsiglio, "Slow to Respond, Workplace Now Confronts AIDS," *WorkForce Training News* (April 1994).
14. "HIV/AIDS in the Workplace—Q&A."
15. The Center for Disease Control, "Morbidity and Mortality Report."

16. Graham Hancock and Enver Carim, *AIDS: The Deadly Epidemic* (London: Victor Gollancz, 1986).
17. American College of Physicians, Medical Knowledge Self-Assessment Program, "HIV Disease," 1994.
18. *Surgeon General's Report to the American Public on HIV Infection and AIDS*, The Center for Disease Control, 1993.
19. Diane E. Lewis, "U.S. Firms Are Faulted on AIDS Awareness," *Boston Globe*, December 2, 1994.
20. DiConsiglio.
21. Barbara P. Noble, "Attitudes Clash on Jobs & AIDS," *The New York Times*, November 7, 1993.
22. Lewis.
23. DiConsiglio.

8

There's No Such Thing as a Stupid Question

In this chapter we provide brief answers to the ten questions most frequently asked about gays and related issues in the workplace. The questions and answers concern laws and civil rights, sexual orientation education, AIDS education, and domestic partner benefits. More comprehensive information about all these matters is included in the previous chapters, and appropriate references are provided here.

1. Do gays want "special rights"?

No. They want the same rights that others enjoy.

The rights of gay Americans, civil and otherwise, are (as of this writing) specifically protected in only nine states. Those states are California, Connecticut, Hawaii, Massachusetts, Minnesota, New Jersey, Rhode Island, Vermont, and Wisconsin. In March 1995, a bill was introduced in Illinois to make it the tenth state that put a gay civil rights law on its books. The protections extended to gay people in the nine states that have such a law cover public employment, public accommodations, private employment, education, housing, credit, and union practices. Where public and private employment is concerned, all of these states' laws specifically exempt insurance and benefits. What this last sentence means is that even in the nine states that specifically grant full and equal rights to their gay citizens, employers in those states (this includes the states themselves as well as anyone else) are not compelled to offer insurance benefits or any other kinds of workplace benefits to the partners or families of gay employees.

In addition to the nine states that have civil rights laws for gay people, there are eighteen states with executive orders on the books that offer some degree of protection to state employees in those places. Between eighty-five and one hundred cities or counties in the United States have civil rights ordinances for gays and at least thirty-eight cities/counties have council or mayoral proclamations banning discrimination in public employment.

Some people argue that gays want "special" rights because their rights are already specifically protected by the U.S. Constitution. They are not. The equal protection clause of the U.S. Constitution is intended to protect all citizens, but there are some groups that fall into what are known as "suspect classes." The suspect classes recognized today are differentiated by race, national ancestry, and ethnic origin.

There is no federal job protection extended to gay and lesbian citizens in the United States. As of this writing, a federal act to implement such protection (ENDA) remains in Congressional committee.

For more information about gays and the law, please see Chapters 1, 2, and the Epilogue.

2. Since gays are such a minority, why should we include them in our diversity plans?

The first answer to this question is that it does not matter whether there are ten gay people in the country or 10 million. It is wrong to discriminate against anyone on the basis of an inherent characteristic that has no bearing on performance.

The most famous of the studies having to do with human sexuality is Dr. Kinsey's in 1948,[1] the findings of which were reiterated in a follow-up study by the Kinsey Institute in 1994. Judging from his continuum of sexual orientation and behavior, Kinsey concluded that 10 percent of the population—male and female—is homosexual.

To understand Kinsey's work demands understanding his belief (shared by the authors of other studies*) that it is necessary to consider

---

* Of all studies done since 1953, despite their more volatile claims that only one to 4 percent of the population is gay, none have done anything to disprove Kinsey's work:

- A study by Janus in 1993 claimed that 9 percent of men and 5 percent of women are strictly homosexual in orientation and behavior.[2] Taken together, this constitutes 14 percent of the population.
- In 1994, the Alan Guttmacher Institute released its study based on a sample of 1,600 men who answered questions put to them by women researchers.[3] This study said that only one to 3 percent of males are homosexual. This finding grabbed quite a few headlines, but the fine print said that the researchers acknowledged that the answers given by the respondents may very well have

a variety of activities in assessing an individual's orientation. You must include fantasies, dreams, thoughts, frequency of sexual activity, and emotional feelings. You must also begin with an agreed-upon definition of homosexuality. This is something that still does not exist because people cannot agree on the degree to which orientation dictates behavior and vice versa. By combining all the factors that contribute to the display of a person's sexual orientation, Kinsey estimated that 10 percent of the general population—male and female—falls into a homosexual continuum.

If you believe that numbers matter, you should recognize that gays are thought to constitute the largest workplace minority.[5] Chances are your organization has a good-size gay constituency in which you have made, and continue to make, a significant investment.

For more information, see Chapter 2.

3. What are the most common objections to including sexual orientation in workplace policies, and how do I deal with them?

The most common objection stems from a misconception of gays' legal rights. Seventy percent of Americans (according to the Human Rights Campaign Fund in 1993 and the National Gay/Lesbian Task Force in 1994) do not know that workplace discrimination against gay people is, to a great extent, legal. Therefore, they believe that gays are trying to get "special rights" or provisions made for them on the basis of a lifestyle choice.

Second, people who do not believe that homosexuality is an inherent characteristic like handedness or eye color believe that gays make a

---

been less than honest, and that the study did not take into account necessary factors such as those outlined by Kinsey.

- In 1994 a survey released at an international statistics meeting in Toronto, Canada, indicated that more than 20 percent of American men and women reported having had homosexual experiences or sexual attraction to members of their same sex. Similar proportions were found in France and the United Kingdom.

- Also in 1994, Sex in America[4] was released. In it, 5 percent of men and 4 percent of women admitted having had same-sex experiences at least once since age 18. Nine percent of men and 4 percent of women said that they had had a same-sex experience since puberty. Just over 4 percent of women and 6 percent of men admitted that they had been sexually attracted to a person of their same sex in their lives. The study found that over 9 percent of men living in the nation's twelve largest cities identified themselves as gay. Among women, the percentage was 2 percent. Taken together, 11 percent of the population self-identify as gay, and this with women constituting less than a third of the total sampling.

conscious choice to be different and therefore are not entitled to minority status.

Third, people hold a belief that lesbians and gays are an economically and educationally elite minority who don't need civil protection or rights because they already have special advantages not available to heterosexuals.

Fourth, people object to anything that might be construed as validation or acceptance of homosexuality because of their religious beliefs. On the other hand, many object to including homosexuals in any workplace diversity programs because there are not enough of them to warrant attention. These are contradictory objections since people with religious or moral concerns spend an inordinate amount of time, money, and energy trying to defeat gay rights initiatives.

Last, people object to inclusion of sexual orientation because of their fear of a human characteristic they don't understand and because of the anger they feel at the discomfort it causes them. Ann Richards, ex-governor of Texas, said in early 1995 that we live in a time when people unfortunately find it easier to blame others than to look for the deficiencies and insecurities in themselves.

When faced with these objections, what does one do to respond effectively? The only effective way is to avail yourself of education and information about this issue so that you can respond with facts to objections usually founded on myths and misinformation. Furthermore, as a manager you can encourage your company to make sure these facts are available through workplace education, and you can encourage people within your sphere of influence to avail themselves of it.

See Chapters 2, 3, and 5 for more information.

4. If I support inclusion of sexual orientation in my workplace diversity programs, will my company suffer in the marketplace?

There is no evidence to suggest that being supportive of sexual orientation in workplace programs, whether in the form of nondiscrimination policies, educational initiatives, or benefits policies, results in loss of market share or revenues for the organization. There is, in fact, evidence to suggest that the opposite is true. The experiences of Lotus Development, IKEA Furniture, Saab, Northwest Airlines, Stanford University, and many others suggest that their support of gay issues in the workplace has been beneficial to the organization as a whole.

AT&T is under extraordinary pressure from groups that don't approve of its gay-supportive policies, and it has been forced to withstand a tremendous amount of negative publicity, which it has done without flinching. However, the company has not reported a loss of revenue. In the case of Apple Corporation, unwillingness to back down to anti-gay agendas has served to increase its market share and employee loyalty from those who understand that if you bow to pressures to discriminate against one group, there will be others targeted next.

Also, both Chrysler Corporation (Saturn division) and Procter & Gamble have recently decided to direct marketing efforts to the gay community. Others who are targeting this market include American Express, IBM, American Airlines, Chase Manhattan, Merrill Lynch, and Paine Webber.

Last, the national gay lobby groups in Washington and employee groups and consortia throughout the United States stand ready to support and publicize the proactive policies of gay-supportive companies. This support on a national level has been known to tip the scales for one company over a competitor. See Chapters 1, 3, and 9 for more information.

5. Must we include sexual orientation in our nondiscrimination policy?

Yes. Because most lesbian, gay, and transgendered people live and work in places without such protection, unless the employer provides some level of nondiscrimination protection, gay people can (and are) routinely separated from their jobs. It's also important that the words in your nondiscrimination policy or code of conduct be *sexual orientation* and not *lifestyle* or *preference*. Please see Chapter 3 for more details on this vital issue.

6. Should our diversity education include sexual orientation?

Yes. Sexual orientation is admittedly a difficult topic to include in diversity education because it raises a number of intensely personal issues and can cause an extremely high degree of discomfort. However, the difficulty inherent in its inclusion pales in comparison to the importance and benefits of doing so. Education is the answer to homophobia, which results in lessened productivity and profitability of the enterprise, as well as lessened productivity and job satisfaction of everyone employed there. See Chapter 5 for a comprehensive look at workplace education specific to sexual orientation.

7. Isn't AIDS a gay disease?

No. Although it's true that the first major outbreaks of AIDS in the United States occurred in the gay male community beginning in the first half of the 1980s, the disease does not discriminate on the basis of sexual orientation. Since the mid-1980s, education in the gay community about AIDS and other sexually transmitted diseases has significantly stemmed the spread of the disease in that community. Of the 200 or more people who become HIV-infected on a daily basis in the United States in 1995, the majority are heterosexuals. Vigilance on the part of all human beings is called for to stop the spread of these devastating conditions. Since there is no long-term effective treatment and no cure, education is the only tool people have to protect themselves. And the first lesson is that AIDS is not a "gay disease." See Chapter 7.

8. If we allow someone who is HIV-positive or AIDS-affected to work here, will we endanger other workers?

No. AIDS is not transmittable through the kind of casual contact that (most) people have at the office or other place of work. Transmission of the HIV virus that can lead to AIDS-defined conditions requires the exchange of blood or other bodily fluids. The virus requires specific conditions to survive, conditions not commonly found in most public surroundings. This means that sharing a keyboard, a telephone, or a bathroom with an HIV-positive person does not put you at risk. For more information, see Chapter 7.

9. What companies are currently offering domestic partner benefits?

Between 1990 and 1995, the number of businesses, universities, and municipalities that have chosen to offer domestic partner benefits inclusive of medical benefits has increased from under five to over 270. As of this writing, a majority of those organizations are in high technology, entertainment, law, education, health and insurance, labor unions, and municipal government. However, the greatest interest in implementing these benefits is starting to come from the communications, manufacturing, financial, and marketing services fields.

The best way to find out whether a particular organization or university has any form of these benefits in place is to call up its human resources departments and ask. Other excellent resources for information and referrals include:

The National Gay/Lesbian Task Force Workplace Project:	202-332-6483
The Human Rights Campaign Fund National Coming-Out Day Office:	202-628-4160
The Society for Human Resource Management:	703-548-3440
The College and University Personnel Administration:	202-429-0311
The Employee Benefits Research Institute:	202-659-0670

See Chapter 6 for a comprehensive examination of domestic partner benefits.

10. What can I do if I want to offer domestic partner benefits but my insurance company says it won't cover the risk?

When an organization tells its employees that it won't offer domestic partner benefits, it will often try to blame its insurer. The employer will say that it would like to offer partner benefits, but the insurance company said it won't or can't write the claim. A disturbing number of these rejections are not true, and as time goes on such statements are even less likely to be true. In those instances where it is true, form a coalition of employers to gain leverage with the insurer.

There is nothing in any state's laws in the United States that precludes any insurer from offering domestic partner benefits to the partners of their employees as the employer defines those people. However, in some states, typically states with greater population densities such as those in the Northeast and on the West Coast, the state insurance departments can stand in the way of such plans being offered by standard insurers.

Some state insurance departments have no regulations whatsoever about partner benefits, so employers in each state have to check. Chances are your insurer already knows the answer to this question on a state-by-state basis. Even in those states where current regulations seem to block partner insurance plans, there are ways around them.

The change in the policy toward domestic partner benefits coverage of most insurers since 1992 has been dramatic. In summary, what most would not do two or three years ago, most will do now. The reason for the change is simple: competition. The insurance industry as a whole acknowledged two things, both related to fears of an increase in adverse selection (read: AIDSphobia). First, insurers recognized they already cover people who could be HIV-positive. Second, an increase in these claims has not materialized in the domestic partner population.

More of the standard insurers such as Prudential, Aetna, and Travelers have lowered or are lowering the threshold on the number of people they will accept as a small group to starting at thirty or thirty-five. This is bound to make the market for partner policies more competitive.

Please see Chapter 6 for more details.

Notes

1. Alfred C. Kinsey et al., *Sexual Behavior in the Human Male and Sexual Behavior in the Human Female* (Philadelphia: W.B. Saunders, 1948, 1953).

2. Cynthia L. Janus and Samuel S. Janus, *Janus Report on Sexual Behavior* (New York: Wiley, 1993).
3. Alan Guttmacher Institute, "Family Planning Perspectives," (March/April 1994).
4. Robert T. Michael et al., *Sex in America: A Definitive Study* (Boston: Little, Brown, 1994).
5. Alistair D. Williamson, "Is This the Right Time to Come Out?" *Harvard Business Review* (July/August 1993).

9

True Stories: People and Companies That Have Been There

All the material contained in this book has been researched and substantiated to the best of our ability to ensure the complete veracity of the facts. But as noted in an earlier chapter, sometimes all the verifiable facts and statistics in the world don't have a tenth as much effectiveness as true stories told by real people.

This chapter offers personal perspectives on five major areas. In the first section, three women, all human resources or education executives, tell their stories about what it's like to be gay in today's competitive world. Two of them tell their stories from out of the closet, and one from inside.

The next section tells what it's like to work at a company that has a recognized gay employee group. Is this group a good thing for those employees and for the company as a whole? In the third section, we hear from one of the men responsible for one of the most proactive and comprehensive HIV/AIDS education programs in the world, and in the fourth section a very senior sales and marketing manager at a very popular insurance company talks about how that company—and he—think and feel about domestic partner benefits.

The last section concerns the viewpoint toward sexual orientation in the workplace of one of America's most recognizable corporate names. In 1995 this company and the HR manager we interviewed have borne and probably continue to bear attack campaigns and very negative press instigated by those vehemently opposed to their inclusive policies. What does a company do when faced with this kind of troublesome and disturbing problem? What would you do?

Cleaning Out Closets, in People's Own Words

People speak about coming out of the closet as if it's something a gay person does once and then forgets about. The truth is, coming out is not done just once, and most gays never forget about it. They forget neither the times they've done it nor the fact that they might have to do it again at any moment. This is not to say that it does not get easier; for most, it does. But the authors maintain after their own ten or more years of "coming-out practice," that the twinge of terror remains and the doubt about "am I doing the right thing?" lingers.

For some, out is out and they are never going back in for anyone or for any reason. For others, out is out most of the time, and there are instances when going back in is considered prudent or necessary. It is not unusual for the workplace to be lodged in either the prudent or necessary category.

What does the ability to come out and be out mean for the individual, and what does it mean for the organization? Three women's experiences serve to answer these questions. Two—Laura Gold, director of diversity strategies at Lotus Development Corporation, and Carolyn G. Rose, vice-president and general manager of education for Novell, Inc.— are outspoken proponents of openness and honesty in their lives, including in their work lives. A third, telling her story using the pseudonym "Britt Dena," is a former vice-president of human resources for a large printing concern in the East. She worked from the closet, but her sexual orientation was revealed to her employer by a third party, and she lost her job. Her closet door, at least professionally, remains closed.

Profile: Laura Gold

Part of the reason that I feel free to be out and outspoken at Lotus is that, from the very beginning, this was an environment very inclusive of different sexual orientations. Protection for sexual orientation was in Lotus's first nondiscrimination policy drafted back in 1982.

The founders of this company were responsible for this inclusiveness. Janet Axelrod established the culture of inclusiveness, and Mitch Kapor invented Lotus 1-2-3. Janet's job was to create a culture that was going to be as progressive and innovative as 1-2-3 was and would be as a product representative of this company. She came to Lotus with a background in social activism, and as a result, had a very nontraditional take on what business was and what it could be. That's why they drafted her for Lotus.

I've been here since 1984, coming from a background in human services. I was in the Peace Corps, and my job just before Lotus was working for a human services agency that was in the process of being defunded. It was my responsibility to ensure that the directors of that agency understood what the defunding meant from a human and cultural perspective. I was neither out nor outspoken about my sexual orientation before joining Lotus in 1984, or until around 1988 for that matter.

My first job here was to help Lotus develop the first set of human resources policies. There wasn't a thing written down about who the company was or wanted to be from a cultural perspective. My job was to research, observe, talk to people, and begin to document the culture as it blossomed. Issues like inclusion of sexual orientation or AIDS awareness in this workplace, which I worked consciously to include, were included without much of a struggle. But that was as much Janet's doing as anyone's.

To a certain extent, I suppose in the beginning (while still in the closet at Lotus) that I felt a bit uncomfortable about being too outspoken or seeming to favor sexual orientation inclusiveness. But I never hesitated to bring up sexual orientation or AIDS awareness when it was appropriate to do so because I trusted that there were people who would support me. On the other hand, I still harbored feelings that try as we might, Lotus as it grew and succeeded would never escape being anything but a traditional business in the end. We were all working for innovation, but in the back of my mind, I wondered if we'd really pull it off. The tide in business and in society was just too strong in the other direction. So I stayed in the closet.

Two things encouraged me to come out. After I'd been here for about four years, in 1988 or so, I took part in our first diversity training effort, and it was very different from any kind of training I'd been exposed to before. We were really talking, honestly, about differences. It was not my plan going in to come out in that class, but I felt the situation required my coming out if I were to get the most I could out of that program. Coming out in that class didn't mean that I had to come out in the rest of the work environment; I absolutely trusted that if I asked the other participants to respect my privacy, they would have. But knowing that this workshop and subsequent diversity efforts would be starting to bloom made me feel more comfortable about coming out, being out, and staying out.

Next, of course, Lotus instituted domestic partner benefits, and that made me more comfortable with my decision to be myself at work. We had public forums about domestic partner benefits at that time to help employees discuss their feelings and opinions, and our senior management was in the press supporting and reiterating Lotus's philosophy of inclusion. That really helped me feel more comfortable and confident in being myself.

Last, in 1990, we were just starting a full-fledged diversity awareness initiative of which I was manager, and I ideally did not want to have outside gay speakers coming into our environment to talk about being gay at work. I wanted our own gay employee constituency to feel comfortable about doing it. So I put the word out that a Lotus Speaker's Bureau was an idea whose time had come and that it was endorsed by the company. I asked someone other than me to actually make it happen, but this was my final push out of the closet with the door slammed shut behind me.

Now I don't spend a lot of energy worrying about whether people feel that I favor so-called gay issues over other issues. Nor do I have to be uncomfortable with explicitly including them. This allows me to do my job better. I'm aware that this double standard exists for other gay members of senior management in my position. Gays are for the most part invisible and remain invisible until they take the bold step to become visible. I think as an "out" gay senior manager, I have a responsibility to myself in terms of being who I am, to others as a role model, and to the organization to bring my best effort to my job unencumbered by any other agendas.

In terms of the effect that being out and outspoken has on me as an individual, it has been positive. My good feelings about being who I am at work have mostly to do with a feeling of inclusion. I found that there was a very tangible difference for me after I was able to be out with the team I worked with, after I came out to my manager, and after I finally attended a social event with my partner here at Lotus. I felt that I was completely free to just speak more freely about everything. As a matter of fact, I was amazed at how relieved I was to feel so free about expressing myself. It was more a weight off my shoulders than I had imagined it could be. The freedom was almost unnerving.

It took me about a year after those events, in 1990 or so, to get to a place where my behavior and attitude about coming out and being out leveled off to the point it is right now—that is, very steady and very dependable both for me and for the people with whom I interact.

In terms of the effect that my being out has on my value to the organization and my ability to do my job, it is also positive. I believe my openness and willingness to be who I am contribute heavily to my creativity on the job. Leading what I understand to be a "nontraditional" life, I've had to figure

> "I don't spend a lot of energy worrying about whether people feel that I favor so-called gay issues over other issues. Nor do I have to be uncomfortable with explicitly including them. This allows me to do my job better."

things out in a nontraditional way. I think that being used to approaching problems with a different perspective, a skill honed from years of careful analysis of almost every situation trying to figure out what is safe and what isn't, affords me creative problem-solving skills not all that common in those who have not had to work so hard at creative solutions in all facets of their lives. This is not a value judgment or a statement about performance; it's a statement about the facts from my perspective. For me, there are no hard-and-fast rules about anything. I'm more free to come up with alternative suggestions because my whole life is about alternatives.

Because I have received promotions and pay increases on a regular basis since my coming out, I can only conclude that the company values me as an employee and a contributor. I feel congruent with this organization and my ability to contribute here. I feel that my opinion is valued, and that I have an ability to do my best because I am in no way limited. I know that when I was in the closet, I could not and did not perform at a level that allowed me to question authority, ask questions, and go that extra mile in the best interests of the organization. I could not push for honesty and best effort from others because I had a secret myself.

Profile: Britt Dena*

I was vice-president of human resources at a large printing company. Ironically, I worked in one of the nine states that protects the civil rights of gay Americans. You would not have known it upon scrutiny of my former employer.

I was originally hired into the company as director of organizational development and was promoted to human resources vice-president within six months of my hire date. I brought eight years of directly related experience to the job. Many things fell under the umbrella of my human resources responsibilities: everything from HR policies and procedures to training and development.

This particular company employed about 500 people and had annual revenues in excess of $30 million. It was a successful printer. It also was, and is, one of the most homogeneous environments I've ever seen, heard about, or experienced. White, male, and Republican were the standards, and everything else was deemed "stupid." This was not a covert opinion; rather, it was blatant and it came from the top.

So how'd I end up there knowing that I was a woman and a lesbian to boot? All HR functions were traditionally female, and the position going in offered a tremendous opportunity and challenge to develop and initiate hu-

---

* Not her real name.

man resources policies, including EEO policies, and training programs. That's what they said they wanted; those stated desires turned out to be far afield from the truth. It took some time before I realized the situation as it really was and not as I wanted it to be. The president of the company liked me, my gender notwithstanding. I believe he thought human resources was "woman's work" anyway. But he told me I was aggressive and I knew my stuff, both of which were true. I was pulling down a six-figure salary and five-figure bonuses. I believe the phrase is "golden handcuffs."

Oppression and hypocrisy were the norm. For instance, all my male peers were under enormous pressure to conform to the debilitating image and behavioral standards of the CEO. They had familial responsibilities that kept them in line. As for the hypocrisy, we were located near several large cities with large gay populations. Our client base included gay men and lesbian business owners who were referred to as "fags" and "dykes" behind closed doors, and whose money was gladly taken. The top sales rep was a gay man. He was also called a "fag," but he was tolerated because he was the top rep.

There was no nondiscrimination policy when I started there, nor one by the time I left. I doubt there's one now. I was in a position to make improvements in the environment for all minority workers, including gays and women. We employed many minority people in the print shop, if not in the white-collar offices. I felt like a fraud and a fake for my entire tenure there. I am a very driven person, and I think my paranoia and powerlessness over the parts of my job supposed to deal with correcting discrimination caused me to overcompensate in all the other areas. I tried to create a less blatantly discriminatory environment because I had a responsibility to people other than myself to do that. I know for a fact that I was completely ineffective in that area.

Unable to address minority issues in diversity work, and for sure unable to address sexual orientation, I looked for other strategies to introduce these topics. I believe that for some people in my position, there are things you can do short of coming out and slitting your own economic throat to insinuate these issues into the fabric of the workplace. One strategy I tried was to introduce AIDS-awareness education for the workforce, ostensibly to get in front of any potential situations and help keep our workforce healthy. This was interpreted by my boss, the president, as a condoning of homosexuality, and he would not have it. My paranoia about my own sexuality did not allow me to fight for this education on the basis of keeping the workforce healthy. I have always regretted that.

I could have lobbied harder for pilot diversity programs that may have included sexual orientation as a module weighted no more and no less than other topics. I did not do that either. I could have encouraged the formation of employee/management diversity task forces that may (or may not) have included gays. There were many things I could have done to affect a positive change in that workforce, which was my job. I did not do many of them, concentrating on everything else but diversity.

After a while I felt trapped, constantly feeling that no matter where I turned, I got caught or was stuck. I made a lot of money and worked out a lot. I had a lot of nice things and I looked good, but my self-esteem and self-respect were destroyed, and I was not performing to my potential. My own paranoia about my situation was not the only culprit in my poor performance. When a company forces a worker into the closet as I was, a lot of time, energy, and by extension money are wasted. In my case, constantly having to find work-arounds or brainstorm alternatives to situations like diversity management was a complete waste of everyone's time. It would be much better for the health of any organization if it would just let its employees concentrate on the task at hand, unburdened by needless prejudice, bias, and the resultant fear.

I was "outed" and I lost my job. I lost a lot of money and whatever self-esteem I had left. I believe that I not only let myself down, but let down other people who were counting on me. I felt the way a parent must feel who has children with expectations and requirements and who is unable, through no fault of her own, to fulfill them. It's not that I'm not culpable; I am. I know in my heart that the money made me stay, but I will not take the responsibility for the homophobia that drove me further into the closet. Other people own that.

It's taken me over a year to get over this experience. My next job will be with a company that is gay-friendly, regardless of what kind of money or opportunity might reside in a homophobic environment. It's not worth it. I'm an HR professional, and I'm a good one. I'm supposed to be a change agent, and that is what I will be. When I left this position, several of my peers told me that upon finding out my sexual orientation, they came to understand that their homophobia and homophobic behavior were unreasonable and unjustified. On the basis of this feedback, even if it came from only a few, I will not waste one bit of my talent, enthusiasm, or energy on a company that will not let me be who I am. If only one person has his mind changed in any place

> "My next job will be with a company that is gay-friendly, regardless of what kind of money or opportunity might reside in a homophobic environment. It's not worth it. I'm an HR professional, and I'm a good one. I'm supposed to be a change agent, and that is what I will be."

I work from now on, it will be well worth it. Sometimes people who are the most oppressed bring real value to a job like mine. We know what it's like to be denigrated. People who know what it's like are unlikely to do it themselves.

People may read this story and think that this sort of thing doesn't go on anymore, not in the East. It does. And employers who think that forcing compliance to standards of morality, religion, politics, or behavior builds team cohesion are sadly mistaken. More than anything else, this experience taught me that robbing people of their individuality robs them of their ability and desire to perform.

Profile: Carolyn G. Rose

I don't think everyone who works for Novell knows that I'm gay, but it's not something that I ever hide. And I'm certainly outspoken in the sense of raising concerns and issues with respect to the individual's ability and right to be out, as well as with respect to corporate policies concerning sexual orientation.

I got a degree in electrical engineering and went to work for a company called Fairchild in its automatic test equipment division. The company was acquired by Schlumberger Technologies. I worked there for three years and was not out to anyone.

When I was twenty-nine, I left Schlumberger to make a career switch over to networking. I was faced with good job offers from Sun Microsystems and from a small company called Excelan. I chose Excelan even though it was smaller and offered less in the way of compensation because I felt it was the kind of company where I could come out. I remember feeling that way very pointedly. And I did start coming out. I made no announcements, I just started doing things like not editing my pronouns. In general, what I was doing at work mirrored how I was conducting myself outside of the office, but I was a lot more "out" out of work than when I was there.

We treat our worlds differently, and until I decided to be more honest about myself at work, I always carried that fear around with me, the fear closeted gays know too well. We are social creatures, and we're all victims of society. Our prejudices, and we all have them, are deeply ingrained. We get bombarded with all kinds of messages day in and day out, of which homophobia is definitely one. I think we as gay people internalize those messages to different degrees. I know I did. I know it's taken me time to get past those negative thoughts about myself.

I had to come out. There's too much energy that goes in to trying to figure out how to answer simple questions. I was at a crossroads in my career, and I couldn't afford the energy I was spending hiding, editing my responses,

> "I think I am a role model, and I think that's appropriate. I think my very existence proves that a person can be out and go far in a company and do well. I believe that my status adds value to this organization, and I think Novell believes it too. This organization understands that hiding wastes time and energy, whereas if you can go about your business with the same level of comfort as straight employees do, then you are automatically contributing more positively to the bottom line."

and changing pronouns from "she" to "he" or "it." People don't realize how even the simplest question like "Are you married?" can be an all-out confrontation to a gay person. I just decided to start telling the truth more often. It was evolutionary, not revolutionary, for me. It took time.

Going to the march on Washington last year was part of my evolution. I read a piece by Anna Quinlan in *The New York Times* called "The Power of One Topples Walls" in which she wrote about how we play the numbers game, trying to figure out how many people are gay, as if it mattered. All that matters is that one person is gay, and by getting to know that person, you destroy the prejudice and bigotry surrounding that person. Coming out allows others to get over their ignorance and their fear. I think gay people need to do that, need to come out. It's the only way.

I've been at Novell for eight years. I see my position here as a senior manager who is gay as a challenge and an opportunity to do a lot of good. The challenges are as much a product of my gender as my sexual orientation, but basically my approach is to simply go about things as I feel I should. If someone's got a problem with me because of my gender or my orientation, the problem rests solely with that person. It is not my problem, and I will not assume it.

The opportunity I have is to raise people's awareness and consciousness around sexual orientation. I think I am a role model, and I think that's appropriate. I think my very existence proves that a person can be out and go far in a company and do well. I am always honest about my orientation if it comes up, and I insist that my staff and people who know me be honest and straightforward about it too. I don't want anyone to feel, ever, obligated to cover for me. I do not actively mentor employees, but I encourage human resources to use me as an example in classes if discrimination on the basis of sexual orientation comes up. Likewise, anyone struggling with coming-out issues here at Novell is welcome to contact me. That offer will always stand. It may not be part of my written job description, but I do believe it is part of it nonetheless.

Insofar as Novell itself is concerned, I believe that my status adds value to this organization, and I think Novell believes it too. This organization understands that hiding wastes time and energy, whereas if you can go about your business with the same level of comfort as straight employees do, then you are automatically contributing more positively to the bottom line. In particular, my experiences as a homosexual in this society have absolutely caused me to develop a greater sense of humility, passion, understanding, tolerance, and acceptance, and I can and do apply that on a day-to-day basis in a managerial function. And the corollary argument is that as more people are out, fewer people will be intolerant and will likewise spend less company time indulging their homophobia.

It is appropriate for people at my level in an organization to lobby internally and externally for the things that they believe in, that matter to them. The support I receive from my peers and my superiors reinforces my decision to be out every day. Bob Frankenberg, our CEO, sent a holiday card to me and my spouse, specifically mentioning her by name and therefore acknowledging our relationship. That means a lot to me, and that translates positively into my performance. I think that gay people don't give other people, specifically straight people, enough credit enough of the time to be able to confront their ignorance and fears and work through them. And we should.

The Ups and Downs for Gay Employee Groups

An employee support group is not a labor union. Employees have a legal right to join together for mutual aid or protection. Whenever two or more employees meet to discuss problems relating to their jobs, or share ideas on ways to promote their common interests, they are protected under the National Labor Relations Act (NLRA). The employer may not lawfully prevent employees from organizing a group on whatever basis they choose. The group does not have the right to exclude other employees from participation in its activities on the basis of race, sex, or other protected characteristics. The employer's basic legal obligation is not to interfere with the efforts of any employee who wishes to take part in the group. The employer must never allow an employee group to pressure it into some action that might constitute discrimination either in favor of a member or against a nonmember. Employers should be scrupulously careful to be even-handed in their treatment of different organizations and groups representing different minority factions in the workplace. Privileges and perquisites granted to one group should be granted to all.[1] Employee support groups can be a real sticking point for management. In many places, employee groups are, for all intents and purposes, banned or nonsanctioned by the organization for fear that they do (or will eventually) constitute a quasi–labor union that will attempt to influence or change corporate policy. In fact, in some places that do allow employee groups to form, it is only with the specific, written understanding that the groups will never attempt to influence or change corporate policy in any way.

Profile: LEAGUE (Lesbian and Gay United Employees) at the Walt Disney Company

At perhaps no place in America is the question of employee groups, specifically gay employee groups, more interesting than at The Walt Disney Company (TWDC). TWDC is a very large organization with different business units and market focuses all over the United States and the world. This profile of its LEAGUE group is representative only of that chapter based in the Los Angeles area.

Although started with some of the angst one might expect at the beginnings of a employee group for those of minority sexual orientations at a company like Disney, whose name is synonymous with "family values" (read: heterosexual, traditional-family values), LEAGUE at Disney has not caused any more turbulence within the organization than any other employee group.

According to LEAGUE's cochair Garrett Hicks, people on both sides of the ideological fence agree that the group contributes positively to the bottom line of the company and the satisfaction of most who work there:

> From our perspective, we contribute to making this a more productive environment for gays and the gay allies who work here by insinuating ourselves into the corporate vernacular. Disney recognizes LEAGUE, therefore recognizing the validity and concerns of its gay employee constituency. Disney has taken and continues to take the position that commitment to a hate-free workplace means putting itself behind its nondiscrimination policy, which includes (as of 1992) sexual orientation, making sure that issues of discrimination and harassment are appropriately dealt with, and that people are aware that there is recourse should they suffer such discrimination.

One of LEAGUE's primary functions, according to Hicks, is to provide a safe haven for all Disney employees who are at various stages of coming out of the closet. Believing beyond a shadow of a doubt that people who feel free to be who they are make healthier, happier and inordinately more productive individuals, LEAGUE believes that message has gotten across to Disney management as well:

> TWDC is still going through its own coming-out process, but it does know that people who feel unencumbered by fear of prejudice, worries about glass ceilings, and threat of verbal or physical harassment will perform better than those who are forced to operate under those constraints. So while the company as a whole continues to look at things it can do to provide even more support to its gay workers, things like implementing domestic partner benefits, for example, we believe its equitable support of the gay employee group is a reasonable demonstration of its commitment to a hate-free work environment.

The question then becomes, is the workplace the right place for such support to be offered to individuals? According to LEAGUE, it is. LEAGUE believes that an employer, regardless of whether it has two people, 200, 2,000, or 200,000 working for it, has an investment in each and every one of them. This is true regardless of industry or of geographic location. If there is a population that is and has been historically raked over the coals by prejudice and that may suffer more than its fair share of distraction from the task at hand, then it is absolutely in the employer's best interests to alleviate as many of that group's concerns as is humanly possible.

But the fear continues to be real that an employee group—especially an employee group so intrinsically connected to a highly subjective, emotional, and volatile issue like human sexuality—could quickly turn into a union or special-interest group with policy change on its mind. Where does the employer draw the line? Hicks countered:

> I just don't get that union argument. Yes, you have a group of people who are joining an organization because they have a common interest or characteristic. They are not joining the group, at least not here, because they want to negotiate a higher pay scale for gays

---

"Regarding policy, what we're trying to do is remedy a disadvantage that has been culturally inculcated within corporate America. Maybe the employer needs to ask itself another question: 'If this group is lobbying for a policy change, is there really a problem that we need to address?'"

or they want special rights. Regarding policy, what we're trying to do is remedy a disadvantage that has been culturally inculcated within corporate America. Maybe the employer needs to ask itself another question: "If this group is lobbying for a policy change, is there really a problem that we need to address?"

This is not to say that LEAGUE in Los Angeles has purposefully steered clear of all possible conflict that could be construed as outside the "normal" interests of an employee support group. In 1994 KCAL, which is a TV station owned by Disney in southern California, decided to carry the Rush Limbaugh TV program. LEAGUE took definite exception to this sponsorship of Limbaugh because of his historically virulent homophobic point of view. As a group, LEAGUE wrote letters to appropriate people at Disney.

LEAGUE's issue was not that Limbaugh should be censored by being dismissed (although LEAGUE's members probably would not have shed any tears for him if he were fired). The issue was that if Rush Limbaugh said in the workplace even half the things he said about gays that Disney was in fact paying him to say on TV, he would be called to task for violating the company's nondiscrimination policy in a heartbeat. LEAGUE's position was that Disney was indulging a double standard based on a profit motive: Limbaugh's show made money, so Disney would tolerate him. Hicks explained:

> We didn't get Rush off the air with that campaign, but I think we opened some eyes and made the decision makers aware that creative choices cannot be made in a vacuum. People will stand up and say something if they feel their dignity and integrity as human beings are being attacked. We don't want to be a watchdog group, and although I think our action made some executives here uncomfortable, I think at the highest echelons of the company it's understood that we are certainly not watching every move that's made by Disney, ready to pounce on the company at the slightest indiscretion. On the other hand, I think top management also understands that even had there not been a LEAGUE to protest Rush en masse, there would certainly have been individuals banded together to mount such a protest.

Disney is not without controversy, nor has it ever been. In the 1940s, when the company released "Song of the South," there was a great deal of disillusionment heard at the top of the magic kingdom from African-Americans even though there was no black employee caucus at Disney at the time. As Hicks concluded:

Corporate America is not above reproach. It needs to consider different constituencies in and out of the organization. It is mistaken to view an employee group as a barrier. An employee group can help it consider different constituencies; it's a two-way street of communication that more often than not is a good one.

The consensus seems to be, at LEAGUE and at other organizations asked about this, that employee groups are good for the employees too. It's good for employees to have an effective mechanism to see and understand the corporate decision-making process. Employee groups represent a way for employees not only to offer advice and information, but to send representatives to task-force efforts and meetings, thereby allowing them to get a sense of the decision-making process from the inside. Granted, what they hear and see won't always be to their liking, but they'll know what it is, not what they imagine it to be. Such efforts can alleviate the "us versus them" mentality that can do unnecessary damage to employer-employee relations. Hicks put it this way:

> I think it's unrealistic for any corporation or employer to think that employee groups, sanctioned or not, are not going to form. Employees are interested in equitable treatment, and as human beings, we have a natural tendency to band together with others like us and go for what we want or need. From our perspective, it's a lot more efficient for this voice to be heard as a single source in the form of an employee group. And from the employer's perspective, if top-level managers are hesitant to see this kind of effort take hold in their work space, then they can make it the responsibility of a group of employees to go to the trouble of forming a concerted effort. They can tell those employees, "Look, if you can't get it together enough to form a group and a consensus around your issues, then we don't feel obligated to discuss them with you. When you do have it together, let us know." I think that such a demand on the part of the employer would be more than fair. And to be quite frank about gay issues in the workplace, I think that the gay community is getting the message loud and clear that legislation for us will be driven by economics. So I think all employers can expect gay employee groups to be forming and to be encouraging the organization to get behind sexual orientation issues and the potential of the gay market in a positive way. This does not mean labor strikes or work actions; this means a concerted effort by a certain employee constituency to gain recognition in the workplace based on the belief that such recognition will eventu-

ally have greater, more positive, societal affect. Employers should not fear this; they should welcome and encourage it for the simple reason that the more employees feel safe and equitably treated at work, the better job they'll do. This can be, should be, a win/win situation for everyone.

LEAGUE in Los Angeles has about 125 members in an employee population of roughly 7,500. Of those, about 90 are out of the closet. The group allows all these people, out or not, to present a common voice when conferring with Disney management. And what would they say if they could get Michael Eisner's ear for ten minutes of uninterrupted conversation? Hicks answered this question as follows:

> Eisner's a smart man, and he's been made well aware of the issues, so I wouldn't waste any of those ten minutes trying to get him to see the facts. I'd spend it trying to get him to see the faces on the issue. A group gives people strength in that there is safety in numbers, but it has a downside in that it also turns individuals into a faceless, nameless mass. So it's almost as if when you succeed in forming a successful group with a recognized voice, when you get the opportunity to exercise those vocal cords, you have to get the powers that be to see the issues in terms of individual people with individual problems looking for a collective solution. I'd try to get Eisner to see that as a man with a wife and kids, he's got a set of concerns. And there is another man, a gay man, with a male partner and kids, who's also got a set of very similar concerns. I think the message from the group goes over much better when it focuses on making sure that management understands completely that the group is no more than a collection of individuals.

HIV/AIDS Workplace Education

Profile: Polaroid Corporation With the Assistance of Dr. Richard Williams, Worldwide Manager, AIDS Awareness Program, Polaroid Corporation

Since 1987 Polaroid Corporation has taken a leadership position in the fight against HIV/AIDS and other sexually transmitted diseases by providing education in the Polaroid workplace. The goals of this ongoing effort are to contribute to preventing the spread of HIV disease, both within the Polaroid community and the wider community; to promote an informed, rational, and compassionate response to those affected by HIV disease; and to minimize the financial impact of HIV disease on the company.

In 1987, a task force commissioned by John Harlor, who was then vice president of human resources, recommended that Polaroid adopt a broad AIDS action plan to include:

- A position statement on HIV/AIDS issued to all domestic Polaroid members, as well as a nondiscrimination policy and a policy banning harassment.
- Management AIDS training.
- AIDS awareness sessions for all Polaroid members.
- AIDS awareness sessions for family members of Polaroid employees.
- An AIDS information office providing employee counseling, management consultation, referrals, and information on a wide range of AIDS issues.
- Individual service coordination with the medical, employee assistance program, and benefits staffs.
- Regular employee communications on HIV/AIDS,, including articles in the company newsletter.
- Voluntary, confidential HIV antibody testing through the medical department.
- Support groups for company members who are caregivers of HIV-positive people.
- An AIDS-related book and video loan service through the Polaroid library.
- An AIDS information telephone line providing information on AIDS training, volunteer opportunities, fund-raising events, timely AIDS information, and so on.
- Promotion of employee community service activities with AIDS organization through the Polaroid volunteer clearinghouse, Skillsbank.
- An active philanthropic program that includes grants to AIDS services from the Polaroid Foundation and corporate contributions to AIDS organizations and fund-raising efforts.
- Participation in community activities.

Dr. Richard Williams explains:

Our efforts to initiate AIDS education and support programs at Polaroid were not because the company experienced HIV or AIDS in the workplace as of 1987. John Harlor was somebody who was pretty savvy about what was going on in the world, and who also is a very decent guy. I think he saw that AIDS was going to have an impact on the workplace. And he saw through the whole issue of homophobia or AIDS being a so-called gay disease, recognizing that it was a health problem, not a gay problem.

In the late 1980s Polaroid's blossoming effort did not have many others to serve as benchmarks against which to measure itself, nor did it have the luxury of using or borrowing previously developed curriculum material from other sources. As Williams continued:

> There's no doubt that by 1987, a group of companies mostly around the San Francisco area had already reached the same conclusion we did about the coming devastation of HIV and AIDS at work and in society, but they hadn't really gotten their programs together yet. So we created our own programs and policies to address these conditions in the Polaroid environment.

Polaroid's commission set up by Harlor to study options to respond to HIV and AIDS in the workplace resulted in the policies set forth above (bulleted items) and a comprehensive education program. Since there was none to borrow, education was developed using materials gleaned primarily from gay AIDS-action organizations that were starting to spring up in ever-increasing numbers in the late 1980s. Because none of the available materials, either from the AIDS-action groups or from the Center for Disease Control in Washington, D.C., dealt at all with HIV issues specific to the workplace, all those materials were developed by Rick Williams and his team at Polaroid.

Polaroid Corporation employs 12,000 people worldwide. Eight thousand of those work in Massachusetts, where the corporation is headquartered, and another 2,000 work in other U.S. locations. The HIV/AIDS education effort began in Massachusetts, and to date 70 percent of Polaroid's domestic workforce has been through the roughly two-and-one-half-hour education program. Williams went on to say:

> One of the clarifying questions for the organization has to be, "What's the definition of education?" When we and some of the AIDS-education coalitions with whom we're affiliated ask other organizations if they've done AIDS education, a fair number will say yes. But the question remains, what have they done *exactly?* In a lot of cases, their definition of this education is that they've distributed a brochure about HIV, AIDS, and maybe some other STDs to their workforce. By that definition, Polaroid has educated 100 percent of its employee population. But we take a much

more holistic approach to this issue. First of all, it takes more than just one education session in a given location to start to educate about HIV and AIDS. We back up our programs with brochures, with resource rooms, with regular features in our newsletter, and with sponsorship of community organizations and events, among other things.

Polaroid's effort is targeted not only at the general goals of keeping the infection rate down, helping employees continue to function cooperatively and productively in the age of AIDS, and mitigating associated expenses. Its messages are also specifically targeted at five specific constituencies with five distinct areas of concern. (This list is not meant to be a ranking of priorities).

The first constituency is those employees who are HIV-positive or AIDS-affected themselves. Second are caregivers of people with AIDS. Next are the co-workers, friends, and family members of those with HIV or AIDS. Fourth are supervisory and management personnel who must consider these conditions in their day-to-day worklife. And last, to a lesser extent, is the general public in the communities in which Polaroid employees work and live.

For the first constituency, those who are HIV-positive or are AIDS-affected, the focus is on communicating that the organization is supportive of them. It's vital that these people know what Polaroid's policies are concerning them, that they know what their rights and responsibilities are, and that they know what resources exist inside and outside the company to assist them.

In terms of the second constituency, Polaroid recognizes that it has a significant population of caregivers—people caring for others who are HIV-positive or who have AIDS. The concerns of these people are likely to fall in line with the concerns of the ill themselves, but caregivers have other questions and issues too. Williams said:

> Our guess is that, in our particular environment, we have significantly more employees who are caregivers to others with HIV or AIDS than who are sick themselves. This is primarily, I think, a function of the average age of our employees. The average Polaroid employee is about 47 years old. These are people more likely to have teenage and young adult children—people between the ages of 25 and 44, who are currently in the highest age group for infection. So our circumstance differs slightly from what a company like Lotus Development might experience, which has an average age of about 30, people who themselves are at risk. Therefore, we make specific provisions for caregivers.

> "HIV/AIDS cannot be swept under the rug, and waiting for a case to appear is the wrong approach to take. Organizations are well advised to be proactive about these conditions. Telling themselves that it is not going to happen to them is a waste of time. With 200 people becoming infected per day nationwide, HIV and AIDS are going to occur in every workplace. An ounce of prevention is worth decidedly more than a pound of cure."

The third constituency, co-workers, friends, and family members of people who are infected, also gets special attention because Polaroid acknowledges that HIV and AIDS engender very emotional responses, both positive and negative. Education about the conditions helps to mitigate the fears of these people, thereby lessening the chance that there will be any destructive or counterproductive behavior among people in the workplace or at home.

What is true for co-workers is also true for the fourth constituency, supervisory and management staff. Supervisors and managers must be given the tools to work effectively with staff who are infected, ill, or concerned about the status of another person. They have to be able to manage teams or groups of people where this additional dynamic may be operating, and they must also be prepared to support their co-workers and staff members, in some cases having to put aside their own concerns and fears about these conditions. Williams asserted:

> Without support and education, this will prove an impossible task and will be to the detriment of the individuals involved and of the entire organization. HIV/AIDS cannot be swept under the rug, and waiting for a case to appear is the wrong approach to take. Organizations are well advised to be proactive about these conditions. Telling themselves that it is not going to happen to them is a waste of time. With 200 people becoming infected per day nationwide, HIV and AIDS are going to occur in every workplace. An ounce of prevention is worth decidedly more than a pound of cure.

Are Polaroid's efforts working? Williams answered this way:

> In some ways we know they are, and in some ways we don't know, but we infer that they are. One thing we can say for certain is that, even though AIDS is the most litigated disease ever, Polaroid has

not had a single negative incident around HIV in the company. Nothing. No work slowdowns even in locations where people have self-identified as HIV-positive or AIDS-afflicted. No job actions, no boycotts, no lawsuits, not even a letter of complaint to the editor of our newsletter.

Further, the research we've done to find out if people actually learned anything from the education efforts indicates that they have. What we measure for is what have people learned about HIV/AIDS and have their attitudes toward the conditions themselves and toward affected people changed because of the information they've received? We do not try to find out if people are engaging in safe sex as a result of the education; we feel that's a bit out of bounds for us.

We conclude that attitudes are definitely shifting for the better as the result of education in the workplace. People usually start the sessions with fears about HIV and AIDS and about people who have these conditions. Truthfully, they also start with some negative attitudes about infected and uninfected gay people in particular. A lot of what they have to say going in actually manifests itself not so much in hateful attitudes about people with HIV/AIDS or gays, but more as insensitive attitudes about these people. They'll say things like "I'm afraid, I don't want to work with them," giving no thought at all to the fact that they are talking about a human being with a serious illness. This is understandable, of course, but we try to overcome it by getting people to understand the facts, which in turn lessens their fears and allows them to feel and exhibit some compassion. We have found that when people are not distracted by fear, they have an enormous capacity for understanding and compassion. We've seen that here in a big way since 1988, and from that, we infer that the program is working.

How much of Polaroid's success is attributable to geography, the fact that it is based in Massachusetts, as opposed to a more conservative part of the country? According to Williams, not much.

The fact of the matter is that there might be something a little more tolerant in the air in Boston, but first, we haven't had any negative incidents around HIV/AIDS anywhere in any branch office of this company, and second, we found that people's initial attitudes and level of information about these conditions were no better or higher in Boston than in any other part of this country. I think geography is less important than is the issue of how you approach the education itself. One of the lessons I've learned is that you have to talk to individuals in a way that recognizes their particular point of view and vulnerability around HIV and AIDS.

For example, in Polaroid's population, our first education sessions comprised more older participants, who were sitting there basically thinking, "Well, I don't really engage in high-risk sex anyway, so why should I be worried about this stuff?" But when you start talking about their children or grandchildren, it becomes a lot more relevant to them. So it's important to figure out where the participants' interests may lie and speak to that rather than trying to impose a particular viewpoint or political agenda.

I've had the opportunity to work with Polaroid and other organizations around these issues on a nationwide level, and I'd say that the kinds of difficulties and challenges people run into around these issues are the same. I think it's a big mistake for an organization to assume that it can't address a difficult subject like AIDS because of where it is located. Companies can be sure that the conditions themselves are not going to pass them by because of geographic location.

In terms of convincing other organizations that ask whether or not they should investigate educational and policy efforts for HIV and AIDS in the workplace, Williams relies on the facts, which are more than adequate information:

I think that Americans in general, and American business in particular, tend very much to be reactive. We are not very good at planning. A lot of people have looked at the difficulty at this notion of getting behind proactive AIDS programs and attributed it solely to homophobia. And while I don't disagree that homophobia plays a part, I think what's happening around AIDS is just typical of how we approach things. We just don't do anything until there's a crisis.

So what needs to be done is to prove there's a crisis, and for that, the numbers speak for themselves. In the United States, one in one hundred workers is infected; 200 people per day become infected, heterosexual transmission is on the rise, and since there are more straights than gays, the numbers of infected people is going up. One to two million people are HIV-positive, and half of them don't even know it. AIDS is the leading cause of death for young people between the ages of 25 to 44 and responsible for more teenage deaths than any kind of accident. The people becoming infected now are the workforce of today and tomorrow. This is a business issue.

And one other thing to consider, the facts and stats aside: This is a business *morale* issue. Polaroid's program's contribution to general morale in this workplace was and is a completely unexpected outcome. Originally, we were worried about talking about HIV and AIDS and sex and death and human sexuality in these sessions, but participants don't get wrapped up in those things at all. For the most part the feedback we get is, "If the company is doing this, it must really care about us." This is a very important point for employers who think their employees are not going to like this education or react negatively to it. In fact, experience proves to us time and again that employees react very positively to a well-done program of AIDS education because they want the information.

Domestic Partner Benefits and the Insurance Industry

Profile: Questions and Answers With Bob Lewis, Senior Vice President, Group Operations, The Prudential

As recently as 1992, we conducted a survey of twenty-four insurance companies and HMO's about their position(s) on writing employer-based health insurance and COBRA benefits for domestic partners. We found that only one would offer it standardly to all its customers across the board. Ten would not offer it and were not contemplating it. Three said customers had asked and they had declined, and one said it was thinking about it. Of the remainder, seven others had recently begun offering the benefits on a request-only basis, and two thought that they would start responding positively to such requests within a few months of the survey.

Were this same survey to be conducted now, less than three years later, the results would undoubtably show that all twenty-four insurers and HMO's were either already writing these policies or would if they were asked to with no special premiums, caveats, or requirements of the participants in the programs.

One company with considerable experience and insight into domestic partner benefits is The Prudential.

Why is there less resistance on the part of insurers like The Prudential to offering these domestic partner benefit programs if the employer requests them?

Domestic partner benefits always were, and to some extent still are, a cost issue tainted by cultural homophobia. There has also historically been a lot of cloudiness in the legal and regulatory environment regarding definitions of partners, financial dependence, and things of that nature, but that cloudiness is starting to clear up. The issues are being clarified state by state. So the issue increasingly really is whether an employer wishes to include partner benefits as a part of its compensation package. Benefits are just another form of compensation.

When did The Prudential start writing these policies?

I think it was 1990. We accommodated a group client that wanted to cover domestic partners.

Why did The Prudential start to offer these benefits?

The principal reason is that we want to be customer-sensitive. We try to work in partnership with our clients (in health insurance and other areas), and if they want to do something, we will try to find a way to do it. That's the simple answer. We try to take the emotion or attitude out of the subject, and this subject can sometimes bring plenty of both. Our health maintenance organization in California uses domestic partners as part of our standard HMO plans. An employer has to specifically tell us it *doesn't* want to extend these benefits out there, not that it does.

Has The Prudential experienced any problems or additional expenses because of its willingness to offer these benefits?

We have had no problems—no client, customer, or market complaints—that I'm aware of. We don't make a premium surcharge but rather rate the overall group. Aside from some additional expense in preparing language for documents or filing different documents with state agencies or for the clients, there are no real additional expenses to us.

How about fraud or the cost of the claims themselves?

We're unaware of any fraud in domestic partner benefits statements of relationships. Fraud is a problem of course in health insurance, but

---

"We're [The Prudential is] unaware of any fraud in domestic partner benefits statements of relationships. Fraud is a problem of course in health insurance, but I'm unaware of any in domestic partner claims. As for the cost of the claims themselves, we have not noticed any spiking in claims cost attributable to domestic partners."

I'm unaware of any in domestic partner claims. As for the cost of the claims themselves, we have not noticed any spiking in claims cost attributable to domestic partners. We don't have any actuarial studies specifically on partners, nor do we have any plans to do any. If the insurance industry as a whole were to investigate doing a study of claims experience attributable to partners, it would probably be done as a coalition effort, and The Prudential would take part, but we've seen no need so far to instigate one.

Does your willingness to write partner benefits constitute a market advantage?

There have been some situations where we have recognized that we were chosen over a competitor because of our willingness to write these policies.

Has there been any resistance on The Prudential's part to extend CO-BRA benefits to domestic partners?

Although COBRA itself doesn't require this extension, we're willing to provide a COBRA-like extension where that doesn't conflict with other legal requirements. Where there are difficulties, there are usually solutions available. A customer can self-fund, for instance, or can apply a more aggressive interpretation of the law, or can ask for a clarification of regulations.

In many instances of resistance, the resistance exists because laws were written without domestic partner relationships in mind at all. It is a question usually of the spirit and intent of a law or regulation. Most of the regulations and laws you run up against didn't purposefully exclude gay couples; they just didn't consider them. So when the question of same-sex domestic partners arises, or even nonmarried heterosexual couples, it just takes a while for people (and institutions) to reprocess things.

How about the insurer's perspective on confidentiality?

I don't particularly personally care for the phrase "coming out of the closet," but for lack of better jargon, I'll use it. The fact is that coming out is sometimes an issue. We as an insurer want to have some evidence to support the definition of domestic partner. That often comes into conflict with the employee's desire to have coverage for his partner, but to preserve his confidentiality and restrict the publicity associated with his need for coverage. Like it or not, there are people in the workplace, whether they are agents of the employer or simply associates, who will not treat the issue kindly.

That becomes a problem because our typical approach is to have some sort of declaration on the part of the employee to satisfy the definition of domestic partner. These declarations are kept in strict confidence, but the fear remains for the employee in some cases. We acknowledge this, and we continually assure our clients and customers that their declarations are kept strictly confidential.

How do you answer people who blame you for their employer's inability to write partner policies?

As insurers, we often feel we're blamed for everything...we learn to live with that. Too often a person's perception of insurance is, "If I have insurance, then everything will be taken care of." They think if they have insurance that anything related to their health, like two aspirin or a vacation to relieve stress, can be submitted to the insurance company. It doesn't work that way, of course, but we don't stand in the way of reasonable accommodations to our customers. Domestic partner benefits are reasonable to us.

What effect does the size of the group have?

The size of a group is really not the issue; it's more how you rate the group. That was one of the significant general issues associated with what the Clinton Administration called health-care reform. It was how insurance would be underwritten.

Our general attitude is that you should not punish an individual by virtue of her association with a small group as opposed to a large group. But the market reality is that until some reform takes place, there will be companies that will go through rather stringent underwriting for small groups, in essence denying people coverage for previous conditions or what have you. Our view is that we ought to try to reach some common plateau on that as an industry and spread the risk across a block of business.

We have some administrative costs to consider, and we do choose to focus our business on larger groups, but that has to do with the type of company we are and not with AIDS-phobia or domestic partner benefits. Our group minimum size ranges from twenty to fifty employees around the country. This is neither a change of direction nor a new market for us. We tend to respond to local markets, and if our reps say there is a need and business we can fulfill, we will do what's appropriate and possible in that market.

What do you think the prognosis is for domestic partner policies?

Large companies tend to be lemmings. Once a couple of them start going toward this ocean, they all will. Any guess at a time frame would be speculative, especially given the recent change in political winds, but I would say that in three to five years, this will start to become a norm.

In employee benefits, things will often break according to the size of a company or the industry a company's in. So, for instance, if two large national banks offer these benefits, pretty soon all banks will follow suit. It's like a product development curve. It starts relatively slowly, then gains momentum very quickly, and then reaches maturity in relatively short order.

What is the biggest holdup?

Part of the holdup is cost and the other, not wholly unrelated, part is AIDS. If you look at recent history from a benefits perspective, two things were happening at the same time that were really unrelated to each other but were perceived as being related. One was the publicity associated with AIDS, and one was a significant spike in health-care costs themselves, of which AIDS was and is only a small part.

So, in the sort of superficial world of the benefits manager, those kinds of things had a connection. But things are starting to change in that now, health-care costs are not spiking, because of other factors like intense competition starting to improve the cost-effectiveness of the delivery system. Prices and costs in health care have been relatively stable in the last couple of years, so the concern about cost is becoming less an issue. Added to that are the longitudinal data now available from organizations that have been offering domestic partner coverage for eight or ten years, none of which point to significantly increased costs for anyone. It's just the cost of adding another person to a plan.

Including Sexual Orientation in Diversity Management Programs

Profile: Questions and Answers With Sheila Landers, Human Resources Manager, AT&T, Andover, Massachusetts

AT&T is particularly outspoken in recognition of its lesbian, gay, and bisexual employee constituency. This is demonstrated by the corporation's support of its internal gay employee group, LEAGUE, and by its financial and philosophical support of groups outside the organization interested in securing more equitable laws and policies for nonheterosexual people.

The corporation enjoys a hefty amount of patronage from the gay community in recognition of its courageous attitudes, and it bears more than its share of criticism from those who do not believe that gays are entitled to this support, especially in 1995. The organization is one of several leading-edge product and service providers that spends considerable time, money, and effort on direct marketing to the gay community. It likewise spends its time, money, and effort addressing the not-always-favorable fallout from these efforts. Clearly there must be a reason why AT&T puts itself in this position.

AT&T is one of the only organizations that offers a full-day or half-day education program on sexual orientation. Why does your corporation do this?

First, for what it's worth, participants tell us they like the full day more. AT&T recognizes that there are a number of gay employees in the workplace and that a full-day workshop allows more time to address those issues that prevent people from being able to work to their full potential. Our feeling is that the extra half day really gets to all the issues. It also allows time in the session to role-play real-life situations and practice the tools that participants learn in the program about how to respond to homophobic comments.

Is sexual orientation the only subject that gets this kind of treatment?

No. We offer other full-day workshops on topics such as sexual harassment, the aging workforce, and disability awareness. Our race and gender programs are several days in length. We run programs on every issue affecting the work environment.

How do you decide what you can and cannot do?

AT&T has employee resource groups that enable liaisons from the employee population to interact with management in order to raise issues that management may not be aware of. And we certainly do targeted work for those groups covered under our nondiscrimination policies and affirmative action statutes. The issue for us is about inclusion. We want everyone to be a part of the business and feel welcomed, not intimidated.

Does AT&T make sexual orientation education available to all its personnel?

The company is set up in separate business units, lines of business. Each organization in AT&T has separate diversity groups, but there is an

AT&T diversity strategy that is supported by all. There's no doubt that some diversity issues are worked more aggressively in some parts of the country than in others. That's probably attributable to the management in each location, the commitment from the people who are in the diversity organization, and also to the employee resource groups in that location. Employees do have a certain amount of responsibility to make their needs known. I would submit, as far as sexual orientation is concerned, that if the education is not offered in a given location, there's probably not a LEAGUE group there either.

How did sexual orientation education get started in your area?

I was invited to a pilot program of a sexual orientation program offered at our headquarters in New Jersey. That class was attended by AT&T diversity managers from all over the United States, along with members of LEAGUE, also from across the United States. I really enjoyed the program and immediately elected to bring it in house at Andover. So far, we've offered this program to over 1,200 of the 6,000 people who work here.

Is this education good for your facility?

This education enhances performance and is very good for us in that it eliminates stereotypes and misunderstandings around these issues and allows people to be more comfortable. It's a time-saver and a conflict-avoidance tool.

For gay employees, this program directly contributes to creation of an environment where they can be themselves, free from worry about hiding. They can produce at their full potential. They no longer have to worry, for the most part, about being harassed because so many people have been through the program here that our gay employees find the environment much more supportive and inclusive.

Some people may be impressed with that answer, others not. Those who are not will insist upon quantifiable evidence of the effectiveness of the program. Can you offer any?

I believe I can. I take a survey after every workshop. Every participant receives it, and it's very open-ended so that participants can feel free to express themselves truthfully. We tell them that we read each and every survey, which is true, we do. And we share the results from each session with the facilitators. The feedback is always incredibly positive. I constantly hear that the program should not only be open to everyone, but should be mandatory for everyone. People report that they found out myths they had held about gays just are not true. They report that they feel sorry about things they had done and said in the past degrading gay people. This is true for everyone who's undergone this program, from the executive staff to all line employees. I can say in absolute honesty that out of 1,200 surveys or so sent out, of which we have a 80 percent to 90 percent response rate, all but one survey came back saying that they felt the session was good for them and had a positive affect on their outlook and attitudes. The one that came back saying there was no effect said that his objections to homosexuality were based on religious beliefs and had not changed. In addition, more employees, both straight and gay, become members of LEAGUE after each workshop is presented. I think this provides additional evidence of the changing environment.

We think one con compared to 1,200 pro is pretty quantifiable.

What originally led to the company soliciting the pilot in the first place?

I think it was an employee group and LEAGUE asking for education around this issue. That took place in about 1988 at Bell Labs in New Jersey. The pilot was very well received.

Was there any management resistance to this education?

Yes and no. No one told me that I could not go ahead and offer it, but a few of our leaders here told me that they did have a problem with it. I had some very frank discussions with some senior people who expressed great discomfort about this education. But to their credit, they trusted me and the credibility had I built up with them to that point, and they told me to go with it. At any point, any one of them could have pulled the plug on this, but I really think that they understood their objections to be their own baggage that they could not and should not impose on employees.

> "Every now and then I do come across a supervisor or manager who has a problem with this. What I say to such people is that they have an obligation to understand what these issues are. If a manager supervises gay employees, and everybody most likely does, and that manager doesn't understand the issues, then he or she cannot be an effective or equitable manager."

Has there been any change in perspectives at the top?

Oh, yes...and then some! One of the senior managers, who told me in the beginning that he was having difficulty getting behind this program, attended it and has since become the management liaison to the gay employee group. His attitude change was 180 degrees in the other direction, and his support of the group today is very active. He is not just a figurehead in that position.

What do you say to management or supervisory personnel who refuse to go to the program or to encourage orallow their employees to go?

Every now and then I do come across a supervisor or manager who has a problem with this. What I say to such people is that they have an obligation to understand what these issues are. If a manager supervises gay employees, and everybody most likely does, and that manager doesn't understand the issues, then he or she cannot be an effective or equitable manager. I tell these people that they don't have to like it, or like all their employees, but they do have to understand differing points of view in order to do the job they're being paid to do.

To me, it's the same as if a manager says that a woman's place is in the home and then expects me to believe that he can be objective about that woman's work at performance review time. I'm not going to believe it and would encourage him to avail himself of some facts about women and the workplace. We are not trying to change beliefs here; we are only trying to send the message that certain behaviors are expected, and if you need more information to help you behave in a certain way toward a certain person or group, we'll gladly provide it.

AT&T gets more than its share of criticism for its progressive policies toward its gay workers. Do you expect that AT&T management will continue to be supportive?

Absolutely. AT&T is supportive of all our employees regardless of race, sex, religion, disability, or sexual orientation. We have an investment in them and we care about them. And if that means that people won't do business with us, then so be it. This organization will not discriminate under threat of boycott or for any other reason.

Change and support come from the top. It's tough for management to take the heat in situations like this, but AT&T senior management is smart enough to know that if it folds in the face of criticism about support to AT&T gay employees, it would be only a matter of time before another minority group would be under attack. At what point do we not stand up for our employees? I don't think I have or want an answer for that. I don't think most people would.

What is the prognosis for this education at AT&T?

I expect that more of our employee base in other parts of the country will avail itself of this program. We have scheduled an advanced-level workshop for management too, to give them additional strategies for diffusing conflict situations involving homophobia. But I'd have to say that many of the people that have gone to the first-level class say they feel very well informed about how to deal with these situations. And I see people putting their training to use all the time...cracking down on others who tell homophobic jokes or use certain derogatory language. And I think the managers, many of them, are really a lot more comfortable around these issues as more employees go through the program and support one another through the process.

Note

1. Robert E. Williams, "Legal Issues Affective Employee Support Groups," Equal Employment Advisory Council, Midwest Meeting (Chicago, October 21, 1988).

Epilogue

More average people, who just happen to be gay, are making themselves known in the workplace. Gays are seizing upon the workplace as the focus of their efforts to achieve equal rights because money talks and because the language of productivity and profitability is universally spoken. It is therefore critical for employers to understand the issues we've discussed in this book. We hope that we have offered insights to promote this understanding, as well as tools to act upon it. We believe that it is in the enlightened self-interest of employers to create a productive environment for *all* their people—including gay people.

We also believe that our society will reject continued attempts to defend discrimination against gays in the name of "family values" or "special rights" or "preservation of morale" or any other meaningless slogan. Such discrimination will be seen for what it really is: bigotry. And history proves that we are right.

The analogies one could make to other types of prejudice also once considered justifiable are startling and deeply disturbing. One would think that after 2,000 years or more, human beings would finally understand that there is no such thing as an acceptable prejudice that results in blatant or benign discrimination against any classification of people. In 1939, just two years before Hitler began the last step in his "final solution for the Jews," 53 percent of Americans voiced the opinion that Jews were different from everyone else, elite and overeducated, and that these differences should lead to restrictions in business and social life.[1] Six years later, ten million people were dead at the hands of the Nazis in concentration camps. Six million of them were Jews.

In 1940 black American citizens still found themselves in the position of having to fight for equal treatment, equal opportunity for advancement, equal facilities, and the equal opportunity to enlist and fight for their country. The armed services were not ordered fully integrated until 1948, when President Truman directed it, and not without a lot of kicking and screaming.

Less than forty years before the armed services elevated General Colin Powell to its highest position as head of the Joint Chiefs of Staff, the army classified blacks as "...not having progressed as far as other sub-species of the human family. The cranial cavity of the negro [standard terminology in the 1930s and 1940s] is smaller than [that of] whites. The psychology of the negro, based on heredity derived from mediocre African ancestors, cultivated by generations of slavery, is one from which we cannot expect to draw leadership material. In physical courage, the negro falls well behind whites. He cannot control himself in fear of danger and is a rank coward in the dark."[2]

When on the eve of America's entrance into World War II, President Franklin D. Roosevelt sought ways to help blacks enlist in the service because America was in dire need of soldiers, he was told that his efforts to integrate the services were detrimental and would cause a complete breakdown in morale and the services' ability to operate. He was further told by the navy that there was no way blacks could be accepted upon ships as anything more than stewards, mess assistants, or janitorial crews to serve the (white) officers. Negroes, President Roosevelt was told, were incompatible with military service, especially in close quarters with whites on a ship.

We would welcome the opportunity to ask General Powell how he—as a black man who less than fifty years ago would not have been allowed to eat with whites, let alone command them—can endorse and further by his own words and actions sweeping discrimination against gay people by saying that their orientation is incompatible with military service and that their presence would be bad for morale.

Regardless of his answer, the die is cast, and all of human history dictates that this "last acceptable prejudice" will not be with us long. It will vanish because it will not stand up to ever-increasing scrutiny. We believe that as more people learn the facts about sexual orientation, they will understand that you should not discriminate against another person on the basis of an inherent human trait that does not remotely affect performance or character. Upon such understanding, we predict passage of civil rights laws applicable to gays in all fifty states, removal of sodomy laws still on the books, court decisions based on the law and not on personal prejudice, and broad extension of domestic partner registration and benefits. We also believe that the federal government will enact something like the Employment Non-Discrimination Act (ENDA) to protect all workers—specifically including gays—in the United States.

ENDA was introduced in Congress with bipartisan support in late 1994. In its current version (March 1995), ENDA exempts small businesses of fewer than fifty employees. ENDA exempts religious organizations, including religious schools. ENDA prohibits quotas for gays. ENDA does not require domestic partner benefits. ENDA does not apply to the armed forces. Even with all these exceptions designed to assuage the fears of the opposition, ENDA is still not law. But then, FDR could never get a federal anti-lynching act passed either, and Mississippi just recently officially abolished slavery in that state! Some things do take time, we agree. Some things take too long.

Is ENDA necessary? Without it, gay people have no effective recourse to fight discrimination, including violence against them on the job, in most states in the United States. There is a 300-day backlog on Equal Employment Opportunity Commission cases where the bulk of such complaints end up and whose decisions in any case carry questionable weight.

What are the two most important things an employer can do right now to further the cause of equitable treatment for lesbian and gay employees? Make sure your nondiscrimination policy expressly includes sexual orientation, and support passage of ENDA.

The next few years will see many legal battles concerning sexual orientation in this society, and most will have a direct effect on business, government, and higher education. As we wrote earlier, employers can expect their gay employees to seek equality in the workplace because the workplace is a fertile landscape in which to plant the seeds of education and coalition building. Sexual orientation is, today, a human characteristic unfairly burdened by discrimination. Lesbian and gay people simply want to incorporate the same rights and responsibilities into their lives as straight people do into theirs, and will expect their employers to be ready to demonstrate on which side of this issue they stand.

Notes

1. Doris Kearns Goodwin, *No Ordinary Time—Franklin and Eleanor Roosevelt: The Home Front in World War II* (New York: Simon & Schuster, 1994).
2. Ulysses G. Lee, *The Employment of Negro Groups: U.S. Army and World War II* (Washington, D.C.: Office of the Chief of Military History, 1966).

Appendix I

Supplementary Information on Domestic Partner Benefits

Please note: Whether you are a company representative or an employee, be sure to consult a tax attorney or expert before making any decisions regarding the taxability or taxation of domestic partner benefits.

IRS Code 162

The employer's cost of domestic partner coverage is a compensation expense under IRS Code Section 162, attributable to the employment of the "employee partner." Therefore, the expense is tax-deductible by the employer.[1]

IRS Code 152

Section 152(a): General Definition

For purposes of this subtitle, the term *dependent* means any of the following individuals over half of whose support, for the calendar year in which the taxable year of the taxpayer begins, was received from the taxpayer, or is treated under subsection (c) or (e) as received from the taxpayer.

1. A son or daughter of the taxpayer, or a descendant of either.
2. A stepson or stepdaughter of the taxpayer.
3. A brother, sister, stepbrother, or stepsister of the taxpayer.
4. The father or mother of the taxpayer, or an ancestor of either.

5. A stepfather or stepmother of the taxpayer.
6. A son or daughter of a brother or sister of the taxpayer.
7. A brother or sister of the father or mother of the taxpayer.
8. A son-in-law, daughter-in-law, father-in-law, mother-in-law, brother-in-law, or sister-in-law of the taxpayer.
9. An individual (other than the individual who at any time during the taxable year was the spouse, determined without regard to section 7703 [former Code Sec. 143] of the taxpayer) who, for the taxable year of the taxpayer, has as his principal place or abode the home of the taxpayer and is a member of the taxpayer's household.

Section 152(b): Rules Relating to General Definition

For the purposes of this Section, an individual is not a member of the taxpayer's household if at any time during the taxable year the relationship between such individual and the taxpayer is in violation of local law.

No states recognize homosexual marriages or marriage-like arrangements as legal spouse status. Therefore, all homosexual employees who receive benefits for their domestic partners have to pay taxes on those benefits unless the partner also qualifies as a dependent under Section 152. Common-law marriage may give legal spouse status to some heterosexual partners.

Caveats for Further Consideration

The "51 Percent Rule"

In addition to the IRS Codes, there is a U.S. Treasury Regulation that has been called out in some instances as a way to declare a partner as a dependent. It's known loosely as the "51 percent rule." The Treasury Regulations state:

> For purposes of determining whether or not an individual received, for a given calendar year, over half of his support from the taxpayer, there shall be taken into account the amount of support received from the taxpayer as compared to the entire amount of support which the individual received from all sources, including support which the individual himself supplied. The term 'support' includes food, shelter, clothing, medical and dental care, education, and the like. Generally, the amount of an item of support will

be the amount of expense incurred by the one furnishing such item. If the item of support furnished an individual is in the form of property or lodging, it will be necessary to measure the amount of such item of support in terms of its fair market value.

This has been taken to mean that your partner can be considered a dependent if you provide more than 50 percent of your partner's support (as defined above), *and* he or she is a member of your household for the entire taxable year.

The "$2,350 Rule"

A $2,350 income limit is one of the criteria for a person to be listed as a dependent on another person's tax return. That is, if you are the employee and your partner whom you want to put on your benefit plan did not make more than $2,350, he or she would qualify as a dependent.

We encourage you to seek counsel if you wish to pursue this line of tax relief.

Calculation of Imputed Income

The fair market value of the benefits is taxable as imputed income to the employee, and the taxable amount is subject to withholding for federal income taxes, state income taxes (where applicable), and FICA. The taxable income will be reported on the W-2 issued to the employee at the end of the calendar year. Employee premium contributions for domestic partners and nonlegal dependents must be paid with after-tax dollars.

The question of what portion of premium is actually paid with after-tax dollars is one of great confusion. To a lesser extent, so is the determination of what portion of a domestic partner benefit and/or nonlegal dependent benefit is imputable. The examples that follow are the result of comparing the methods used by several providers of domestic partner benefits. As stated above, because there are no official rulings on these issues, a tax attorney should always be consulted.

The fair market value of the benefit is defined in one of two ways. In the *premium model*, it is the full unsubsidized individual rate for insurance, less the remainder of subtracting the employee's individual rate from the employee's family rate. In the *actuarial model*, it is defined as the actual value of the coverage, usually in a model such as:

Employee
Employee + spouse or partner
Employee + children
Employee + family (adding a partner to a family plan)

Sample Calculations Using Premium Model

Situation 1. You have coverage for yourself and are paying for it on a be-fore-tax basis. You add your domestic partner, so your premium changes from the cost of individual coverage to the cost of family coverage. Imputed income is the unsubsidized cost of the individual coverage less the difference between your premium for family coverage versus individual coverage.

Example:

Employee individual premium is	$30/month
Employee family premium is	$120/month
Full unsubsidized individual rate (paid by employer) is	$160/month

Calculation:

Employee family premium:	$120/month
Less employee individual premium:	−30/month
Difference, paid with after-tax dollars:	$ 90/month
Employer's unsubsidized cost for coverage, which is monthly taxable amount:	$160/month
Less difference above:	− 90/month
Imputed income:	$ 70/month

Situation 2. You have coverage for yourself and are paying for it on a be-fore-tax basis. You add your domestic partner plus his or her dependent chil-dren, so your premium changes from the cost of individual coverage to the cost of family coverage. Imputed income is the cost of the full unsubsidized family rate less the difference between the individual employee rate and the family employee rate.

Example:

Employee individual premium is	$30/month
Employee family premium is	$120/month
Full unsubsidized family rate (paid by employer) is	$450/month

Calculation:

Employee family premium:	$120/month
Less employee individual premium:	−30/month
Difference, paid with after-tax dollars:	$ 90/month
Employer's unsubsidized cost for coverage, which is monthly taxable amount:	$450/month
Less difference above:	− 90/month
Imputed income:	$360/month

Situation 3. You already have family coverage, covering your dependent children and paying for it with before-tax dollars. You add a domestic partner. There is no change in your premium because you are already paying the cost of family coverage. Imputed income is the full unsubsidized cost of individual coverage.

Example:

Employee family premium is	$120/month
Full unsubsidized individual rate (paid by employer) is	$160/month

Calculation: Monthly taxable amount: $160

Note: In this case imputed income (amount to be paid with after-tax money) is a matter of great confusion. Either no after-tax assessment is made, or the company divides the amount of the employee's contribution by the number of people on the plan and uses that number to represent the monies going toward the partner's insurance.

Situation 4. You already have family coverage and you add a domestic partner plus his or her dependent children. There is no change in your premium rate because you are already paying the cost of family coverage. Imputed income is the full unsubsidized cost of family coverage minus your contribution.

Example:

Employee family premium is	$120/month
Full unsubsidized family rate (paid by employer) is	$450/month

Calculation:

Full unsubsidized family rate:	$450/month
Less employee family premium:	−120/month
Imputed income:	$330/month

However, see note for situation 3 above for after-tax monies ramifications of this example.

Sample Calculations Using the Actuarial Model

Value of Insurance in Acme HMO:

Employee:	$1,000
Employee + spouse/partner:	$2,000
Employee + children:	$3,000
Employee + family:	$3,500

1. Employee has insurance for himself only. There is no imputed income, and all of his premium contribution is paid with pre-tax dollars.
2. The employee has no other dependents and adds his partner only. The value of the insurance is $2,000, divided by two people on the plan, one of whom is a nonlegal dependent. Imputed income is $1,000. After-tax contribution is figured as the difference between what the employee contributes for employee + spouse/partner coverage minus what he would contribute for individual coverage.
3. The employee has a dependent child (or some number of children) on his plan. He adds his partner. Imputed income is figured as the difference between employee + family and employee + spouse/partner cost. And as above, the after-tax contribution is figured as the difference between what the employee contributes for family coverage and what he would contribute for individual coverage.

Note from authors: Assuming benefits for a domestic partner carries with it financial risk and tax implications. By no stretch of the imagination are these benefits fair and equitable when compared with what legal spouses and dependents get on the basis of current marital status provisions and definitions of *family*. Adding to the risk is the fact that many organizations are unfairly calculating and assessing imputed income and after-tax deductions. Caution and research by all is advised.

Sample Affidavit for Domestic Partner Benefits

A domestic partner benefits agreement should always be made by affidavit between the partners and the company. In this sample, we've used CBKB, Inc., as the company name.

CBKB, Inc.

Affidavit of Domestic Partnership

We, [employee's name] and [partner's name], certify that we are Domestic Partners as described in the benefits enrollment material of CBKB, Inc., and that we are therefore eligible for benefits.

Note: If you have a Certificate of Domestic Partnership from a city or municipality authorized to grant same, no other proof shall be necessary. If not, the employer and/or its agents or insurers reserve the right to request proof(s) of the nature described in our domestic partner policy as relates to the definition of a domestic partner.

1. We have an exclusive committed relationship and we have been in such a relationship for at least six months [could be one month or twelve months; any time frame within that range is common].

1a. We are of the same sex. (This is sometimes included when partner benefits are offered to same-sex partners only).

2. We are responsible for each other's common welfare and financial obligations. We are liable to third parties for any obligations incurred by each other and will continue to be so liable during the period that the nonemployee partner is covered by the CBKB, Inc., benefits program.

3. We share the same principal place of residence with each other and intend to do so indefinitely.

4. We are at least eighteen years old and are both mentally competent to consent and enter into a contract.

5. Neither one of us is legally married to anyone else, or has had another domestic partner within the last one [six, eight, twelve] month[s].

6. We are not related by blood to a degree of closeness that would prohibit legal marriage in the state in which we legally reside.

7. We agree to notify CBKB, Inc., if our partnership status changes to such a degree that the nonemployee partner would no longer be entitled to benefits under the plan definition. We agree to notify the company in writing within one month (31 days) of such a change.

8. If such termination of relationship occurs, the employee partner agrees that he/she will not file a subsequent Affidavit of Domestic Partnership for a period of [six to twelve] months from the date of notification in writing of the existing partnership's termination *unless* the Affidavit is filed for the same nonemployee partner.

9. We understand that CBKB, Inc., is not liable or forced to extend COBRA to the nonemployee partner, but does so by its own choice. [This is applicable to those companies that so extend COBRA.]

10. We understand and agree that the employee partner can and will make health plan elections on behalf of the nonemployee partner.

11. We understand that under applicable state and federal income tax laws, employer contributions for the nonemployee partner's health benefits can result in additional imputed income to the employee and that such tax may not be paid with pre-tax dollars.

12. We understand that any fraudulent claims of partnership, or any failure to comply with the requirements for plan qualification of CBKB, Inc., can result in loss of employment and/or civil action against us to recover losses, fees, premiums, and so on.
13. We understand that some courts recognize nonmarriage relationships, not limited to opposite-sex common-law relationships or opposite-sex domestic partnerships, as the equivalent of legal marriage in terms of establishing and dividing community property.
14. We understand that this document is filed confidentially but may be subject to subpoena.

We have read and we understand the terms and conditions under which this coverage is offered and accepted. We declare all statements assigned to by us are true and that all documents submitted to support these statements (if requested) are also true and verifiable.
[Signatures and dates]

[In some cases, a notarized copy must be filed.]

Note

1. IRS Private Letter Ruling PLR 9231062, May 7, 1992.

Appendix II

AIDS Testing, Resources, and Policies

The screening test for HIV/AIDS is designed to detect the antibodies that are formed by the immune system after the body is infected by HIV.

Who Should Be Tested for AIDS?

People need not be tested who have been celibate or in completely monogamous relationships for fifteen years or more, starting from roughly 1978 or so, and who have not had blood transfusions or misused IV drugs.

It is a good idea to be tested if:

- You are male and have had sex with a man in the past fifteen years.
- You use IV drugs or have ever shared a needle.
- You have had sex with a prostitute in the past fifteen years.
- You are female and have had sex with a bisexual male in the past fifteen years.
- You have had sex with someone from a country where AIDS is epidemic.
- You received a blood transfusion between 1978 and 1985.
- You are a woman thinking of becoming pregnant, regardless of your sexual history (as per the Surgeon General's recommendation in 1987).

How Are AIDS Tests Performed?

The AIDS test itself is called the ELISA, or Enzyme-Linked Immunosorbent Assay, test. Half an ounce of blood is removed from a vein and is tested in a lab to see whether antibodies to HIV are present.

If your ELISA test is negative, it should mean that you have no antibodies against HIV and are not infected. *However,* false negatives can occur when the sensitivity of the test or the ability of the test to recognize a person infected with HIV is too low.

There are several brands of the ELISA test, each made by a different company. The sensitivity of most brands is greater than 98 percent, which means that if one hundred infected people are tested, two of them will be erroneously told that they are not infected.

False negatives can also occur if the lab makes a mistake, if you are tested too soon after your contact (six months is a standard), or if your body failed to make antibodies against the virus, which is an extremely rare thing.

If your ELISA test is positive, more testing must be done before a conclusion is reached, because the ELISA test has a false positive rate of 2 per 1,000. The fact is that the ELISA is so sensitive that it can pick up an infection where none is present.

If your test comes back positive, have the original specimen tested again. If it's still positive, another more specific test called the Western Blot test can be performed. If that is also positive, it confirms the presence of the virus in that specimen of blood. At that point, you should consider having another specimen tested, have a new sample drawn, and go through the two rounds of testing again. This is to eliminate the human error factor that your blood was mislabeled.

The ELISA and Western Blot tests will tell you only whether or not antibodies to HIV are present. There are many questions they won't answer, such as when you got your infection, or from whom, or what your chances are of ultimately developing AIDS.

Tests for AIDS are now available everywhere: through doctors' offices, public health departments, hospitals, community labs, and at special AIDS testing centers in some larger cities. Make sure you know the circumstances and rules under which the location you choose performs the test. Most important to most people is whether or not the test becomes part of a permanent record (anywhere) and who has access to it. Make sure that only you or someone you designate will be given the test results, and that you receive counseling about the test and what the results do and do not mean.

All cases of AIDS must be reported to one or more governmental health agencies, but there is a wide variation in this reporting from one state to another.

Resource and Reading List for HIV/AIDS Information

- AIDS Action Council: 202–547–3101
- AIDS Medical Foundation: 212–949–7411
- American Red Cross, National Headquarters,
  Office of HIV/AIDS Education: 1–800–434–4074,
                                                          202–737–8300
- Center for Disease Control and Prevention,
  Business Responds to AIDS, Resource Service: 1–800–458–5231
- Common Ground: 508–651–1476,
                                 Common-Ground@WORLD.STD.COM

- Federal AIDS Information Database: 1–800–272–4787
                                                          (modem connection)
- Federal AIDS Information Line: 1–800-HIV-0440
- Lambda Legal Defense and Education Fund: 212–944–9488
- Mothers of AIDS Patients: 619–234–3432
- National AIDS Network: 202–347–0390
- National Coalition of Hispanic Health and
  Human Services: 202–371–2100
- National Gay Task Force AIDS Hotline: 1–800–221–7044
- National Hemophilia Foundation: 212–219–8180
- National Leadership Coalition on AIDS: 202–429–0930
- National Sexually Transmitted Disease
  Hotline: 1–800–227–8922
- New York Business Group on Health, Inc.:   212–808–0550
- Public Health Service Hotline: 1–800–342–AIDS

Specific Workplace Policies Concerning HIV/AIDS and STDs

As stated in Chapter 7, workplace policies* concerning HIV/AIDS and other STDs generally fall into two categories: the life-threatening illness approach and the HIV/AIDS-specific approach.

* This section of Appendix II adapted from National Leadership Coalition on AIDS, Sample Policies. Available from the CDC and National AIDS Information and Education Program.

The Life-Threatening Illness Approach

Organizations using the life-threatening illness approach treat HIV/AIDS as part of the continuum of all life-threatening illness or disabilities. These policies usually state that HIV/AIDS will be handled as are all other serious illnesses—that is, sensibly, compassionately, and without discrimination.

Example of a Life-Threatening Illness Policy

CBKB, Inc., is sensitive to associates with disabling and life-threatening illnesses. Because of the seriousness and sensitivity of disabling and fatal diseases such as and not limited to, certain cancers and HIV, CBKB will treat any inflicted associate with the same dignity and compassion as any CBKB associate who suffers permanent disability from any cause.

We will not knowingly permit any associate with a life-threatening illness to be discriminated against or terminated solely because of his or her illness or disability.

HIV/AIDS is not a food-borne illness, nor can it be transmitted in the workplace through casual contact such as sneezing, coughing, breathing the same air, sharing eating utensils, or using the same rest room facilities. Periodically, education via newsletter articles, guidelines, education video and awareness sessions will be made available through CBKB's Home Office and designated AIDS Program Representative.

Strictest confidentiality will be maintained when a CBKB associate advises of his or her life-threatening condition. Absolutely no information regarding the person's history, diagnosis, and other medical information will be shared with any other associate.

Associates who have contracted a life-threatening disease may seek help or information confidentially through the HR Department. Associates who need help and/or information regarding HIV/AIDS may contact the AIDS Program Representative confidentially to provide individuals with an in-depth and clear understanding of their illness or concerns, and referral to agencies and organizations that offer supportive services for life-threatening illnesses.

The HIV/AIDS-Specific Approach

In an HIV/AIDS-specific approach to policy, these conditions are specifically acknowledged and addressed as major health issues with potential impact on the workplace. In addition to the policy statement itself, these policies often contain an educational component stating that HIV/AIDS is not trans-mitted through casual contact, and that employees with HIV/AIDS are not a health risk to their co-workers.

Example of an HIV/AIDS-Specific Policy:

CBKB, Inc., has a continuing commitment to provide employment for physically disabled people who are able to work. CBKB's AIDS policy is a direct outgrowth of this commitment, and it provides guidelines for managing employees and situations when a question of AIDS or HIV disease arises.

CBKB employees who are diagnosed as having AIDS or other HIV-related medical conditions may continue to work if they are deemed medically able to do so and can meet acceptable performance standards. If considered necessary by a physician, the employer will provide reasonable job accommodation to enable these employees to continue working. (In these cases, Employee Assistance Services may choose to obtain a second opinion from another medical expert.)

CBKB's AIDS policy protects employee privacy by keeping personal medical information confidential. The employee has the legal right to choose who may know the cause of his or her illness.

CBKB provides AIDS education for all employees to help them understand how AIDS and other HIV-related conditions are spread and to reduce unrealistic fears about contracting the virus through normal work practices.

The Ten Principles for the Workplace

Sometimes, in lieu of a workplace policy, employers choose the Ten Principles for the Workplace, which were developed by the Citizens Commission on AIDS of New York City and Northern New Jersey. Specifically, these principles are:

1. People with AIDS or HIV infection are entitled to the same rights and opportunities as people with other serious or life-threatening illnesses.
2. Employment policy must, at a minimum, comply with federal, state, and local laws and regulations.
3. Employment policies should be based on the scientific and epidemiological evidence that people with AIDS or HIV infection do

not pose a risk of transmission of the virus to co-workers through ordinary workplace contact.

4. The highest levels of management and union leadership should unequivocally endorse nondiscriminatory employment policies and educational programs about AIDS.

5. Employers and unions should communicate their support of these policies to workers in simple, clear, and unambiguous terms.

6. Employers should provide employees with sensitive, accurate, and up-to-date education about risk reduction in their personal lives.

7. Employers have a duty to protect the confidentiality of employees' medical information.

8. To prevent work disruption and rejection by co-workers of employees with AIDS or HIV infection, employers and unions should undertake education for all employees before such an incident occurs, and as needed thereafter.

9. Employers should not require HIV screening as part of preemployment or general workplace physical examinations.

10. In those special occupational settings where there may be a potential risk of exposure to HIV (for example, in health care, where workers may be exposed to blood or blood products), employers should provide specific, ongoing education and training, as well as the necessary equipment, to reinforce appropriate infection control procedures and ensure that they are implemented.

Bibliography

"AIDS Education in the Workplace: What Employees Think." *Report of a Study by the New York Business Group on Health, Inc.* New York: New York Business Group on Health, Inc., 1990.

Alan Guttmacher Institute. "Family Planning Perspectives." March/April 1993.

Altman, Lawrence K. "AIDS Is Leading Killer of Those 25–44 in U.S." *The New York Times*, January 31, 1995.

Bartlett, John G., and Ann K. Finkbeiner. *The Guide to Living With HIV Infection.* New York: Johns Hopkins University Press, 1991.

Blumenfeld, Warren J. *Homophobia: How We All Pay the Price.* Boston: Beacon Press, 1992.

———. *Speaking Out: A Manual for Speaking on Gay, Lesbian and Bisexual Issues.* Boston Speaker's Bureau, 1993.

Bordwin, Milton. "AIDS: The Disease for Which You Call Your Lawyer." *HR Focus* (January 1995).

Byham, Kim. "Episcopal Dioceses Back Gay Rights." *The Lesbian and Gay Press*, February 7, 1994.

Caudron, Shari. "Training Can Damage Diversity Efforts." *Personnel Journal* (April 1993).

———. "Valuing Difference Not the Same as Managing Diversity." *Personnel Journal* (April 1993).

Coren, Stanley. *The Left-Hander Syndrome: The Causes and Consequences of Left-Handedness.* New York: Free Press, 1992.

Cox, Taylor. *Cultural Diversity in Organizations: Theory, Research and Practice.* San Francisco: Berrit-Koehler, 1993.

DiConsiglio, John M. "Slow to Respond, Workplace Now Confronts AIDS." *Work-Force Training News* (April 1994).

Finamore, Frank, et al. "Managing HIV/AIDS in the Workplace: A Resource Guide for EPA Managers and Supervisors." Washington, D.C.: Environmental Protection Agency, September 15, 1994.

"Gay in Corporate America." *Fortune* (December 1991).

Gebhard, P. *Sex Offenders: An Analysis of Types.* New York: Harper & Row, 1985.

Goldberg, Suzanne B. "Employee Benefits and Insurance: Working With Your Client to Achieve Full and Equal Benefits." *Tax Law & Estate Planning Course Handbook Series, Estate Planning & Administration.* New York: Practicing Law Institute (April/May 1994).

Goodwin, Doris Kearns. *No Ordinary Time—Franklin and Eleanor Roosevelt: The Home Front in World War II.* New York: Simon & Schuster, 1994.

Gossett, Charles W. "Public Sector Patterns—Domestic Partner Benefits." *Review of Public Personnel Administration* (Winter 1994).

Greenberg, Eric Rolfe. "1994 AMA Survey on HIV- and AIDS-Related Policies." New York: American Management Association, 1994.

Hancock, Graham, and Enver Carim. *AIDS: The Deadly Epidemic*. London: Victor Gollancz, 1986.

Haseley, Kenneth. "Raising Awareness Precedes Changing Attitudes." *Public Relations Journal*, September 10, 1994.

Heery, William. "Corporate Mentoring Can Break the Glass Ceiling." *HR Focus* (May 1994).

Henry, William A. "Pride and Prejudice: Bumping Up Against the Limits of Tolerance." *Time* (June 27, 1994), pp. 56–59.

Hentoff, Nat. "A Case of Loathing." *Playboy* (September 1992).

"HIV/AIDS in the Workplace—Q&A." New York and Washington, D.C.: New York Business Group on Health and National Leadership Coalition on AIDS, 1993.

Janus, Cynthia L. and Samuel S. *Janus Report on Sexual Behavior*. New York: Wiley, 1993.

Kinsey, Alfred C., et al. *Sexual Behavior in the Human Male and Sexual Behavior in the Human Female*. Philadelphia: W.B. Saunders, 1948 and 1953.

Kinyon, John. "Out on a Job Interview." *Gay Chicago Magazine* (May 12–22, 1994).

Lee, Ulysses G. *The Employment of Negro Groups: U.S. Army and World War II*. Washington, D.C.: Office of the Chief of Military History, 1966.

Lewis, Diane E. "U.S. Firms Are Faulted on AIDS Awareness." *Boston Globe*, December 2, 1994.

Lovelace, Kay, and Benson Rosen. "Fitting Square Pegs Into Round Holes." *HR Magazine* (January 1994).

Lynch, Frederick R. "Demystifying Multiculturalism." *National Review* (February 21, 1994).

Lyndenberg, Steven, Alice T. Marlin, and Sean O. Strub. *Rating America's Corporate Conscience: A Proactive Guide to the Companies Behind the Products You Buy*. New York: Addison-Wesley, 1986.

McNaught, Brian. *Gay Issues in the Workplace*. New York: St. Martin's Press, 1993.

Marcus, Eric. *Is It a Choice: Answers to 300 Most Frequently Asked Questions About Gays and Lesbians*. New York: HarperCollins, 1993.

Michael, Robert T., et al. *Sex in America: A Definitive Study*. Boston: Little, Brown, 1994.

National Leadership Coalition on AIDS. "Sample Policies." Washington, D.C., 1992.

New York Business Group on Health, "Discussion Paper," Volume 9, Supplement No. 2 (May 1989).

———. "HIV/AIDS and the Workplace: What Employers Need to Know and Do!" New York, 1992.

Noble, Barbara P. "Attitudes Clash on Jobs & AIDS." *The New York Times*, November 7, 1993.

Reichheld, Frederick F. "Loyalty Based Management." *Harvard Business Review*, March/April 1993.

Reynolds, Larry. "ADA Is Still Confusing After All These Years." *HR Focus* (November 1994).

Riddle, D.I., and B. Sang. "Psychotherapy With Lesbians." *Journal of Social Issues*, 34(3), 1978.

Robbins, Stephen P. *Organizational Behavior*. Englewood Cliffs, N.J.: Prentice-Hall, 1989.

Rynes, Sara, and Benson Rosen. "Profiting From Other's Experience: A Diversity Training Checklist." *HR Magazine*, October 1994.

———. "What Makes Diversity Work." *HR Magazine*, October 1994, pp. 68–70.

Signorile, Michelangelo. *Queer in America: Sex, Media, and the Closets of Power*. New York: Random House, 1993.

Surgeon General's Report to the American Public on HIV Infection and AIDS. Atlanta: The Center for Disease Control, 1993.

Thomas, R. Roosevelt, Jr. *Beyond Race and Gender: Unleashing the Power of Your Total Work Force by Managing Diversity*. New York: AMACOM, 1991.

Thompson, Cooper. "A Guide to Leading Introductory Workshops on Homophobia." Chicago: Campaign to End Homophobia, 1990.

"Trendy Miami Beach Area Owes It All to Tolerance." *Miami Herald*, November 14, 1994.

U.S. Census Bureau. *Statistical Abstract of the United States, Household and Family Characteristics, Marital Status and Living Arrangements*. Washington, D.C.: U.S. Government Printing Office, 1992 and 1993.

U.S. Department of Agriculture. "Sexual Orientation: An Issue of Workforce Diversity." A Report by the Ad-Hoc Committee of the Regional Civil Rights Committee Prepared for the Regional Forester, Washington, D.C., September 1992.

Van Sluys, Loralie. "Domestic Partner Benefits Study." Chicago: Hewitt Associates, 1991.

Walsh, Pamela M. "Growing AIDS Epidemic Becomes More Diverse." *Boston Globe*, February 7, 1995.

Wellman, Senator Paul. From "Employment Non-Discrimination Act Hearing," July 29, 1994. Taped in Congress and distributed by the Human Rights Campaign Fund.

Williams, Rick. "When a Co-Worker Is Living With AIDS: A Guide for the Workplace." Cambridge, Massachusetts: New England Consortium for AIDS Education, 1994.

Williams, Robert E. "Legal Issues Affecting Employee Support Groups." Equal Employment Advisory Council, Midwest Meeting (Chicago, October 21, 1988).

Williamson, Alistair D. "Is This the Right Time to Come Out?" *Harvard Business Review*, July/August 1993.

Woods, James D. *The Corporate Closet: The Professional Lives of Gay Men in America*. New York: Free Press, 1993.

Index